Calling Detective Crockford

Calling Detective Crockford

THE STORY OF A PIONEERING
POLICEWOMAN IN THE 1950S

Ruth D'Alessandro

WELBECK

Published in 2023 by Welbeck
An imprint of Welbeck Non-Fiction Limited
Part of the Welbeck Publishing Group
Offices in: London – 20 Mortimer Street, London W1T 3JW &
Sydney – 205 Commonwealth Street, Surry Hills 2010

www.welbeckpublishing.com

Design and layout © 2023 Welbeck Non-Fiction Ltd
Text © 2023 Ruth D'Alessandro

A CIP catalogue record for this book is available from the British Library.

ISBN 978-1-80279-368-0

Typeset by Roger Walker
Printed in Great Britain by CPI Books, Chatham, Kent

10 9 8 7 6 5 4 3 2 1

To my husband Paul, always my first reader

Contents

Author's foreword

by Ruth D'Alessandro

"Your mum was the first woman detective in the Berkshire Constabulary!"

This was a phrase I heard so often growing up in a police family that I became immune to its impact and significance. It was only when I was an adult that I truly appreciated what an extraordinary achievement that was for a plumber's daughter from Wokingham.

My mum, Gwendoline Crockford, was one of the first women police constables in the Berkshire Constabulary in the early 1950s, and so good at her job that, in the mid-1950s, she was the first-ever woman police officer to be sent to the Metropolitan Police Detective Training School at Hendon. She served as the force's only female detective until 1960, when she was promoted, back into uniform, to woman police sergeant. Following an unusually long (for a woman at that time) 11-year career, she left the force when she married my dad, a police constable, in 1962.

How did I come to write my mum's story? When International Women's Day came round in 2017, I wanted to post something on social media celebrating women. Whose achievements needed to be highlighted?

Who had inspired me? Who did I admire? Then it struck me like a lightning bolt – my mum. She was amazing, and I probably hadn't appreciated that enough – until now.

I dug out one of my treasured black-and-white photos of her, and posted it with the caption, "So on International Women's Day, here's a pioneer – the first-ever woman detective in the Berkshire Constabulary – and my mum. If only she was still around to write her memoir, *Call the Sergeant*."

The likes and comments on my post rolled in. My friend Pippa wrote, "OK, sadly she couldn't write *Call the Sergeant*... However, nothing stopping my creative Ruthie from doing so...!!!!"

The seed was sown. I *had* to tell my mum's story. How on earth was I going to do that? Cancer had taken her suddenly and unexpectedly in 2004, and while it had always been my intention to sit Mum down and get her to tell me all about her police career in chronological order, we'd never got round to it.

What Mum *did* leave, however, was a small file of newspaper cuttings, papers, photographs, some books, and – most importantly – the stories she told me, which were seared into my memory from an early age. Mum had had a hotline to Scotland Yard, and rubbed shoulders with the eminent "rock star" pathologists of the day – how cool was that? You see, when you grow up in a police family, you grow up listening to stories. The same stories are told over and over, to anyone who'll listen. They're unforgettable because they're powerful, funny, shocking, rude, sometimes upsetting, and unembellished over time.

I spent thousands of hours in the British Library researching local Berkshire newspapers of the time, and anything about policing Berkshire in the 1950s and 1960s that I could lay my hands on: out-of-print books, journals, academic papers and online forums, to build up as complete a picture as possible of the Berkshire Constabulary (now part of the Thames Valley Police), and my mum's career at that time. What really shocked me was how little was written about 1950s policewomen – footnotes here and there, if I was lucky. It's almost as if they had been airbrushed out of history. This made me even more determined to share the stories Mum told me, set within the context of that fascinating period of British social history when the country emerged from post-war austerity into a social revolution, with the formation of the NHS and the welfare state.

All my memories and research resulted in three books about my mum's astonishing police career. *Calling Detective Crockford* begins in 1956 and follows on from *Calling WPC Crockford* – the story of my mother's WPC years from 1951 to 1955. At the end of that book, we left Gwen, recommended for detective training after identifying a decomposed body *and* for her stellar work pioneering interview techniques for at-risk children, musing, "I wondered what 1956 would bring."

In this second book, we follow Gwen into 1956 when, after some frustrating false starts, she becomes Berkshire's first woman detective. Her CID service (1957 to 1960) spanned an important, but often overlooked, period of social history that took tentative baby steps towards the groundbreaking policy changes of the revolutionary late

1960s regarding the decriminalisation of homosexuality and the legalisation of abortion (1967), and divorce reform and the abolition of capital punishment (1969).

The Wolfenden Committee (1954 to 1957) examined the treatment of gay men and sex workers. Suicide and attempted suicide were still illegal. Teddy boys with their "subversive" rock and roll music and gang fights stuck two fingers up at the crumbling Establishment; and the sun was finally setting on the British Empire.

Be warned – you may find some of this book shocking and upsetting. The treatment of gay men by the police and authorities in the 1950s was truly appalling, there's no getting away from that. I've used the word "homosexual" throughout the book, as although the word "gay" was beginning to be used by the community, its use wasn't widespread then.

Similarly, attempting suicide was a felony that was only decriminalised in 1961. There's an account of an attempted suicide in Chapter 18, the details of which you may find distressing. Mum came across many suicides and suicidal people in her police career, and the memory of every single one stayed with her.

And of course, the maltreatment of children is, tragically, nothing new. Mum investigated child abuse and deaths throughout her career – they were part of her remit as a "specialist in women and children". There was little regard for how repeated exposure to such horrors would affect investigating police officers, and no support.

I have painstakingly and exhaustively researched *Calling Detective Crockford*, but I appreciate that some details may be wrong. From my research and conversations with Mum, I learned that procedures and inter-agency collaborations were much looser back then, and Mum's position as a female detective was unique, so she really could do things her own way.

While *Calling Detective Crockford* is closely based on real events that my mum experienced in the late 1950s, it is a work of storytelling. I have fictionalised the majority of characters and relationships – apart from direct Crockford family members and well-known historical figures. I changed some names, locations, incidents and timescales to protect any relatives and individuals still connected with Wokingham, Newbury, Windsor and Maidenhead. However, much of the events you will read is true, and a reflection of a time long gone. And if you think that some of the stories are a little far-fetched, shocking or incredible, those are probably the true ones.

PART 1

CHAPTER 1

Why on earth did
I become a detective?

Wokingham
January 1956

The Webley .32 revolver felt leaden in my hand as I held it barrel-down by my side. My finger lightly caressed the trigger as I stood, feet planted hips-width apart, rocking slightly, feeling for that midpoint of steadiness and control. My target was well within sight, standing stock-still, and gazing in my direction. It was time to take the shot, but I needed a few more seconds.

WPC Pattie Baxter, standing next to me, breathlessly murmured, "Gwen, you've got to take the shot."

"I know," I murmured back, "but I've only got one chance and I don't want to blow it."

Inhaling, I raised the Webley to my eye line and straightened my arm. Lining up the iron sights and training them on the centre of my target's forehead, I curled my finger back against the trigger. I began to exhale, my breath vaporising in the cold January air.

"He's starting to move! Just do it!" whispered Pattie.

I squeezed the trigger. The shot rang out, the pistol kicked back, and my target fell to the ground backwards, a bullet between his eyes. My best shot yet.

"I can't believe you just did that!" cried Pattie.

"Bullseye." I smiled, and resisted the temptation to blow the vapour theatrically from the barrel.

The tannoy crackled into life. "And with that winning final shot from WPC Crockford, Wokingham police are champions of the Divisional Shooting Competition for the fourth year running."

Cheers and applause broke out among the Wokingham contingent, and the Newbury team shrugged in resignation.

Pattie jumped up and down like a small child who's been told she's going to the funfair. "We did it again, Gwen! Four years in a row!"

You weren't expecting me to be a pistol-packing WPC, were you? I hadn't had the opportunity to mention it before. It was something I'd taken up recreationally in 1952, soon after I joined the force, and I'd built up a reputation as one of the best shots in the Wokingham Police shooting team. Pattie was pretty good too.

"Bit touch and go this year, Pats," I replied. "The wind was wobbling the target and I wasn't sure of my aim."

Our sergeant, Bob Hartwell, a big grin on his face, strode towards us holding the target – a life-size cardboard model with a cartoon Hitler face glued onto it. We used something fun like this for a tiebreaker.

"Got Adolf right between the eyes, Gwen. Well done!" he said, "And you did well too, Pattie. Great shooting from both of you."

"Thanks Bob!" I replied. "We make a good team, don't we? I'm rather liking these revolvers. Firing the real thing rather than the .22 air pistols."

"Yeah – I don't know where the guv'nor got those from. I think the Met might be upgrading their service weapons and we've got their old stock. They do the job, that's for sure."

As always after the Divisional Shooting Competition, we ended up crammed into a police club bar, where Pattie and I hadn't had to buy our own halves of light ale for the last four years. It was comforting and familiar, like having an inky police blanket wrapped round us – the warmth of colleagues following a sporting triumph. All that was about to change this year.

"I hear you're off to Hendon soon, Miss Crockford," said Dick Baker, Newbury's superintendent, offering me a cigarette and lighting it. "We haven't had a woman detective in Berkshire before. Long overdue in the county forces."

At the beginning of the year, at the behest of our own superintendent, I'd attended a CID selection board. I'd had my usual sleepless night beforehand, but it turned out to be more of an informal chat with some top CID brass than an interview.

"We're particularly impressed with the work you did with some local 'problem families', Miss Crockford. Would you like to tell us a little more about that?" asked Detective Superintendent Wilkins.

"Yes, sir," I replied. "I'm afraid my interview technique was a little homespun, getting the children to open up to me by playing with their toys, but it helped unravel an incest case involving their father."

"The Carroll case, sir," added DCI Heath.

"Ah yes, I remember it well," said Wilkins.

"And quite by chance, and an unconnected case, one of the Carroll children had possession of a driving licence that he'd found on a skeletonised body, and this helped us identify the deceased," I explained.

"Sergeant Robertshaw told us about that," said Wilkins, "saying that you're one of the least squeamish people she knows."

Scenes from my WPC years that had tested my strong stomach flashed through my mind: my first post-mortem, which turned out to be on a lady I knew well; removing that skeletonised body from the woods, so decomposed he first broke in half and then his head fell off; processing casualties after the Ascot races lightning strikes; the snot-streaked face of the abusive father finally brought to justice – to name but a few.

"I'm not sure about that, sir," I replied. "I think all us police officers are trained to deal with some pretty dreadful things, and you can never guarantee how you're going to feel when you come across a nasty incident. I will say that I find forensics absolutely fascinating, so I'd always put my hand up to attend a post-mortem."

Wilkins scribbled some notes, chuckling. "I know plenty of teams who'd be grateful to have you, Miss Crockford. Believe me, there are even senior officers who would do anything to avoid attending a PM…" He gave Heath, who avoided his gaze, a significant stare "…but others who love 'em. I'd put you in that latter category."

"Love may be pushing it, sir, but I find it so interesting that I forget about the smells and the fluids and the strange contortions and the wounds as the pathologist gets stuck in."

"Quite, Miss Crockford." Heath wrinkled his nose. "Now answer me one last thing. Why do you want to become a detective?"

Why indeed? I hadn't sought to become a detective, detective work had sought me, with our superintendent suggesting it might be a good thing for me to do. I hadn't really prepared an answer to this question, so I just spoke from the heart.

"I suppose I just want to get to the truth of crimes and misdemeanours, and bring the criminals to justice. Uniform do this as well, I appreciate that, but detectives can go deeper, into more complex investigations. And I also think it's important to put the victim at the centre of any investigation, to remember you're doing it for them. I've found so many victims are inspiring, and I believe getting justice served for them would motivate me to do my best as a detective."

Phew – did I really say all that?

There was a short silence as Heath and Wilkins blinked at me.

"Any particular victims that have inspired these detective ambitions?" asked Heath.

I wasn't ready for this question, but in a split second, and somewhat unwillingly, I was transported back to 1953 and a condemned slum house in Wokingham's Rose Street.

"Yes, sir," I replied. "Miss Robertshaw and I had been called, with a doctor and an NSPCC inspector, to a shocking case of child cruelty. A father – Saul Felton his name was – had systematically beaten, punched and bitten his young sons, Carl and Dennis, black and blue."

Heath and Wilkins exchanged glances as I continued.

"Felton had been put on probation for three years for that, then breached it by beating up his wife Dorothy, although she had asked the Bench to withdraw those charges against her husband, 'for the sake of the children'. I don't feel that justice was done in the Felton case – he really just got a slap on the wrist for the terrible abuse he meted out to his family, and I think he should have received a custodial sentence. The only saving grace for those children is that soon after, Saul Felton left Dorothy, and Wokingham, for another woman. Although I fear for *her*, I really do."

I took a deep breath. I hadn't had to think about the Felton case for a long time, and it still had the power to stir horror and anger in me whenever I did. In my line of work, the sight of every single bruised, terrified child you meet is seared into your memory, and has a habit of popping up to trouble you from time to time.

"We don't always agree with the magistrates' decisions, do we, DCI Heath?" said Wilkins.

Heath rolled his eyes. "Too many do-gooders these days being soft on crime and soft on the causes of crime for my liking," he replied, "although Saul Felton is one of our more, shall we say, *well-known* characters…"

"Do you know where he ended up?" I asked.

"Some council estate in Maidenhead," replied Heath, "but he's kept his nose clean so far. I haven't heard any-thing untoward about him since he's been there."

And long may that continue.

Unfortunately for his new family, as I was to find out, it didn't.

My interview with Wilkins and Heath ended with smiles and handshakes all round. A week later, I'd received a letter saying that I had passed selection board and I was to be on the next training course at Hendon Detective Training School.

In the police club bar after the shooting competition, I replied to Dick Baker, "Yes, sir," before taking a drag on my cigarette. "I'm off for 10 weeks residential at Hendon quite soon."

"I wonder if they're still using Mary?" mused Dick.

"Mary, sir?"

He chuckled. "You'll find out soon enough, Miss Crockford."

I couldn't even begin to imagine who or what "Mary" was, but I was intrigued to meet her.

On the bus back to the police station, Pattie cuddling our trophy, I noticed something glint on her left hand. Two small diamonds and a sapphire adorned her third finger. I hadn't noticed them before, but then I had been wrapped up in the shooting competition. I knew that she'd met a Metropolitan Police officer at her uncle and aunt's pre-Christmas party in Kensington, but I had no idea it had got this serious, this soon.

Pattie saw me looking at her ring, and blushed. "George asked me to marry him on Friday night," she whispered. "We got the ring in Bracher & Sydenham's jewellers in Reading on Saturday."

"Oh congratulations, Pats!" I whispered back. "You don't hang about!"

Hanging about wasn't something that came naturally to Pattie. Still carrying that wartime "live for the moment" attitude that had led so many people to have flings, affairs, trysts and shotgun weddings, she loved being in a relationship. She'd had a few – some riskier than others – during her WPC years with me.

Nowadays, few people would bat an eyelid at a sexually confident single woman serial-dating different men, but Pattie found out the hard way that some men brag about their exploits, and it was all too easy for a WPC to get a reputation that could besmirch her good name. In the uptight 1950s, a reputation as a "station bike" (a repellent expression meaning "because anyone can ride her") could supersede all the great attributes a woman officer had, and stymie her chances of getting on in the police. Pattie had blotted her copybook more than once.

"And we've set the wedding for eight weeks' time," whispered Pattie, her eyes twinkling. "It's only going to be a small family do after the registry office in Hackney near where George is stationed."

"You're definitely leaving the police, then?"

"Yes, I've given in my notice to the superintendent," she replied.

"I guess that means you're going to be moving to London permanently?"

My mind flipped back to a conference for women police we'd been on where some chief constable type posed the question, "What is the most serious occupational hazard in the ranks of the women police?"

Several hands shot up.

"Being beaten up while making an arrest?" suggested one WPC.

"No," said the chief constable type.

"Being sexually assaulted on solo patrol?" asked another.

"No."

"Being run over while directing traffic?" asked yet another.

"Nope. I'm going to have to tell you, aren't I?" He grinned. "It's marriage. Marriage is the most serious occupational hazard for women police."

We looked at each other, trying not to snigger, while some senior women officers from Reading Borough seated behind him on the stage rolled their eyes.

The chief constable type continued, "The risk is never more acute than during the 13-week training period, when fit, healthy, fresh-faced young women are thrown together with fit, healthy, fresh-faced young men at training schools up and down the country, and some, inevitably, forge relationships."

I'd looked at Pattie and she'd blushed beetroot red. She had consummated her feelings for Jim, another PC, during training school, and dated him for a long time after, but he had never proposed marriage.

"But it is you women who generally don't continue with your career when this happens," the chief constable carried on. "Marriage is no longer a bar to the police service. Indeed, we have two married policewomen who have found it possible to continue their duties, er, satisfactorily."

"Well, if that's their major concern about us over and above being assaulted, raped or run over, God help us all," a sergeant from the Oxfordshire constabulary behind us had mumbled.

On the bus, Pattie looked at me, then out of the window. "Yes, I'm leaving, Gwen. I've probably gone as far as I can in this force. I've seen and done enough to understand the job and that will come in really handy when I support George in his job. I think the Met's a lot harder than our cosy little Berkshire Constabulary, so he'll be tireder and more stressed, and I can just do my bit to make it easier for him when he comes home."

I was sorry that Pattie would be leaving. My endearingly clumsy, warm friend I'd known for the last four years, who exasperated me one minute then touched my heart with her sensitivity the next, wouldn't be there to leave her mess in the women's office any more. Thinking about it, I probably wouldn't miss that.

"You'll come up to London and visit us though, won't you?" asked Pattie. "Who knows, I might even get myself a little part-time job as a store detective in one of those posh department stores. I'd know when all the good stuff comes in, and the sales and all that, and we could go on shopping sprees together. After all, once you're a detective you're going to need some smart plain clothes. Are you excited?"

I was certainly excited, and more than a little apprehensive about the detective training. I'd heard the

18

criminal law we had to learn was 10 times harder than the police law we had to learn by rote at training school, and there was advanced self defence and practical sessions. I just hoped I could keep up with the men and not let the women's side down.

CHAPTER 2

Death of a (newspaper) salesman

Windsor with Kinch
Summer 1959

"Smelly Eddie's dead!"

DS Stanley Kinch's deadpan Brummie tones interrupted my concentration on the cheque fraud report I was reading, bringing me back into the reality of the CID office. I'd heard the phone ring, but Kinch's characteristic silence as he listened to the call went on for so long that I had returned to my paperwork. If there was anything important, he would tell me. If there wasn't, he wouldn't.

Turns out, the call *was* important.

"Smelly Eddie?" I replied. "The grubby old newspaper seller who peddles his papers around town in that battered old pram?"

"The very same." Kinch rose from his desk, drew himself up to his full six feet and reached for his jacket.

"He's dead? How? Where?"

"Yep. That was the woodentops[1] on the blower. A bloke walking his dog in the meadows by the railway arches

---

1 CID slang for uniform officers.

found him. Usual scenario – dog ran off, owner followed it, found it under the arch growling at Eddie's body just lying there. He checked for a pulse, but it seems that Eddie was well and truly deceased, so he ran and found the nearest copper. Get your coat, Hepzibah[2], we've got a death to investigate."

It was midsummer, but I knew from experience to take a cardigan and my mackintosh; serious crime scenes always feel cold, whatever the weather.

"And can you grab the bag too? We're going to need it. Hurry up, I'll meet you downstairs."

I stood on tiptoe to reach for our "murder bag", which was kept on top of our tall filing shelf. The murder bag – which was actually a wooden briefcase – was an important piece of our investigation kit. It contained rulers and measuring tape, thermometers, probes, lancets, pliers, rubber gloves and aprons, test tubes, glass boxes, labels, polythene bags, disinfectant... everything you needed to investigate a murder scene, really. I didn't have time to check the contents and just had to hope that those officers who would periodically raid the murder bag for scissors to cut their toenails, or tweezers to pull splinters out of their fingers, had bothered to put them back. There were some finger marks in the layer of dust on the top of the bag, which made me wonder who'd been rummaging recently.

I headed out after Kinch.

We drove in our black unmarked CID Austin to the outskirts of Windsor, where the line of Victorian brick railway arches stretched from the station across the

---

2 You'll find out why he calls me this later.

meadows towards Eton. It seemed to go on forever, like some vast brown caterpillar marching away from the town. As we tramped across the dewy grass in the morning sunshine, noting the weather conditions like the observant detectives we were, we could see a uniform bobby guarding the scene. A ruddy-faced man with a border terrier on a lead stood nearby.

"DS Kinch and WDC Crockford, Windsor CID," said Kinch to the man and our uniform colleague.

"PC Adrian Weir, sir."

"Robert Leigh-Temperley, officers," said the man, shaking our hands.

"I understand, gentlemen, we've got a body in there?" said Kinch.

"Yes, sir," said the PC. "This gentleman found him. It's always been well known to us that Eddie's got a little hideaway out this way where he can shelter from bad weather and store his papers in the dry. We just left him to it. He wasn't doing anyone any harm."

Kinch turned to Robert Leigh-Temperley. "What time did you discover him?"

"About eight-thirty, officer. I'd lost Sparky here in the meadows around eight. I eventually heard him barking and followed him over. He was growling and snarling at something and I thought he might be worrying a rat, but when I got here, I saw it was a little man, lying face down..." Robert's voice caught in his throat. "He... he looked strangely flat, and when I touched his neck to feel for a pulse, he felt stone cold, and that's when I realised he was dead, and I ran to find a policeman. He must have been murdered, mustn't he?"

"We can't draw any conclusions at this stage, sir," said Kinch. "We'd better take a look. WDC Crockford, shall we?" Kinch waved me through as nonchalantly as letting a lady go through a door first.

Leaving PC Weir and Mr Leigh-Temperley outside, we stepped carefully into the gloom of Eddie's hideaway, hands firmly in our overcoat pockets as we conducted the first visual crime scene sweep. Windsor's railway arches were open to the breeze on both sides, and always smelt chalky and fungal, and today this was combined with the sour, greasy, urinary odour of someone unwashed.

Eddie seemed to have built himself a little fortress inside, with what looked like old wooden laths, wood-wormy timbers and ancient tarpaulin, probably scavenged over the years from derelict buildings. It looked neat and felt oddly homely: a moth-eaten tapestry button-back armchair stood next to a tatty square little chest of drawers with a paraffin lamp on top, and a stained, threadbare oriental rug covered the whole of the floor area. Some bundles of newspapers tied with string sat in a corner, next to his old pram, and on top of them some loose *Health and Strength* bodybuilding magazines, their covers featuring muscly men flexing in the great outdoors.

Kinch saw me looking at them. "Clearly he had delusions of giving himself the body beautiful, the daft old sod," he said.

And in the middle of the rug, face down, lay the flat, diminutive body of Eddie, dressed in a grubby shirt and stained tweed trousers, his head pressed against the chest of drawers. Some dark blood had dripped onto the carpet from a cut under his eyebrow.

Kinch kicked him – unnecessarily hard, I felt – with the toe of his boot, then went through the motions of feeling for a pulse in the wrist above Eddie's nicotine-stained fingers, and his neck.

"I'm not expecting to find one," he said. "Looks like rigor mortis has set into his arms and hands."

"So that means he's probably been dead for at least 10 hours?" I asked, remembering Dr Keith Simpson's lecture at training school.

"Looks like it," said Kinch. "And I don't think we're going to have much joy extracting fibres, hairs or skin from under his fingernails. Look how bitten down to the quick they are – nothing would get under those."

We won't need the tweezers and test tubes quite yet, then.

I knelt down to take a closer look at Eddie's face, and spotted a cluster of what looked like tiny grains of rice in the corner of his eye. I flinched as an angry bluebottle buzzed out of nowhere into my face.

"The blowflies have started laying eggs on him already, Stan," I said.

"The sooner we can get him out of here, the better," said Kinch. "Then we can properly search this place."

He went outside to PC Weir.

"Officer, could you get a message to the superintendent and update him, and we'll need a doctor and a photographer down here as soon as possible?"

Shortly after, a small professional hubbub turned up: our police surgeon Dr Welby, a photographer and our guv'nor – portly Detective Inspector Cockerill of Windsor and Maidenhead. A familiar figure waved at me. The photographer was none other than PC Bennett, who had been our clues officer for Wokingham and now worked with the photographic department at Sulhamstead County HQ. He'd graduated to his own vehicle now, no longer having to wobble to crime scenes on his bicycle with a wooden forensics box strapped on the front. He set up a plate camera with a bellows lens on a tripod.

"That's a very modern camera, PC Bennett," I commented.

"All state-of-the-art at HQ now," he said. "We've got technical cameras, enlargers, infrared and ultraviolet ray lamps... You name it, we've got it. Forensics is coming on in leaps and bounds."

Kinch opened the murder bag and took out some chalk. Once Bennett had taken his photographs from various angles, he made some marks around Eddie's body.

"Just so we can orientate ourselves once the body has been removed."

I took out the fingerprint kit, dusted the chest of drawers, the lamp and the pram handle for prints, and Bennett photographed those too. Then we stepped outside again to let the surgeon assess Eddie's body.

DI Cockerill pulled us to one side. "What do you think, chaps?"

"Hard to say at this stage, guv," replied Kinch. "No obvious signs of foul play, and we can't rule out suicide or natural causes until we've been able to PM him, obviously."

"Well, I think it's a case that you two are more than capable of handling between you," said Cockerill. "I'll go ahead and receive the body at the morgue, and we'll take things from there."

Dr Welby came over, peeling off his rubber gloves. "Well and truly deceased, I'm afraid, not that this will come as any surprise. Poor old boy. By his body temperature I would estimate that he died around 11 o'clock last night. I'm not satisfied yet that the cause of death is a natural one, so I'm not going to issue a certificate. You'll need to refer this one to the coroner, officer."

While we waited for the undertakers to arrive, I took a statement from Robert Leigh-Temperley, who'd been good enough to stick around as we went through our procedures. He was signing the bottom of it as the private ambulance approached, bumping across the meadow.

"I'll let you go now, Mr Leigh-Temperley," I said. "Thank you for your help. If we need you again, would you be willing to pop into the police station?"

"Absolutely. Glad I could be of some help, and you catch the blighters who did this."

"Blighters?"

"Those Teddy boy[3] hooligans who are hell-bent on causing disruption and destruction all over the place. You police need to crack down on them much harder than you do. Bloody ridiculous that national service is being wound down now. Spell in the army, like I had, would do all these yobboes the world of good," he spluttered.

"You didn't see anyone out here while you were walking Sparky that would give you that idea, did you?" I asked.

---

3 A youth subculture of the 1950s that embraced Edwardian fashion, Brylcreemed quiffs and US rock and roll music.

"Well, no. But surely it's only a matter of time before those reprobates kill someone."

The private ambulance drew up beside us. Two smartly dressed undertakers got out and unloaded polythene sheeting and a coffin shell.

"What state's the body in?" the older man asked.

"Doc thinks he died last night before midnight," said Kinch. "Minimal blood and gore, but rigor mortis has set in."

The younger undertaker cast a worried glance at his colleague. We watched the undertakers prepare to remove Eddie, Kinch nodding with approval at their professionalism.

"Aww, he's only a little bloke and he's passed away in a fairly straight position," murmured the older man reassuringly to his whey-faced assistant.

I knew exactly what he was referring to: sometimes people died in the strangest of positions before their bodies went into rigor mortis. It was then necessary to "break" the stiff limbs to extract or remove the cadaver, a process that produces slightly nauseating crunching sounds.

The undertakers lifted Eddie's rigid body, keeping him in exactly the same position as he was on the rug, and placed him gently face down in the coffin shell. He fitted perfectly. They then trundled him off to the mortuary.

Kinch and I took the torches out of the murder bag. Mine switched on and illuminated the scene immediately; his made a dead click.

"Bloody hell," he swore and unscrewed the bottom of

27

the torch. "Look! Nothing there! Some bugger's pinched the batteries out of this one... again."

My torch was adequate, and I shone it around Eddie's den. Apart from the blood spots and a damp patch of moisture, presumably urine, on the rug, the place seemed in order. But we did look in dismay at the piles of shattered laths and timbers making up the "walls".

"Will we have to remove all these for examination, Stan?" I asked.

"Not necessarily. We'll examine everything in situ, preserve the scene, and see what the PM reveals. We might not need to toothcomb all this."

I must have let my face look relieved.

Kinch grinned. "But then again, we might have to."

Blood and urine swabbed, the crime scene measured, sketched and examined carefully, and a small bundle of papers, a snuff box and a tobacco pouch removed from the chest of drawers, we were ready to return to the CID office, leaving PC Weir's relief to supervise the boarding up of Eddie's den.

Back in the CID office several hours later, we opened a file for Eddie, and held our first case conference with DI Cockerill and PC Weir.

"So, what do we know about the deceased?" asked Cockerill.

PC Weir put his hand up like a small boy answering an arithmetic question.

"PC Weir, you kick us off."

"Well, sir. Smelly Eddie – I mean, Eddie – has been a fixture in the town for as long as I've been a beat officer.

He, shall we say, didn't pay a great deal of attention to his appearance or personal hygiene, and we sometimes got complaints from members of the public that there was a tramp wandering about. He's not one of the official paper sellers, but he does, I believe, have a valid pedlar's certificate for hawking his newspapers and magazines."

As Weir had been talking, I'd been rummaging through the papers we had removed.

"This is it," I said, holding up a stained, creased piece of paper.

```
BERKSHIRE CONSTABULARY
PEDLAR'S CERTIFICATE No. 720

In pursuance of the Pedlars Act 1871 and
1881, I certify that
Edward Rooke of Sheet Street Windsor in
the Royal County of Berkshire, is hereby
authorised to act as a Pedlar for One Year
from the date of this Certificate.
Description of Pedlar -
Age: 64 Years    Height: 5ft 4in.
Complexion: Swarthy    Eyes: Brown
Hair: Grey    Figure: Slight
Marks: British bulldog tattooed on right arm
Certified this 1st day of January 1959

Signed: The Chief Constable of Berkshire

This Certificate will expire on the
31st day of December 1959
```

"I never knew his surname," said Weir.

"And he has a fixed abode – Sheet Street, Windsor," said Kinch.

"Has he had any brushes with the law before, do we know?" asked Cockerill.

"None of his own making," continued Weir. "A few months back, I remember, PC Collins reported he'd had to intervene when a local Teddy boy gang had been teasing Eddie, taunting him and throwing his papers around. He'd given as good as he got, apparently, for a little bloke, although the yobboes ran off when they saw Collins. Eddie wasn't hurt, and once he'd picked up his papers, he just carried on shuffling along with his pram."

"Teddy boys, eh?" said Kinch, scratching his chin. "Weren't they kicking off over the weekend?"

"Yes, sir, there were some pockets of violence with rival Teddy boy gangs from Cookham, Maidenhead and Windsor fighting in the streets and breaking a few shop windows," said Weir. "And they're not just using their fists any more; one lad got his face slashed with a bicycle chain. And in a nasty new development, some of the Teds have taken to lining the undersides of their velvet coat lapels with fishing hooks. So any rival gang member grabbing another Ted by the lapels finds their fingers impaled on the barbs, unable to move without ripping their skin to shreds, rendering themselves sufficiently stuck and incapacitated to get an up-close thumping."

It took us a couple of moments to appreciate the unpleasantness of this.

"Less Peaky Blinders[4], more Hooky Lapels, then," said Kinch.

"It's all become a far cry from my encounters with the early days of the Teddy boys," I added, "where the worst thing they did was disrupt meetings of the Wokingham Women's Institute by messing about outside the village hall."

"Make no mistake, Miss Crockford, these gangs crossed the line into criminality long ago," said Cockerill.

"Eddie had that cut over his eye," said Kinch. "We didn't see much evidence of bloodstains inside the den, did we?"

"Apart from that one stain on the rug under his eye, no," I said.

"Could it be possible that a gang went out as far as those railway arches and attacked Eddie?" suggested Kinch. "Maybe robbed him? We didn't recover a wallet, purse or watch from the scene, did we?"

"That's assuming Eddie even had a wallet, purse or watch," I replied, "but he must have had some money on him from his newspaper sales. We didn't find any."

"I'm not liking the sound of this," said Cockerill. "As-yet-unexplained head injury, lack of valuables..."

"But no signs of a struggle, sir, and his place didn't look as if it had been ransacked."

"Something still doesn't feel right," said Cockerill, rising from his chair and heading for the door. "I'm going to get on to Scotland Yard and ask if they can

---

4 The Peaky Blinders were a turn-of-the-century Birmingham gang who, legend had it then, stitched razor blades into their peaked caps as illicit weapons.

send down a Home Office pathologist[5] to do the post-mortem on Eddie... Mr Rooke. I don't think we can rule out foul play."

Kinch flicked a cigarette out of the packet and into his mouth, then proffered me one. I'd been gasping for a ciggie all through the meeting, and took a deep draw as he lit it for me with his silver Zippo lighter.

Kinch had a worried look on his face and his shoulders twitched. "You'll be OK attending Eddie's PM for us, won't you, Hepzibah? I think I've got an appointment coming up that I can't miss..."

You don't even know when the PM's happening, Stan. But I do know how squeamish you are...

"Absolutely! Favourite part of my job," I replied. And it was true. I couldn't think of anything I found more fascinating than investigating a human cadaver to determine cause of death. If I hadn't joined the police, I'd have loved to have been a pathologist, but you needed a medical degree to even think about that.

"Do you reckon these Teddy gangs are capable of crossing the line from street fighting to murder?" Kinch asked, blowing the smoke sideways.

"I really hope not," I said. "I guess we'll just have to see what the Home Office pathologist – whoever they send – says after the post-mortem."

---

5 In England and Wales, the Home Office maintains a restricted list of forensic pathologists, with specific qualifications and approved training, to perform autopsies in cases that might result in criminal proceedings, e.g. murders.

CHAPTER 3

Hendon detective training school

January 1956
Hendon, London

It was 5 a.m. and still pitch black when I tiptoed out of Mrs Cunningham's boarding house where I lodged with my friend Suzette McDaniel, an NHS nurse from Barbados. I clicked the door shut and hauled my suitcase, overnight holdall and handbag to the front gate to wait for Henry.

Murdoch Road was silent, the streetlights haloed with fog, as I looked up and down for his car. I shivered despite my woollen overcoat as I stood for a while, deep-breathing in the damp midwinter air to calm my racing heartbeat, when I spotted headlights in the distance. I checked my watch; 10 minutes late.

I had admired PC Henry Falconer from my very first day as a Wokingham WPC back in 1952. A tall, decorated war veteran, we'd been friends and colleagues at the station; we'd grown closer as he recovered from a serious car accident, and worked together on the day of the Ascot Races lightning strike. He'd bared his soul to me one night about a tragic wartime episode that haunted him to this day, and we'd been dating since Christmas.

Henry's Hillman Minx drew up outside Mrs Cunningham's gate. He got out, gave me a hug and loaded my luggage into the boot.

"I'm going to miss you for the next 10 weeks," he said, squinting through the misted-up windscreen at Wokingham's deserted town centre as we drove through it en route to the train station.

"I'm going to miss you too," I replied, "and I'm a bit nervous about what to expect at Hendon..."

"You'll be just fine." Henry chuckled. "Just don't go falling for some dashing Sherlock Holmes type and forget about me, that's all."

He swung the car into the forecourt of Wokingham station and cut the engine, glancing up and down the road.

"Higgsy's on this beat tonight, but I can't see him, so..."

Henry gave me a lingering kiss goodbye. He glanced up and down the road again, and jumped out to offload my luggage. I waved from the station door as he spun the wheels in his haste to get away before the beat officer came along and noted his registration plate as a "car driving during the hours of darkness". Relationships between police officers, while not forbidden, were frowned upon, and we'd kept our courtship very discreet; only my closest friends knew Henry and I were stepping out together, and we kept a professional distance at work.

The early Waterloo train drew into the station. A kindly builder on the platform lifted my heavy suitcase into the train, and I headed towards Hendon. My detective adventure was about to begin.

The Metropolitan Police Training School was situated just across the road from Hendon Airfield. As I walked through the brick-pillared gateway towards an imposing three-storey red-brick Victorian building, I gasped at the sheer scale of the place: vast playing fields, sports courts, lecture theatres, a parade ground, forensic laboratories, a driving school, skid pan...

University must feel like this – a haven of learning, activity, healthy mind, healthy body – that sort of thing. I couldn't wait to step through the porticoed entrance of the college to start my studies.

"CID training, miss?" A man in a mackintosh with a clipboard in his hand beckoned to me. "Round this way!"

"Hello, yes," I replied. "WPC Gwendoline Crockford?"

He consulted his clipboard. "Ah, yes. Follow me."

I trundled my luggage after the man, and as we approached the grand entrance, my heart swelling with pride, he turned a sharp right down the side of the building. I found myself in a tarmacked alley, lined with asbestos-roofed, single-storey prefabricated huts, some dustbins and, bizarrely, a London bus and coach request stop. At the end was a small, squat brick building with a white sign: "DETECTIVE TRAINING SCHOOL OFFICE".

"Go inside and register, Miss Crockford, then you'll be shown to your room."

I queued with three serious-looking men, also in mackintoshes, to fill in some paperwork. Then our greeter led us through the grand entrance into the Victorian building, part of which was a residential block for detective trainees. We trailed through dingy corridors and up some backstairs to a series of rooms along a wide landing.

"And here's your room," the greeter said to the group of three.

"It's nice and big. Charlie, where's yours?" joked one.

"Yeah, where is ours?" asked the other two.

"It's three to a room here, gentlemen," said the greeter.

"You're kidding us? No way are we bunking up together! Not with his bleedin' snoring!"

My own stomach lurched. Sharing a room with a stranger hadn't crossed my mind. Even at Mill Meece Police Training School, where I did my initial 13 weeks basic in 1952, all us girls had our own study bedrooms.

Leaving the three men muttering, I followed the greeter to the end of the corridor.

"This is your room, miss," he said, opening the door to a tiny room with an even tinier window and a narrow bed, wardrobe and desk.

"Afraid you'll be sharing the bathroom with this lot," he jerked his thumb towards the triple rooms behind, "but at least you've got your own space here."

I didn't mind. I was brought up in a family of six sharing a tin bath and an outside lavatory, and we'd had shared bathrooms at Mill Meece. I was just excited to meet the other trainee detectives.

Once I'd unpacked my clothes into the small wardrobe and arranged my reference texts – *Moriarty's Police Law*,

Moriarty's Questions and Answers, *Stone's Justices' Manual* and *The Essentials of Magisterial Law* – on the desk, I was ready to go downstairs. Looking in the mirror, I reapplied my lipstick, tugged down my suit jacket, took a deep breath and stepped out onto the landing.

You've got this, Gwennie.

The three detectives I'd met earlier were coming out of their room.

"Can I follow you down?" I asked.

"Of course, love," said one. "I'm Charlie Haynes from Hertfordshire, and these two reprobates here are Dick Jarvis and Hedley Haddon from Kent."

"Gwen Crockford from Berkshire. How do you do." We shook hands.

"You're a brave lady," said Hedley, "having to put up with all us blokes. But I guess you got used to that as a WPC? I think you'll find we're a bit more civilised in CID."

We assembled in a lecture hall, and I cast my eye around the room filled with men wearing smart suits with ties and waistcoats. Then I noticed some permed dark hair. Another woman was there, deep in easy conversation with some men she seemed familiar with and comfortable around, laughing uproariously and punching their arms. She clocked me looking over at her. I smiled and nodded. She smiled and nodded back, then continued chatting.

There were 28 of us in my class: nine from the Metropolitan Police, two from the City of London and 17 from the southern provincial forces, stretching from Hertfordshire in the north, to Brighton and East Sussex in the south, and Kent and Southend in the east. Twenty-six men and two women.

After a dizzying day of course outlines, introductory lectures in the schoolroom-like hut, and a tour of the Hendon site, it was time for dinner in the cavernous Victorian refectory. Charlie, Dick and Hedley seemed quite convivial company, so I sat with them, opposite some trainees from the Met that included the only other woman, whose name was Irene.

"So you lot are from the county forces, eh?" said one. "Isn't it all catching apple scrumpers over in Kent and chasing runaway cows in Berkshire?"

"Oo arr oo arr, that be rural crime, that be," joked another.

Irene cackled, and I sensed Charlie take a sharp intake of breath.

"Well, I've never chased a cow, but I did once chase a zebra," I said. "I've removed a skeletonised body from woodlands, dealt with the aftermath of the Ascot Races lightning strikes, chased a child sex offender over a weir before he was apprehended, and helped search for Straffen[6] when he escaped from Broadmoor..."

I paused. Six pairs of eyes were staring at me, and six mouths hung open.

"Straffen? And the Ascot lightning? You were involved with those?"

"Urgh! What was it like handling a decomposed body?"

6 John Straffen was a notorious serial child murderer who escaped from Broadmoor hospital in April 1952 and murdered another little girl in the four hours he was out.

"Where on earth did a zebra come from?"

The questions came thick and fast, and very soon The Met versus provinces preconceptions broke down as we shared our respective local experiences of policing. The Kent boys dealt with ports and smuggling, Hertfordshire had more than their fair share of London criminals on the run, and Irene was highly experienced with runaways and East End prostitutes, or "Toms" as she called them. She even knew Lottie, my friend from training school who was now a woman police sergeant in a big London station.

There was a lot to fill up 10 weeks of training. Our required knowledge of criminal law went deeper than anything I'd needed in uniform, and I regularly gave myself headaches studying beyond midnight in my little room. Lectures also delved deeper into their subjects than uniform training, and CID was a lot more grown up than uniform.

Sex Crime Week at Mill Meece had been uncomfortable, as our immature, sniggering male trainee PCs had seemed more interested in us WPCs' reactions to the subject matter than the matter itself, whereas I sensed nearly everyone at Hendon had had some sort of dealings with such crimes. The lecture on incest drew some gasps and head shakings of disbelief, yet this was familiar territory for me, having brought an incestuous father to justice in 1954.

Being homosexual in 1956 was still illegal, and our spluttering, red-faced lecturer didn't even try to hide his prejudice. "What you need to remember is that the homosexual practices of buggery and gross indecency –

despite what Mr Wolfenden[7] and his cronies would try to have us believe – are still indictable misdemeanours under the Criminal Law Amendment Act 1885, Section 11. Whether behind closed doors, in dubious pubs and clubs, in the bushes or around public lavatories, we must continue to crack down on this perversion!"

As he ranted on, I gazed out of the window and my mind drifted back to an incident in my childhood, when I was 12. I had been to Wokingham Library and borrowed a book of Oscar Wilde's short stories, which I devoured in a single afternoon, hiding in the bedroom. I had read the final paragraphs of *The Happy Prince* in floods of tears.

> *"What a strange thing!" said the overseer of the work-men at the foundry. "This broken lead heart will not melt in the furnace. We must throw it away." So they threw it on a dust-heap where the dead swallow was also lying.*
>
> *"Bring me the two most precious things in the city," said God to one of His Angels; and the Angel brought Him the leaden heart and the dead bird.*

The moving story of the friendship between a little swallow who would never fly south for the winter and the fading statue of a young prince touched me like few other stories ever had, and I found myself ugly-crying at the ending, when my mother came into the bedroom to strip our beds.

---

7 The Wolfenden Committee was set up in 1954 to make recommendations about the laws governing homosexual offences and prostitution. The Wolfenden Report, published in 1957, recommended that private homosexual activities between consenting adults over 21 should be decriminalised, but it was not until 1967 that these recommendations were enacted in law.

"There you are, Gwendoline!" she snarled. "Wasting your time reading again? And what are you snivelling about?" She snatched the book out of my hand and screwed her face up in disgust. "No wonder – it's by that disgusting man!"

"But it's Oscar Wilde, Mum! Why is he disgusting?"

She had already stomped off downstairs with my book, intending to return it to the library that afternoon. I lay on my bed, still weeping from the impact of that ending, and wondering how on earth someone who could write such beautiful stories would be a disgusting person.

Undeterred, the next time I was in Wokingham Library, I thought I would ask the new young librarian.

"Miss Marsh, you know Oscar Wilde?"

"Yes, dear, I do."

"My mum says he was a disgusting man. Why would she say that?"

Miss Marsh hesitated, clearly choosing her words, before lowering her voice.

"I think, dear, knowing your mother, it's because Oscar Wilde was a… a… *homosexual*."

"A what?"

"A homosexual. He loved other men."

Someone coughed in the queue that had built up by the issues desk and Miss Marsh turned away to deal with them.

So he loved other men. But that's a nice thing, not disgusting.

The only person left to ask was my dad, who was in the garden, pruning roses.

"Dad?"

"Yes, Gwennie?"

"What's a homosexual?"

Dad's secateurs halted mid-cut. Colour rose in his face and his jaw twitched.

"Don't ask me to ask Mum because she won't tell me," I ventured.

Dad puffed out his cheeks. "Homo... means man."

I looked at him blankly.

"HOMO... MEANS MAN!" he almost screamed at me. I sensed a potential flashpoint and walked away, leaving him to his roses and me none the wiser.

And that's all I really knew about homosexuality before I joined the police force in 1951 and found out it was a crime, punishable by up to two years' imprisonment.

We learned many practical skills at Hendon, one of which was to identify suspects with only a description to rely on. To do this, we stood in a circle on the parade ground while several volunteer "criminals", only one fitting the exact description, ambled round us.

Could it be that woman? She has a blue handbag, but her shoes are brown, not black. Here's another woman with a blue handbag and black shoes, but she's a redhead, not a blonde. Now, here's a blonde lady with black shoes and a blue handbag but she's tiny and the description said she was "very tall". At last! A tall blonde with a blue handbag and black shoes... Bingo!

"Excuse me, madam, may I ask you to turn out your coat pockets?"

I thought of PC Bennett as we visited the Forensic Science Laboratory. He loved the forensic part of the job as much as I did, and I scribbled him a postcard telling him how modern science can match fibres and particles, identify bloodstains as human not animal, and the incredible things that glow under ultraviolet light.

The ballistics demonstration fascinated us; we learned how scratches on a fired bullet matched unique markings inside a firearm's barrel.

"So when we recover a weapon," said our expert, "I fire a bullet from it, point blank, into a box of wadding, like this…"

We jumped as he discharged a handgun into an impossibly small wooden box.

"We then compare my sample bullet to one recovered from the crime scene – or body – using this double microscope," he'd explained. We all peered down the microscope. "If they match, we've got our murder weapon."

The Fingerprint Department was like taking a journey into the Dark Arts. As a WPC, I'd smugly thought I knew all about the loops, whorls, arches and composite features of fingerprints, but I had no idea these had to be analysed and formulated. We blinked in sheer incomprehension as our teacher covered the board with a mess of fractions.

"…but the total of possible combinations is 32 squared, and our fraction formula does not cover the possibility of 10 fingers with no whorls at all, or 0/0. For convenience, we write this as 1/1 and add 1 to the final numerator and denominator in all other cases…" he explained. He may as well have been speaking Mandarin.

"Thank God there are people out there who understand this bloody stuff, as I sure as hell don't," whispered Charlie, and I had to bite my cheeks to stop myself laughing.

In the days before computers, the humans, or should I say superhumans, of the Fingerprint Department could take a crime scene fingerprint photo and somehow match it with any one of a million and a quarter other fingerprint images held in the collection. It was a miracle of eyesight, memory and filing, and I still don't know to this day how they did it.

We had much more fun investigating mock-up crime scenes. At last, I got to meet Dick Baker's legendary Mary, the Met's Most Murdered Mannequin. Mary was really a glorified shop dummy representing a murder victim. She could be reported dead anywhere on the Hendon training school site – in a copse, on a road, at the foot of a fire escape, down a back alley – and, in pairs, we had to investigate.

With a detective inspector trainer, Hedley and I were called out to Mary's murder scene, driven there in a CID vehicle with a rudimentary "murder bag". We screeched off to a thin copse of trees just behind a prefab building where Mary was lying primly on her back, clothes intact, a splodge of red paint on the back of her head. Today's forensics officers would be horrified as we were encouraged to rush up to her body, trampling the scene.

"Crockford, will you send for the doctor immediately?" ordered the trainer. "And I need a photographer, and alert the chief inspector, and I want some ropes round her to secure the scene." We scurried about, and a "photographer" arrived and set up his tripod.

"Well, well, well, what do we have here?" Hedley pointed at an incongruous patch of mud on the otherwise dry ground that had a huge, obvious footprint in it.

"Cue the plaster of Paris for a footprint cast." I sighed, pulling a ring mould out of our murder bag.

"Good of the killer to leave us a bucket of plaster mix just next to the murder scene." Hedley laughed as I placed the ring mould round the footprint, sprayed it with fixative and mixed up and poured the plaster provided onto it.

As it set, we examined the crime scene. I found some short, blond, upholstery horsehair glued to a low-hanging tree branch, and 20 feet away, Hedley discovered a lump of wood with a blob of red paint on it.

"I think we can deduce Mary was beaten to death with a stick by a Palomino pony," I whispered to Hedley.

"Wearing size 12 wellingtons." He giggled.

At dinner that evening, we compared notes with our fellow trainees.

"Poor old Mary was the victim of a sex maniac for us yesterday," said Charlie. "She was left behind the dustbins, clothing ripped and covered in wallpaper paste."

We screwed up our faces in disgusted amusement at the technicians' resourcefulness.

"I wouldn't want to come across the bloke who could produce that lot," added Dick, and we laughed and laughed, although it wouldn't be remotely funny in real life. Because Mary was for crime scene investigation only, with no follow-up; she was a mannequin for whom justice was never served.

"Have I got a treat for you all this morning," gleefully announced our inspector about halfway through our course. "A day trip to New Scotland Yard's Black Museum!" He cackled like Vincent Price doing a Hammer Horror voiceover, which didn't help.

I was a little apprehensive about the legendary Black Museum. It was purported to have all manner of murder weapons, gruesome photographs, things pickled in jars and killers' death masks[8], with all the evil auras that surround such artefacts. I wasn't sure how I'd feel being in the presence of that much malevolence.

We got off the bus in front of the ugly Victorian pile on the Thames Embankment that was New Scotland Yard, trooped inside, and down to the basement rooms. As we walked down the stairs, the air became warmer and dustier, and my palms sweatier. I could barely hold the pen to sign into the visitor's book.

Nowadays, museum curators create for their visitors an engaging journey and narrative with their artefacts. Whoever collated The Black Museum was firmly in the stuff-it-all-in-glass-cases-or-bung-it-on-the-wall camp. Cramped, glazed table cases held disjointed displays of burglars' implements, forged money and forgery equipment, poisoners' pestles and pill boxes. From the ceiling hung housebreakers' rope ladders and hangmen's nooses. Photographs of unfortunate victims, including women murdered by Jack the Ripper, jostled

8 Likenesses of dead people's faces, made from wax impressions or plaster casts of the corpse.

for space next to portraits of infamous killers. On a shelf above cases crammed with flintlock pistols, a row of death masks of hanged criminals, including Heinrich Himmler, gazed blankly at all this clutter. People talk of the "banality of evil", and this was it. Stuff in a basement with no narrative, the means to lots of historic unpleasant ends. With a sense of anticlimax, we all got on the bus back to Hendon.

At Mill Meece, the closest we got to death was attending a morgue to be shown a deceased elderly lady. At Hendon, we went a step further, naturally. One of our guest lecturers was the rock star Home Office pathologist Dr Keith Simpson, who had been the expert witness for many high-profile murders since the 1940s. He was a particular hero of mine, and I had a bit of a crush on him.

He would always open his lectures with the same line, "Well, you have only come to see my dirty pictures, so let's get on with them!" before giving the most absorbing talk about some famous murder case, or his pioneering work on forensic dentistry.

So, it was as if all my Christmases had come at once when we were invited to Guy's Hospital to watch Dr Simpson perform a post-mortem. Some of the trainee detectives mysteriously came down with "tummy bugs" the night before our visit to Guy's, so my depleted party only included Charlie, Hedley and Irene, who were uncharacteristically subdued on the way to the hospital.

"Anyone been to a post-mortem before?" asked Charlie.

Everyone but me shook their heads.

"The first one I went to was a lady I knew," I said, to murmurs of sympathy. "One of my neighbours. Poor soul had psychiatric issues and hanged herself."

"So what's a post-mortem like, then?" asked Irene. "I can't say I'm looking forward to it."

"It's absolutely fascinating!" I enthused. "The one thing you have to get over is the smell. Human bodies, no matter how fresh they are, always smell pretty disgusting, like gone-off pork left out of the fridge too long. Then there's the lymph fluid, stomach and bowel contents, congealed blood... but you'll find it so interesting you'll soon forget about that."

In the white-tiled mortuary of Guy's Hospital, the neat, dome-headed figure of Dr Keith Simpson greeted us. My heart raced in the presence of such greatness, and I blushed beetroot red. He pulled the sheet off the plump, naked body of a middle-aged man.

"This gentleman collapsed and died suddenly in the street yesterday, and it's now my job to find out why, and tell you why too."

Charlie managed to stay in the autopsy room for the Y-incision, and up to the point where Dr Simpson lifted the clipped-off ribcage to expose the internal organs. Hedley tried his hardest to tough out the stomach contents, but those tested even me.

"Well, good to know this gentleman enjoyed a hearty meal before his demise." Dr Simpson's eyes twinkled. "As you can see, he had clearly eaten a large roast dinner with carrots, peas and what looks like apple pie and custard."

Hedley exited, his hand over his mouth, and Irene moved away from the overflowing kidney dish, retching.

"Time to look at the brain now."

Dr Simpson made an incision and peeled the scalp down over the man's eyes, like a rubber mask.

I felt Irene swaying next to me and grabbed her arm. "Deep breath," I whispered, and she nodded, eyes closed.

Dr Simpson sawed off the top of the cranium, exposing pink brain tissue and a dark red mass of what looked like bramble jelly sitting on its surface.

"Aha!" he exclaimed. "I think it's fairly safe to say that a particularly large subdural haemorrhage has caused this gentleman's death." After some snipping, there was a sucking sound as he eased the wobbling brain and its blood clot out of the skull. "Ladies! Here we see the most complex object in the universe, the human brain. Or as I like to call it, magical blancmange."

"I'm never going to eat pink custard and jam ever again," murmured Irene.

As the mortuary technician slopped all the innards back inside the cadaver and began to stitch up the Y incision with thick thread, we had a few moments to chat with the great man.

I have never forgotten his parting words: "As a pathologist, I have to remember that I am hugely privileged. I'm the last person to properly look at someone deceased, to take in their curves and imperfections, their operation scars and moles, any tattoos and physical vestiges of what life threw at them. I see only a snapshot of a person's life, but it's an important snapshot. And this is why every deceased body must be treated with the utmost respect."

Ten weeks of detective training flew by, and we sat our final examinations in the theory and practice of criminal investigation. All of us passed, and it was time to bid farewell to Hedley, Charlie, Dick and Irene and disperse to our respective police forces, promising to write to each other. As I sat on the train back to Wokingham, I couldn't wait to put everything I'd learned into practice.

CHAPTER 4

Back to Wokingham

Wokingham

Spring 1956

I'd only been away for 10 weeks, but Wokingham station felt different as I walked through the main door the first morning back. It felt like coming back to school in September; the building and the headmaster (The EF[9]) were the same, but you had different responsibilities, a new curriculum and gaps where some classmates had left. Absent were Pattie, who was enjoying newly married life in Bermondsey with her Met officer, and Sergeant Lamb, our gruff-but-avuncular station sergeant.

On the front desk instead was newly promoted Sergeant Willoughby. I had never seen this grey-faced officer smile, even when I'd done my probationary tour with him in 1952, so he was a strange choice to be Wokingham's public-facing front-of-house man.

"Sergeant Lamb in today?" I asked him. I'd been looking forward to seeing Lamby.

"Haven't you 'eard?" mumbled Sergeant Willoughby. "'e took early retirement because of ill health a month or so ago. Some sort of lung disease."

---

9 Superintendent Barker – nicknamed "The EF", short for "Eternal Flame" – because he never went out.

Poor Lamby. Puffing on 40 Woodbines a day since 1914 had probably done him no favours healthwise, and with the government sitting on the fence about any link between smoking and lung cancer, most of us puffed away too, in blissful ignorance.

I had a choice to turn right into the CID office, but instead turned left into the women's office to check in with my sergeant, Miss Robertshaw. Variously described as "fearsome", "tough but fair" and "Genghis Khan" (by Pattie, who else?), she was a formidable policewoman who didn't suffer fools or small children gladly. We worked surprisingly well together, probably because I liked small children, and still had some tolerance for fools, freeing her up to tackle the knottier cases. And I had a lot to thank her for – she had recommended me for detective training, after all.

Miss Robertshaw sat at her desk, a sea of paperwork and several empty teacups in front of her, rubbing her eyes.

"Ah, Miss Crockford," she greeted me, "our very own female sleuth returns! How was Hendon?"

We chatted for a while about my detective training – the thrill of meeting Dr Keith Simpson, the anticlimax of the Black Museum, and the unlikelihood that a real-life murder victim would in any way resemble Mary the Met's Most Murdered Mannequin.

"What's been happening while I've been away, miss?" I asked. "What's all this?" I pointed to the papers covering the desk.

Miss Robertshaw sighed. "If you'd been here, you'd probably have been dealing with this one with me.

Nasty, nasty case of interfering with a 13-year-old girl," she explained. "The girl and her mother came in to report that an old man had attempted to have carnal knowledge[10] with her in the woods behind his house while she was playing there with a friend. Here's the statement I took."

I braced myself for what I was about to read. In my experience, children's statements were often unflinching in their detail.

SG: So there we was, playing in the woods behind the big house. Me and Marlene were building a den and Marlene had gone off to get some more big sticks for the walls. I saw the man on the other side of the hedge. He looked over and called to me. "Hello there, young lady! What's your name?" I told him, then he squeezed through a gap in the hedge and came over to me. He looked around and said, "Are you here on your own?" I said, "No my friend is coming back soon." Then he bent right down, kissed me on the mouth, unbuttoned his trousers and…

I shuddered as I read her account of what happened next. How dare he?

SG: I think he saw Marlene coming towards us with the sticks because he jumped away, doing up his buttons. I was very frightened and embarrassed and pulled my dress back down. Then he gave me 4s. and said, "Thank you. Give two of these to your friend." Then he went back through the gap in the hedge into his garden.

---

10 An archaic term for rape, used by the police until the 1950s.

"Marlene's statement corroborates hers," added Miss Robertshaw. "And of course we had to get her physically examined by a doctor." She handed me another report.

I examined this young girl seven days after the alleged incident, and found her to be virgo intacta, i.e. there was no evidence that carnal knowledge had taken place. As a week had passed since the incident, it would be impossible to detect if physical contact of a lesser degree had happened, although something could have – that cannot be ruled out. Signed Dr J Wickes, GP.

"You know, the carnal knowledge charge won't stick with this medical evidence," I said. "Offences against the Person Act 1861, Section 63. We would need proof of penetration."

"You can tell you're all fresh out of Hendon and able to remember your Acts and Sections," said Miss Robertshaw, giving a rare laugh. "Poor girl probably didn't have a clue what was happening. I think we'll be looking at a lesser charge of indecent assault."

"And why don't we have a female doctor to examine girls in cases like this?" I asked. "Dr Wickes is a kind man, but I can't help feeling that we really should have a woman."

"I've been on at Berkshire health services for ages," said Miss Robertshaw. "They keep telling me we don't have enough cases like this to justify having a dedicated woman doctor in the county. Anyway, want to read the accused's statement?"

"Yes. Who is the accused, anyway?"

My eyes widened as Miss Robertshaw told me who he was. He couldn't have been a bigger pillar of the community: a high-ranking wartime leader, distinguished colonial officer, and an active member of every local organisation from the Conservative Association to the Boy Scouts.

"I would never in a million years have had *him* down as someone who interfered with children[11]!" I exclaimed, aghast. I usually had a pretty good radar for creeps, and it hadn't picked him out. "Why would he besmirch a distinguished reputation by doing something as stupid as this?"

Miss Robertshaw narrowed her eyes. "I think it's precisely because he's such a pillar of the community that he thinks he can get away with it. His word against a 13-year-old girl's? Either that, or he has such a sense of entitlement that he thinks his friends in high places will protect him. And this isn't the first time that he's been done for indecent behaviour."

"Really? He's done it before?"

"I checked him out with the Criminal Records Office. In 1950 he was convicted of indecent exposure, but got an absolute discharge, and some medical treatment to 'curb his exhibitionist urges'."

"Well that worked," I said.

"And an escalation from indecent exposure to attempted carnal knowledge," added Miss Robertshaw. "It pains me when I see people making light of indecency, as it can be a gateway to more serious sexual offences."

---

11 This was the term for child sex offender used in the 1950s.

"Flashing can be incredibly upsetting," I added, remembering the victims of indecent exposure I had taken statements from.

"Quite. Well, first of all he denied everything; then he claimed the girls had only asked him for sweets, and as he had no sweets, he gave them money; then this." She handed me a statement.

GR-W: I was trimming the back hedge with shears when I heard a female voice saying, "Mister! Hello, mister!" I looked over the hedge and there was a girl there calling to me. I said, "Hello, what's your name?" And she told me. Then she said, "Do you want to know a secret?" And just to humour her, I went through the gap in the hedge and said, "All right then." She beckoned me over, and made to whisper in my ear. I bent down to listen to her, and she made an indecent suggestion... "Did I fancy a bit?" "Well," I said, "how do you know about things like that?" and she replied, "I've done it loads of times, how about it?" Then she kissed me, pulled up her dress, grabbed at my trousers and tried to force herself on me. She only stopped when another girl approached. Well, of course, I didn't want these types hanging around so I gave them some money, hoping they would go away.

"Hmm..." I said. "He's now blaming her! A 13-year-old girl trying to seduce a crusty old general? His story's unravelling, isn't it? A decent prosecution should pick it apart further."

"I think it will get sent to a higher court," said Miss Robertshaw. "But he's got a lot of friends in high places who will no doubt put their two pennyworth in about what a sterling character he is. We've got until July before he appears in court again – Inspector Beeton has asked for a remand, giving us time to prepare, and the man's on bail until then. I'll let you know how it goes."

"Anything I can help with?" I asked.

"We've pretty much done the legwork on this one," said Miss Robertshaw, "but I'll try and wangle you witness escort duty on the day, maybe accompanying Marlene. I'll be accompanying the complainant myself. I just hope the defence doesn't tear her to pieces. Now, much as I'd love to chat all day, I know DI Dankworth is keen to see you." She turned back to her papers.

I knocked on the door of the CID office.

"Come," droned a monotone from within.

Larry Dankworth sat with his feet up on the desk, riffling through some files, a cigarette hanging from the corner of his mouth.

"Crockford! You're back! Now we're all detectives together, I can call you Gwen." He hesitated, looking for a reaction. "But you can still call me 'sir', haha!" I must have looked blankly at him. "Only joking. I think we've known each other long enough to be on first name terms, don't you think?

"Yes, sir... I mean, Larry... sir." *This felt weird.*

"Congratulations on graduating from Hendon. Are they still using that... what was she called... Martha the Murdered Model?

"Mary? Yes, they are. She'd been bludgeoned to death for us."

"Aha! She'd been shot dead at the top of a fire escape when I was training. Had to retrieve a bullet and get ballistics involved and everything. Fascinating."

It was actually great to talk to someone else who had been through Hendon, and we exchanged stories enthusiastically. When I was a WPC, I'd found Larry Dankworth to be a bit of an ass, full of himself, at first. He wasn't a terrible detective; he listened to other people more now, and I had warmed to him a little more over the years.

"So, Gwen, I expect you're wondering what you're going to be doing now you've passed detective training?"

I was. I'd mentally said farewell to my uniform and bought a couple of expensive, smart grey skirt suits, and shoes I could run in.

"Yes, I'm really looking forward to CID."

"Well, as you know, with Chief Constable Waldron's police budget cuts, detective constable positions are as rare as hens' teeth in Berkshire. The simple fact is, there are no vacancies for another DC – either male or female."

"So, what does that mean?" I felt my shoulders sinking.

"I've talked to Superintendent Barker and WPS Robertshaw, and the consensus is that we're going to share you!"

Hmmm. She didn't mention that.

"So, for some cases you'll be working alongside me as an aide in plain clothes, and others you'll be working with Miss Robertshaw in uniform. You'll be doing fewer uniform patrols, as Miss Robertshaw would like to get another WPC, if budget allows."

So, even though I had been through all that detective training, I wasn't a proper detective yet, and it didn't sound as if I would be a proper WPC either. I'm not sure that Wokingham police really knew what to do with me – I was an anomaly after all – but at least I was continuing to have CID involvement. And Waldron was a brute with his cuts. Whereas WPCs of my 1951 vintage had been taught and encouraged to drive, Waldron stopped that, and any women police who joined during and after 1954 had to walk, cycle or hitch lifts.

I'd said to Mum and Dad that I would pop in and see them in Seaford Road after my first day back at work. I'd figured I would be in a really good mood and able to tolerate Mum's inevitable barbed remarks, but the truth was I felt a little deflated about my indistinct status. All I really wanted to do was go straight back to my lodgings and have a cup of tea with Suzette. But never one to shirk the "Honour thy father and mother" edict from Sunday School, I felt duty-bound to keep my appointment.

The front door was on the latch, so I walked in. "Cooee! Hello! Only me!"

Mum was in the scullery clearing away their tea things. She had, as Dad would say, "a mouth like a rat trap", so they had either just had a row or were about to have one.

"You're early," said Mum. "Wasn't expecting you until later."

"I got out of the station on time today." I went to give her a kiss on the cheek, but she moved and I ended up pecking her ear instead.

"How have you been, Mum?"

"None the better for your asking," she grumbled, and launched into her usual catalogue of gastrointestinal complaints, things my sisters had done wrong, the things my brother had done right, and the rising prices of food.

"Eggs have gone back up again."

"It's the chickens I feel sorry for, then."

Nothing. Not even a twitch of a smile.

I heard Dad clumping down the stairs and into the front parlour, followed by a woody waft of Palmolive aftershave, a scent from my childhood that signified one or both of my parents were going out, out.

I followed him into the front room. Dressed in a white shirt and black tie, he was rummaging in the dresser for his rectangular briefcase.

"Hello, Dad! Off out to a lodge meeting?"

"Hello, Gwennie!" Dad stumbled up from his squatting position, knees cracking, briefcase in hand.

"I'm dining there after the ceremony tonight, but don't tell your mother," he whispered. "How was your detective training?"

As Dad checked his masonic regalia of a square apron, pointed collar and jewels, and slipped a square and compasses signet ring onto his little finger, I told him all about Hendon and my disappointment that I'd have to wait for a DC position to come up.

"Something will turn up, love. The constabulary will want to get their money's worth having spent all that on training you."

"I hope so, Dad."

Mum stomped in. "You never told me you were out tonight, Wally?"

"I did, Aggie. Told you on Tuesday. And it's in my diary."

"Well, I never check your diary, do I? You and that wretched pinny club! You spend more time there doing funny handshakes and boozing in the bar than you do here. That bathroom tap has been dripping for a month and I keep asking you to change the washer. Call yourself a plumber?"

"Ah, give it a rest, Aggie. You don't complain when you get to go a classy dinner dance at our Ladies' Night, do you? A chance to hobnob with the posh wives of the great and the good of Wokingham – you love all that…"

And they were off. Like a spectator at Wimbledon, my head flicked from side to side as I watched the verbal brickbats fly. Not being able to get a word in to intervene, I tiptoed into the hall and took my mac off the coat stand.

"Well, I am bloody going out and that's final!" roared Dad, grabbing his jacket and hat.

"I'll walk with you as I need some fresh air," I said, feeling the need to go and sit in peaceful Joel Park for a while, as well as having Dad to myself for a few minutes. "Bye, Mum!" All I heard was the bedroom door slam shut.

Walking along Westcott Road, Dad's puce face returned to its usual colour.

"I'll swing for your mother one day, I swear I will," he huffed.

"Honestly, just don't rise to it, Dad. She just wants a row to let off some frustration."

"I'm damned if I know what she's got to be frustrated about, Gwennie. Nice home, four grown-up kids, husband in a job, Mother's Union and church. Honestly, sometimes I think she's deliberately trying to drive me round the bend. You know, like that film where Charles Boyer cuts Ingrid Bergman off from her friends, then tries to drive her insane and get her put into a mental asylum so he can get his hands on her jewellery?"

"*Gaslight*?"

"Yeah, that's the one."

"Firstly, Dad, you're no Ingrid Bergman. And secondly, you don't have any valuables."

We laughed at last.

"Anyway, what's this freemasonry thing all about? What do you actually do?"

"If it's good enough for Churchill, it's good enough for me," he said, chin jutting. "You've probably heard that we bare our breast, roll up a trouser leg and meet in a pitch-black room with a swordsman guarding the door? Well, yes, we do. But the craft also develops our moral fibre, helps us be better people, with civic responsibilities. And we do a lot for charity."

I wanted to delve deeper into what Dad was saying – *how* did it develop "moral fibre"? – but we were nearly at Wokingham Masonic Centre. He skipped across the road with a "Cheery-bye, Gwennie," to join his brethren. I recognised most of the men filing in: a butcher, a baker and a candlestick maker (honestly), several senior Wokingham policemen, a few old colonel types, some bods from the council and corporations, and finally, slimy Basil Gill; one of those types who had a finger in every local pie.

I had a personal reason to dislike Basil Gill – he had complained to the hospital authorities about my housemate Suzette nursing his father-in-law, saying he would be more comfortable with an "English" nurse rather than her. With his thin moustache and combover hair, there was just something about him that made my creep radar blip. Call it a detective's hunch.

CHAPTER 5

Needy, greedy or bored

Wokingham
1956

So. Much. Shoplifting.

When I look back on that funny old year of 1956, I must have spent most of my time dealing with shoplifters. It was a crime as old as shops themselves, but it was having a post-war resurgence with the new ways of shopping. When traditional shops had counters with the goods on shelves behind them, and the grocer, baker or tailor served you individually, there was little or no opportunity to steal things. And maybe the assistant's friendly face and eagle eye had made people less inclined to thieve.

The fifties brought American-style self-service shops and supermarkets to Berkshire, with their wide aisles and opulent displays of goods stacked high, just waiting to be hand-picked and dropped into wire baskets, trolleys, pockets, or in the case of my first shoplifter, somewhere else.

"Can you go to the Pioneer Supermarket, Miss Crockford?" asked Miss Robertshaw. "I've just had a call from the manager. Their store detective has apprehended a woman shoplifter."

Rarely would us police do observations for shoplifting, even in plain clothes. In a small town like Wokingham, we would be far too recognisable. Most of the new self-service stores belonged to chains and employed their own store detectives who travelled between the branches, and even the managers often wouldn't know who was coming or when.

The Pioneer's front-till cashier escorted me through to the manager's office at the back where a tough-looking woman in a headscarf towered over another woman, short and tubby, almost as wide as she was tall, and wearing a voluminous buttoned overcoat that made her look upholstered.

Mr Pritchard, the manager, sat behind his desk. "Ah, there you are, officer," he said. "Thank you for coming. Mrs Donaldson, our store detective here, observed this woman – a Mrs Clark - moving round the store taking various items off the shelves and pushing some of them inside her coat. She paid for the cauliflower and bag of sugar in her basket at the till, then she left the store, and that's when we apprehended her outside."

Mrs Clark peered at me through dusty pebble spectacles.

"I aint got nothin' under me coat." She unbuttoned it and flashed it open to reveal nothing but a bobbly beige jumper and a long, gathered skirt. There were no deep inside pockets to conceal things in either.

Mr Pritchard flashed a concerned look at the store detective. "You are 100 per cent certain you saw this lady secreting items about her person, aren't you?"

"Absolutely, I am."

I could understand Mr Pritchard's concern. If they had wrongfully detained an innocent customer, the reputational and financial damage of any legal action would far outweigh the value of any pilfered goods. This need for certainty was why so many shoplifters got away with it.

"Well, you're wrong, and I shall be speaking to me son about this," said Mrs Clark. "He's in the law, you know."

I was about to say something when we heard a muffled snap and some thuds. A tin of peaches rolled out from underneath Mrs Clark's skirt. Huffing, she stepped backwards to reveal a parcel of pork chops, and a packet of dried peas on the floor.

"Have you got anything else under there you'd like to tell us about?" asked Mr Pritchard.

She pulled up her skirt to reveal a pair of old-fashioned bloomers like my granny used to wear, the elastic on one knee dangling down, and the other leg bulging with groceries. She reached down through her elasticated skirt waist into the bloomers and extracted a pound of sausages, two pairs of nylons and a strawberry mousse.

"That's where she'd been putting them!" said the store detective.

The woman started to cry. "It 'asn't been the same since my 'usband died. It ain't easy making ends meet these days. We was 'ungry."

Tragic figure that this lady presented herself to be, I had no choice but to escort her back to the station and charge her, to appear before the magistrate the next morning.

"Well done on bringing in that 'needy', Miss Crockford," said Miss Robertshaw.

"Needy?"

"Mrs Clark. In my experience, shoplifters fall into three categories: needy, greedy or bored. You can tell by the sorts of things they steal. Your lady just now really only stole necessities – some food and some nylons."

"Although she was clearly a habitual shoplifter who had adapted her clothing to facilitate her pilfering," I added. "She wasn't destitute."

"Sometimes it's more psychological. I'd say she was needy, and the magistrate will probably be quite kind to her. Greedies tend to pinch luxury items – chocolates, potted shrimps, sirloin steak, that sort of thing. They can afford enough food, but would rather steal expensive items than pay for them."

"And who are the bored ones?"

"You'll see them in a wealthy town like Wokingham, maybe even more in posh areas like Henley, Windsor and Maidenhead," replied Miss Robertshaw. "They're generally wives – nine times out of ten, shoplifting is done by women – who have little else to do apart from swan around their big houses, lunch out with friends and go shopping. They need a thrill in their dull, privileged lives, and sometimes they get it by doing something illegal.

"I had a case in Maidenhead while you were away at Hendon. Mrs Cantley-Davis, the wife of an investment banker stole a raincoat valued at £1 7s 6d that she would have easily been able to afford, and claimed black was blue that she'd bought it but lost the receipt. The store detective had watched her snip off the price and manufacturer's tickets, put the hood into her handbag and carry the coat round the store over her arm. Then she walked out of the store, put the raincoat on and hurried away before the detective caught up with her. Fined £5 and ordered to pay £5 costs."

"Probably could easily afford the fine, and costs too," I said.

"Don't forget the reputational damage to her husband, especially as he works in finance," replied Miss Robertshaw. "The newspapers print the names and addresses of defendants, after all."

"You're right – I wouldn't have wanted to have been her when he got off the London train that night," I replied.

Not long after, I had to deal with someone who Miss Robertshaw would probably categorise as a "greedy".

"Child caught shoplifting at Woolworths," said Miss Robertshaw. "Can you pop round and deal with her?"

The set-up was depressingly familiar each time, and I was getting bored with it. A sullen or sobbing apprehended shoplifter sitting on the chair of shame in a back office with the store manager playing gaoler.

"Ah, officer," said grinning Mr Byrne, the new Woolies manager. "I have apprehended this felon – one Marcia Lucas – under the Larceny Act of 1926, and told her that anything she says will be used in evidence against her."

I cringed. What was it with some people when they had a brush with crime that they had to turn into amateur policemen and get it all wrong? Anyway, the Larceny Act was 1916, not 1926, and the caution says just "used in evidence", not "against you[12]", but I had bigger things on my mind just now.

Sitting cross-legged on the chair was Marcia, a small, pale, forlorn-looking girl, stringy blonde hair hanging down and arms firmly crossed. She was staring at the floor. A paper carrier bag sat on Mr Byrne's desk and an array of items: two boxes of chocolate, a bag of peanuts, some birthday cake candles, a brush-and-comb set, and two jumpers were neatly lined up beside it.

"Do you want to dust these for fingerprints?" asked Mr Byrne.

"That's really not necessary," I replied, "but you can tell me what happened."

"So, officer, I noticed this young lady take the chocolates from the confectionery counter and put them in her paper carrier bag – Item One on the desk here – not her wire basket. Then I watched her leave the store without paying for them, so I apprehended her outside and asked her to accompany me to my office. When I searched her bag, I discovered Items Two to Eight inside. She said she'd bought them at another shop, but what she'd failed to realise... you're not going to believe

---

12 Despite nearly every television cop show of the 1970s and '80s using the line "anything you do say will be taken down and given in evidence *against you*", we never said "against you". To say this might prevent an innocent person making a statement that would help clear them of a charge.

this… was they all still had their Woolworths labels on them!"

"She may have bought them earlier," I said, trying to hide my irritation at his smugness. "Did you ask her if she had a receipt?"

"Well, no, I…"

I turned to the girl. "Marcia, did you buy these things before and get a receipt?"

She shook her head.

"So did you intend to take them without paying?"

She didn't reply.

I thought I'd try one more thing. "Did your mummy ask you to get these things and didn't give you enough money?"

"I ain't got no mummy."

"How old are you, Marcia?"

"I'm 18."

Well, that was a surprise. I was usually quite good at guessing ages, and I would have put her at around 12, so elfin was she.

"Where do you live?"

"In a rented room above the newsagents in Broad Street."

"And do you work?"

"I've got a job at the ironmonger's. But please don't tell 'im or I'll lose my job."

"Well, I'm definitely pressing charges now, as she's a grown woman and a shop assistant to boot." said Mr Byrne. "We need some sort of deterrent against these dishonest people, officer."

"YOU'RE A WANKER!" Marcia burst out, making both Mr Byrne and me jump. I couldn't disagree with her sentiment, though.

I had no choice but to arrest her. Now she was facing a larceny charge, I cautioned her before I could ask any more questions.

"Marcia Lucas, I am arresting you on suspicion of shoplifting, contrary to the Larceny Act of 1916..." I put extra emphasis on the "16" "...Section 1. You are not obliged to say anything, but anything you say may be given in evidence."

"AND YOU'RE A BLOODY LEZZA!"

I had to disagree on that one.

I walked back to the station with Marcia now cussing and chuntering, carrying her bag of shoplifted items for her, where Sgt Willoughby formally charged her.

"AND YOU LOOK LIKE SODDING FRANKEN-STEIN!" she yelled at him.

He barely blinked.

In front of the magistrate the next day, Marcia pleaded guilty to shoplifting and was remanded on bail, pending a probation officer's report.

I sat in the women's office on my own on a drizzly Monday afternoon, bored, chain smoking, and staring out of the window. Miss Robertshaw was out escorting a female prisoner to Holloway, and Dankworth was giving evidence in a fraud trial.

I missed Pattie on days like these; her saucy humour and willingness to get stuck into whatever she was doing had carried both of us, whatever we were investigating. I missed the laughs. I still couldn't believe she'd gone from dating her Met officer to marriage in three months, and had given up all her police training and experience after just four years. That damn chief constable type had been right: "Marriage is the most serious occupational hazard for women police."

I looked at the Bakelite telephone on my desk and was tempted to pick it up and dial her London number, but using the phone for private calls could get me put on report so I resisted.

Only one person could pick me up out of my gloom this afternoon, I decided. On the pretext of checking up on the Marcia Lucas case, I walked through the deserted station to the adjoining probation office and knocked on the door.

"Komm in," said the instantly recognisable Germanic tones of Hilda Bloom.

I'd worked alongside Hilda on some complex child care or protection cases while I was a WPC, and with her university background, immense humanity and spot-on sense of social justice, she was one of those rare people who nourished the soul.

"Hello, Gwen, how are you?" Hilda peered over the top of her glasses and smiled at me.

"Bit of a slow day today, Hilda. I've typed up all my reports. I could go out on patrol, but I don't really feel like it."

"When are they going to get you that detective constable slot? You're clearly just marking time here."

"I don't know. I've just got to wait, I guess. Anyway, tell me how my sweary shoplifter, Marcia Lucas, is getting on."

Hilda pulled a file out of a cabinet.

"Despite the fact she called me a Nazi..." she said. *Ouch, that must have stung Hilda since she's Jewish.* "...I'm going to do the best I can for this young girl. She hasn't had the best start in life."

"Oh?"

"I talked to children's services. Poor love was in a Barnardo's home from the age of five until she turned 18. She's had some typing and telephonist jobs but was dismissed from them. Bad attitude, apparently."

"You don't say?"

"I think putting Marcia Lucas on the telephones is like putting King Herod in charge of the kindergarten, no?" We both laughed. "She's been able to hold down the job at the ironmonger's for a few months though, and it would be a shame if she were to lose that. I'm going to speak to the chairman of magistrates and see if he can be a little lenient."

"That would be great, Hilda."

"And it has stopped raining, so I think you and I deserve a break away from this place. Fancy a teacake?"

Sitting in the window of the Galleon Tea Rooms, Hilda and I agreed that we were dealing with more shoplifters than ever before, and we were as bored as each other with them.

"There must be a way to rationalise why shoplifters do what they do," said Hilda. "Let's make up a game!"

73

She took a piece of paper and a ballpoint out of her bag, and using our experiences, we drew up a game of Shoplifters' Excuse Bingo:

"I was in a hurry and meant to come back and pay another day."	"Can't I pay you for it and leave it at that?"
"I must have lost the receipt."	"I'm taking medication for a nervous condition."
"I just stepped outside the store to see my daughter / husband / mother." (Delete as appropriate)	"I put it in my pocket and must have forgotten about it."
"I put it in my bag by mistake."	"Why don't you catch real criminals?"
"I've had a bad day and my mind was elsewhere."	"My husband / Mum / Dad is going to kill me."
"I bought these in another shop."	"I didn't have the right money."
"I have had an abscess in my ear for a week and it's driving me mad."	"I didn't use the wire basket because carrying it makes me short of breath.
"There was no one on the till to take my money."	"Why didn't you tell me I'd forgotten to take it out of my bag?"

"I wonder how long it will take us to get a full house?" I mused.

We pinned the grid to the station board, and within the year we'd crossed off every excuse.

Spending time with Hilda had cheered me up somewhat. As we walked back to the station, we spotted a familiar figure sitting cross-legged by the old horse trough in Market Place. A lad of about 12, a brown leather bag slung across his body, was selling something from a cardboard box. A hand-scrawled sign said:

Grass snake eggs
Will hatch and make good pets
1 shilling each

"Hello, Charlie!" I said. "What on earth are you doing here?"

"Hello, miss, my pet grass snakes laid some eggs and I thought people might like to buy them and hatch them. They make really nice pets, honest."

"You're not *really* allowed to sell things in the streets at your age," I said. "But tell me, how are you all doing?"

"All right, miss," said Charlie, getting up and closing the box. "We're doing good, thanks. Dora and me, we're doing all right in school, and Bernie has got a job teaching horse riding at the stables that she really loves."

"That's great to hear! And what about John? Do you see him much?"

Charlie was silent for a few moments.

"He's in Maidenhead still. He got a job as a labourer, and he's really into his Teddy boy stuff, dances, all the fashion. We don't see him very much, no."

"It's good to hear things are working out for you all. Why don't you run along to the pet shop and see if they're interested in your snake eggs?" I couldn't imagine they would be, but it was hard not to admire Charlie's resourcefulness.

And with a smile, a cheery wave and his box, Charlie Carroll skipped off towards the pet shop.

"I think those children will be all right, you know," said Hilda.

"The Carroll case will stay with me as long as I live," I replied. "Even two years on, I still have nightmares about their horrible abusive father and Bernie having to give birth to his baby, and then it dying."

"They were horribly abused and neglected children, weren't they?" replied Hilda. "But they've got a chance to make something of their lives now in foster care. I think we really made a difference there, Gwen."

"I'll catch up with you next week sometime, Hilda," I said. "Thanks for the teacake and the bingo."

I tidied my desk in the women's office and checked there was nothing urgent in my CID tray. I was looking forward to having a few days of annual leave away from this place, and I was going to spend them with my lovely Henry.

CHAPTER 6

A ton of surprises

Not Berkshire
June 1956

"Pack an overnight bag, and wear trousers," Henry had instructed a few days previously.

"May I ask where we're going?"

"You may ask, but I'm not going to tell you." He grinned. "Mystery tour. Meet me on the corner of Murdoch and Easthampstead Roads at 6 a.m."

"I reckon it's meet-the-parents time, Gwen," teased my housemate Suzette. "A polite dinner with your potential in-laws, then you get to sleep in his childhood bedroom with model aeroplanes hanging from the ceiling, while he has the lumpy Z-bed downstairs. You won't sleep because it will be too weird and you're worried what sort of impression you made on his mother, and he'll be all grumpy because the Z-bed collapsed in the night and he had to sleep in the armchair. It's a recipe for disappointment."

"Well, thanks for that, Suz."

All I knew about Henry's family was they lived in Crystal Palace, and I wasn't remotely ready to meet them just yet. As I packed a couple of pretty floral dresses and some gift-wrapped Woolworths chocolates, just in case, I wondered whether I should just have said no when he mentioned the overnight bag.

I'd watched my siblings and friends play out the classic 1950s courtship rituals: first dates at the cinema; subsequent dates meeting up with other couples to jitterbug Saturday night away at either California-in-England Holiday Park, or the Waterloo restaurant dance hall. If your beau had a car, you might divert to a secluded rural spot on the way home from the date for some kissing and light fondling, before progressing to that final rite of courtship passage for "nice girls" – the swimming date. This was the only acceptable way to check out each other's bodies before engagement, and tough on couples who started courting in November. It would be at least the following May before the temperature of Martin's Pool[13] was anything above subarctic.

I slept fitfully the night before my trip with Henry, my mind wrestling with excitement, apprehension and fear of divine retribution. It simply wasn't the done thing to go away overnight with a member of the opposite sex you weren't married to. My mother, if she knew where I was about to go, would consider me a "scarlet woman", no matter what I did (or most probably didn't do) on this jaunt with Henry. I was 26.

I stood on the corner of Murdoch Road in my ski pants and light summer coat with my overnight bag heavy in my hand, listening to the distant clatter of a train heading to London and some sparrows squabbling in a hedgerow. I

---

13 Wokingham's outdoor lido.

scanned the deserted length of Easthampstead Road in both directions for Henry's car.

Six o'clock seemed far too early to be heading to southeast London. I dismissed Suzette's suggestion that it was "meet the parents". Perhaps we would be driving down to the coast to a seaside B&B? Would he have booked us in as Mr and Mrs Jones? I wasn't ready for any of that just yet.

I checked my watch: 6.15. A passing Cliffords Dairy milkman gave me a cheery wave as he trundled by in his float.

In the distance, I heard a growling sound, getting louder as it approached. I glanced up the road to see a motorcycle coming towards me fast, the begoggled rider hunched over the handlebars.

I would flag him down if he was going at that speed during school hours, I thought.

The motorcycle slowed and slid to a halt next to me, sending a shower of twigs and gravel chippings over my Chelsea boots. *Who does this chap think he is?* I thought, clicking into police mode and about to reprimand him for dangerous driving.

"Hello, darling, fancy a ride?" said a familiar voice. The motorcyclist pulled his goggles up onto his helmet to reveal Henry, grinning like a schoolboy who thinks he's just played the best prank on his favourite teacher.

"Henry! What on earth's this?"

"It's a 1955 Norton 500 Dominator Model 7, that's what. Beauty, isn't she?"

"Well, yes… but how… why?" Words wouldn't come out of my mouth properly.

"Couldn't let my accident insurance money[14] sit burning a hole in my bank account for too much longer, so I figured I'd treat myself, and we could have a bit of fun at the same time."

"So, we're going to have a spin around on this and then back to yours to get the car, aren't we?" I asked.

Henry climbed off the Norton, but didn't reply. He too had a weekend holdall, fixed to the back of the bike with a bungee cord. He took my bag and fastened it on top of his with a second cord.

"So why is your bag on the back?" I asked.

He looked at me and grinned. "Have you ever been a pillion passenger before?" he asked, climbing astride the bike again.

"No..."

"Right then. Let me run through some safety tips. Don't get on until I tell you."

"OK."

"Those things sticking out at the sides, they're pegs, and your feet need to stay on them at all times, even when I stop. And make sure those smart new boots – and your ankles – don't touch the hot twin exhausts underneath. They'll scorch leather and skin. Now, let's get this helmet on you. Nobody can do up a crash helmet on their own if they've never worn one before. And I'm guessing you haven't?"

"You're right, I haven't."

Henry scrunched the helmet onto my head and

---

14 In 1953, Henry had had a serious car accident with a drink driver in a flatbed lorry. He'd received a substantial insurance payout.

fiddled about fastening the pinchy chinstrap. I regretted yesterday's expensive salon shampoo and set.

"You can get on now."

I was supple back in those days. I swung my leg over and eased myself into the tiny space between Henry's back and the bags, wriggling to get comfortable.

"No wiggling like that when we're moving!" ordered Henry. "I might lose control!"

"OK," I squeaked.

"And before we set off, sit so that I can feel you're there. But don't crowd me, and don't lean on me."

"Er, how do I..."

"Now, corners. We lean through them on the same side. Don't go the opposite way to me, no matter how much you want to. When I lean to the right, you lean to the right. When I lean to the left, you lean to the left. You must not lean more than me, and you must not lean less than me. And when I stop leaning, you stop leaning."

I think I got that.

"I'll take it steadily through Wokingham so you can get the feel of the bike. Let's go! Hang on tight to my waist."

"But you said not to crowd you or lean on you..."

Too late. Henry had pulled his helmet on over his ears, adjusted his goggles, and couldn't hear a word I said. With a lurch that cracked our helmets together, we roared off along Easthampstead Road, me clinging to Henry's back like a baby marmoset, trying to remember if I should or shouldn't be leaning, crowding, moving ... It was all rather bewildering, and we'd only just gone past the police station.

On the A321, Henry put his foot down (*Do you put your foot down on a motorcycle?*), and the countryside through Hurst and Twyford flew by in a blur of green, the roar of twin cylinders and me gritting my teeth. All too soon, I saw the Thames glistening on our left-hand side as we approached Henley, and in less than an hour we were skirting Oxford's dreaming spires. Perhaps we were going to loop round that ancient city and head back to Wokingham. But Henry kept going.

Burford, Stow-on-the-Wold, Worcester, Kidderminster. Signs indicating turnoffs right to Birmingham rushed past. I was beginning to chill in my flimsy summer coat and stiffen up all over. My thick ski pant seams dug viciously into my groin, and the insides of my legs had developed a terrible itch. I didn't dare move my hand from round Henry's waist to scratch them, or wriggle, for fear of spilling us all over the tarmac, so I sat frozen like a statue in eternal torment. There was no point trying to shout over the roar of the engine. I shut my eyes and prayed we would soon need to pull over to refuel so I could ask Henry just where the hell we were going.

Along a straight stretch of road somewhere between Cressage and Shrewsbury, Henry shouted something about a ton. I thought he was referring to the coal lorry we had just overtaken, but he hunched over the handlebars and increased the throttle. We roared ahead; the cars we overtook hurtled unsettlingly towards us.

I clung on tighter. I couldn't decide whether the new vibration beneath my nether regions was agony or ecstasy, but factoring in my ski pant seams and spasming muscles, I came down on the side of agony.

Henry whooped something else incomprehensible and dropped his speed, pulling into a petrol station café next to a group of leather-jacketed biker boys.

When I went to unclasp my hands, I couldn't, and my heart raced. Henry removed his helmet and prised my fingers apart. Shakily, I lifted off my helmet, revealing a flat hairdo that King Henry V would have been proud of. The biker boys made appreciative comments about the Norton's chrome exhausts, until one said, "Oh, there's *old* people on it," before turning back to his mates.

"We did it!" cried Henry.

"Did what?"

"The ton!"

"What's that?"

The biker boys peered over with renewed interest now.

"Gave this baby a handful of throttle and got her to touch 100 miles an hour! Admittedly on the downhill, but over her top speed of 95!"

"Is that good?"

"Good? It's a triumph! Or rather, a Norton."

The biker boys laughed at his joke, which went straight over my head. Then they all started talking about their own motorbikes while I heaved myself off the seat and tried to get enough circulation going in my deadened hands to light a cigarette.

Over a cup of tea in the caff, I begged a beaming Henry to tell me where we were going.

"All right. I'll put you out of your misery. We're going to the Isle of Man TT races. I've got tickets for the Lightweights and Sidecar Internationals tomorrow."

I'd never given the Isle of Man much thought. If I'd had to stick a pin in it on a map, I'd have put it somewhere off the north-east coast of Scotland. And I had even less idea what TT races were.

"We carry on up to Liverpool and get the ferry across to Douglas, then it's a short ride to our B&B. I'm amazed you haven't heard of the TTs. They're the world's most famous – and dangerous – open-road motorcycle races."

I can't say all things motorcycle have really been on my radar before today.

"So how far is it to Liverpool?"

"A couple of hours, but I could shorten it by doing another ton." He grinned.

"Don't you dare!"

"I wouldn't risk blowing a gasket. Might push her too far next time."

It's not just the bike that's going to blow a gasket.

I've never been so grateful to get on a ferry in my whole life. As the Royal Liver Building faded into the distance, I swore I would never again take for granted a mode of transport that you can move around on. When we docked in Douglas, it was as much as I could manage to clamber back on the bike.

"Ah yes, Mr Falconer and your sister Geraldine, the Miss Falconer," chirped the pub landlady, checking the reservations book. "Your rooms are straight up the stairs, next to each other, numbers 1 and 2."

"Geraldine? Really?" I whispered as we unlocked our doors. "Isn't that a name you'd give a nanny goat?"

Over a dinner of cauliflower cheese and spotted dick with custard in the chintzy pub dining room, Henry took out his *TT Races Official Guide and Programme* to outline next day's plan.

"Tomorrow's on that new 10.7-mile Clypse course. The first race is the Lightweight International 250 cc, and we'll be looking out for Brits Albert Jones and Frank Cope on the Nortons. That starts at 09.30, so we'll need to be in position well before they close the road at 08.20…"

I could barely keep my eyes open as he droned on.

"Looks like Keppel Gate and Creg-ny-Baa is one of the most exciting sections of the Clypse – the riders come in at top speed, then they brake to 30 miles per hour for a nearly 90-degree bend, and immediately accelerate down to Brandish Corner. We'll go there. It'll be popular, so we need get to the Keppel Hotel parking at seven-thirty to secure a good spot."

I stifled a yawn.

"What time do I need to set my alarm for?" Henry consulted his map.

"I reckon about 15 minutes on the bike from here to Creg-ny-Baa, half an hour for breakfast, however long it takes you to get ready before that."

I'd better set my alarm for six.

"At around 12, there's the Ultra Lightweight International 125 cc. Frank Cope's in this one too – what stamina that man has! And at half past two, the sidecar races start."

"How long are these races?" I asked.

"Each one's about two hours."

I felt my stomach lurch. *Six hours of watching motorcycles go past. Great.*

We retired to our rooms. On the landing, Henry leaned over to kiss me on the lips. I dodged away from him.

"You can't do that! Someone might see! I'm your sister, remember…"

He leaned against his doorpost, smiling adoringly.

"I booked two rooms for decency's sake," he whispered, taking my hand, "but we don't actually have to use both of them…"

How dare he assume such a thing!

"Absolutely not! You know I'm not that kind of girl!" I blurted.

"Ah, well. Can't blame a chap for trying, can you?" He kissed the top of my head just above my new Plantagenet fringe. "Night night, Gwennie… er… I mean Gerry."

I closed my door and flopped down on the powder-blue candlewick bedspread, wide awake now and fuming with disappointment, every fibre of my body still humming from the Norton's bone-jangling vibrations. I ripped the gift wrap off my Woolworths chocolates and wolfed half the box. If I'd known this was the trip Henry was planning, I'd have given him a firm "no". And even if I *was* that kind of girl, a 200-mile pillion journey was the ultimate contraceptive: you really wouldn't want your chap anywhere near you.

My alarm clock rang at six the next morning, rousing me from a dead, dreamless sleep. Blearily, I contemplated the clothes I'd brought. The dresses would be useless on the bike, so it would be those wretched ski pants again, now covered in road dust.

I nibbled on toast as Henry tucked into a full English before we headed out. Sunshine over the pretty seaside town of Douglas was deceptive, as a strong, biting wind blew off the Irish Sea. Granted, on a warmer day, it would have been a lovely spot for sunbathing on the beach. I shivered in my summer jacket, even with a cardigan underneath, wishing I'd brought my big coat.

We rode out of Douglas with other bikers and up onto Creg-ny-Baa, a bleak moorland landscape of yellow gorse and drystone walls, to the Keppel Hotel vantage point. In the hotel car park, motorcycles of every era and horsepower were lined up, creating a pop-up museum of speed for the spectators to mill around for a couple of hours.

"Look! Look!" enthused Henry, hurrying over to an admittedly impressive, shiny machine. "It's a Vincent Black Shadow!"

I nodded along as Henry and the Vincent's owner waxed lyrical about dry sump lubrication, Lucas electrics and how coil ignition[15] had developed.

"That was a £600 machine right there!" gushed Henry, as we squeezed onto a viewing stand. "No difficulty doing a ton when that's got a top speed of 125 miles per hour."

"What happens now?" I asked, pulling my coat round me against the blustery wind.

"We sit and wait."

At around 9.45 a.m., the competitors started roaring down towards the bend, perilously braking and cornering on what looked like half an inch of tyre. I could barely watch, and my squeamishness was not unfounded: every year since the war there had been multiple fatalities at

---

15 I don't know either.

the TTs. Even the jaunty race programme carried a disclaimer that spectators were there at their own risk, landowners, riders and vehicle owners absolved from all liabilities.

To me, all the bikes and riders looked the same, moving too fast to see their numbers on the front, but the other spectators seemed to know who they were. Loud cheers went up for the five British riders and the one from Czechoslovakia, but a small group of men booed the Germans and Italians.

"How rude!" I said. "That's not very sportsmanlike."

Henry didn't reply. He'd got chatting with the man sitting next to him about the relative merits of MV Agusta Italian bikes versus the Nortons, and I had absolutely nothing to add to their conversation – even if they had included me. After the first few laps, I was getting bored seeing the same bikes going round again, and again, and again, and of holding my breath, praying that nobody came off on our watch. By the fifth lap, a devil inside my head willed someone to fall off just so Henry and I could leap into police first-aid mode and actually do something interesting. No one did. I counted the remaining laps, wishing my life away to the ninth.

Over the tannoy came the news that the Italians had taken first and second places, the Germans third and fourth and the Brits had come last. More booing.

"You give the best years of your life to their liberation, then they go and beat you," said Henry. I wasn't sure whether he was joking or not.

The next race, the Ultra Lightweight 125cc, was even more boring – slightly smaller motorbikes also going past nine times. With no Germans in it, there was less booing, and the same Italian – Carlo Ubbiali – won it, with most of the Brits coming last again.

I expected the sidecar race to be a dull, sedate affair, akin to taking Granny out for the afternoon, but the day at last had a highlight. The single-wheel racing sidecars were a surprise – little more than tea trays welded to the side of the bikes. The real revelation was the passengers. Nothing passive about them; like leather-clad ninjas, they'd be all over the bike pillion one second, flipping to the other side of the "chair" the next, fully hanging out parallel with the road round the sharp corners, and then back over the pillion again. No belts, no safety bars, and barely four inches off the tarmac. It was genuinely thrilling.

As these physics-defying lunatics threw themselves round our bends, I could barely stay seated on my hard wooden seat, and kept gripping Henry's arm so hard he cried, "Ouch! Get off!"

By 4.45 p.m., two Germans had won the sidecar race on a BMW, the group of blokes had sung "Hitler has only got one ball" several times, and I was developing a shivery, one-sided exhaustion headache. Henry milled around the parked motorbikes commiserating with his fellow Norton owners, as one by one they moved off back to Douglas.

At dinner, Henry seemed somewhat subdued. I tried to make the best of the day by focusing on the sidecar race, which was like nothing I'd ever experienced before.

"I really thought this was going to be the year of the Brits," he huffed.

"We did come second and third in the sidecars," I responded.

"Bloody Krauts beat us to it," cut in a rough-looking man on the next table. I recognised him as one of the booing crowd. I excused myself to powder my nose, and while in the ladies, felt overwhelmingly tired.

When I returned, Henry was sitting at the man's table with a large glass of whisky, obviously midway through a war-related anecdote.

"You'll relate to this, Ken. When we got home, there was little recognition of what we did, we just had to slot back into civilian life as if nothing had happened. Everything had changed, yet nothing had changed."

"Yeah, mate. I often think about that at three in the morning, y'know."

"Give you an example. I got on the usual bus to go and visit Mum and the same miserable sod of a bus conductor who knew me from before the war was still on it. I gave him the penny h'apenny fare. He just looked at me, held out his hand and said, 'Tuppence,' nothing more. I had to rummage around in my pocket to find another h'apenny."

"'No 'Welcome back from the war, thank you for your service, and by the way, sorry the bus fares have gone up'?" asked Ken.

"Nothing like that," replied Henry. "Miserable old sod."

I patted him on the shoulder. "I'm going to turn in now. See you in the morning."

"Night, love. I mean, sis."

Henry still smelled of whisky when I forced myself back on his bike the next morning for the 11-hour return journey, which was every bit as gruelling as getting here, only at least with home at the end of it. He dropped me back on the corner of Murdoch Road.

"I'll see you at the centenary parade on Saturday. Thanks for a wonderful trip." He blew me a kiss.

I just about managed to peel my near-catatonic body out of my filthy, tarry ski pants and fall into bed, where I slept until 11 o'clock the next morning.

CHAPTER 7

Centenarians

Sulhamstead HQ
9th June 1956

I dragged myself up and sat motionless on the edge of the bed, paralysed by an unwelcome mixture of fatigue, what my granny would call "a touch of the melancholies", and a gloomy foreboding that anything I tried to do ended in disappointment. My throat was starting to feel sore, and I rubbed my scratchy eyes.

I glanced at the picture above my headboard of Beatific Jesus blessing the birds. *Don't worry, I didn't get up to anything,* I told Him.

Pulling myself together, I limped to the bathroom and sat wearily on the edge of the bath, contemplating two large fluid-filled blisters on the insides of my ankles. I must have touched the Norton's exhaust pipes at some point during the gruelling trip home. Great.

"How were the parents?" trilled Suzette from the landing as I shuffled out of the bathroom.

"No parents, thank goodness," I replied. "You don't get blisters like these..." I showed her my ankles "... walking around Crystal Palace Park."

"Ouchy," said Suzette. "I'll take a look at those for you. I've got some dressings in my room. And, honey, if you don't mind me saying, you look worn out. I thought you were supposed to be having a relaxing break away?"

"I thought so too." I rolled my bloodshot eyes. "You'll never guess where we ended up."

As Suzette bandaged my ankles, I told her about the TT Races.

"I can't believe (a) Henry's bought a motorbike, (b) drove at 100 miles per hour with you on the back and (c) didn't tell you where you were going!" she exclaimed, wide-eyed.

"He probably thought I would refuse if I knew we were going on a 400-mile motorcycle round trip."

"Would you have done?"

"Probably. But thinking about it now, as a traffic officer he knows all about speed and can read the roads. He went fast, but didn't take risks. In fact, I felt uncomfortable rather than unsafe. What I was more bothered about was his moods – boyish exhilaration one minute, then disproportionately down in the dumps the next, just because the Italians and Germans won. Haven't we all got over the war by now?"

"Well, we all *should* have done, but there are plenty of people who haven't, I fear," replied Suzette, packing up her first-aid kit.

On Saturday, the Berkshire Constabulary was going to be 100 years old. *I know how it feels*, I thought. Aching all over and with a cold coming on, I gingerly pulled thick stockings over Suzette's bandages and polished my shoes, ready for the centenary parade at Sulhamstead County HQ. Half the constabulary – 210 of us – were to be inspected and then march past the Lord Lieutenant of Berkshire[16] and sundry other dignitaries on the manicured sports field. I was dreading it. I could barely walk, let alone march.

After being bussed to Sulhamstead, we were split up into our sections in true police fashion: uniformed policemen at the front, then CID men in trilbies and raincoats. *I should bloody well be marching with them*, I thought, surprised at the depth of my bitterness. Then came the uniformed policewomen, followed by the Special Constabulary (*Hello, Dad*), motorcyclists (*Seen enough of those for one week, thank you*), patrol cars, and three police dogs with their handlers. Finally, there was a new, much heralded piece of cutting-edge technology – a mobile police station on wheels, aka the "incident van", which was a rickety thing trundling along behind.

I didn't mind the standing to attention parts of the parade. The portly, diminutive Lord Lieutenant, barely shoulder-high to the strapping rank-and-file policemen, and wearing a pretend army uniform with ludicrous scrambled-egg epaulettes, ambled up and down our rows with the simpering chief constable strutting along behind.

"Jolly good show, gals," blethered the Lord Lieutenant into the middle distance, as he toddled past Miss Robertshaw and us WPCs.

He clambered into the incident van, stumbling up the wobbly steps, and attempting to look interested as

---

16 The Queen's representative in a county, responsible for arranging and escorting Royal visits and presenting decorations, among other things.

he inspected it. That would have triggered the sniggers in Pattie, and I felt another stab of missing her. At the same time, I was sort of glad she wasn't there to make me disgrace myself by catching uncontrollable giggles.

My eyes unexpectedly welled up with tears when the Lord Lieutenant handed out bravery awards. Blaming my cold, I blew my nose on a hankie. Two of our PCs, Ernest Nobes and William Griffiths, received British Empire Medals for their heroic rescues of injured passengers following the terrible Milton derailment last November. A train travelling from Wales to Paddington, diverted between Steventon and Didcot because of engineering works, derailed and fell down a 20-foot embankment, killing 11 people and injuring many more.

Another two traffic PCs, George Kerr and William Phillips, received recognition for stopping a van filled with stolen ammunition raided from our local Arborfield REME depot and arresting a pair of IRA men armed with revolvers. I hadn't appreciated how close we'd come to IRA criminal activity in sleepy Wokingham last summer.

"Really brings home the variety of work us police do, and the dangers we deal with, doesn't it?" whispered Miss Robertshaw. "Wish our MPs could see this."

My ankles throbbed as we listened to the chief constable's centenary speech delivered from a podium in front of HQ, that went something like:

"When I survey such a fine force assembled in front of me, I see that we have come so far from those 97 men, dressed in frock coats and tall top hats, who first went on duty to protect and serve the public in 1856. What would those Victorian gentlemen have made of this magnificent police station on wheels..." he gestured towards the rickety van "...that will be our nerve centre at events such as Ascot Races and Henley Regatta Week?"

"They'd have turned their noses up at the shite build quality for starters," muttered gruff Inspector Gregor McTavish behind me, and I had to bite my lip.

The chief constable continued, "This is *the best* illustration of the innovation and progress we have made over the last century. Today, we are a police force 420-strong, and every man is supported by highly advanced technical and scientific aids..."

"Whereas us women still have to use the Victorian kit," quipped an auburn-haired WPC standing next to me, and I stifled a laugh. I recognised her as Heather Newman from Maidenhead station.

"Ye'd probably be better off with that, lassie," chuckled Gregor. "At least ye'd get a truncheon."

We glanced at Miss Robertshaw, and she rolled her eyes.

"If Miss de Vitré[17] were here, he wouldn't get away with that," she murmured.

The band of the Life Guards struck up a jaunty tune and we marched pointlessly round the sports field and back up towards HQ's big white house. I have never been able to march properly, and my blisters and aching muscles made me more ungainly than usual.

"You all right?" asked Heather Newman, pinching my

---

17 Miss Barbara Denis de Vitré OBE (1905–1960) was Britain's first woman Assistant Inspector of Constabulary for the whole country, a formidable and much-loved advocate for women in policing.

arm. Goodness, I must have looked bad, waddling around.

"Yes thanks, I'm fine. I just overdid it hiking on my day off," I fibbed.

"As long as you are," she said, nodding kindly.

"Eyes right!" called a voice.

We saluted the small group of dignitaries ranged in front of Sulhamstead House and the CID men raised their trilbies, then we peeled off to the tea tent for some much-needed refreshment. As police officers were moved around the county frequently, events such as these were always a networking opportunity and a welcome chance to catch up with old friends.

It was packed in the tea tent, and, being unsteady on my feet, I stepped backwards like a clumsy oaf, straight onto the toes of the previous chief constable, Humphry Legge.

"Oh, I am so sorry, sir! I've trodden on you," I apologised.

"Not at all. It's very crowded in here," responded Commander Legge in his aristocratic tones. "It's WPC Crockford, isn't it? I interviewed you for your selection board back in... 1951, I believe?"

"Yes, sir. Well remembered!"

"Didn't I hear you went to Hendon?"

"That's right, sir."

"So why weren't you marching with the CID boys?"

Ouch. That hit a nerve. The touch of the melancholies washed over me again and I took a deep breath before I replied.

"I-I honestly don't know, sir. I don't think a detective constable position has become vacant yet."

"Well, yes, they are indeed as rare as hens' teeth. I'll see if I can have a word. In the meantime, just as a heads-up, it looks as if the British police unit over in Cyprus might be needing a woman's touch in the near future."

Just as I hadn't really taken much notice of the IRA arrests – those had been very much the men's territory – I hadn't taken a lot of notice of what was currently happening in Cyprus. The newspapers always carried accounts of scuffles and skirmishes in the British colonies, but I rarely read them in detail. I knew that the island was in the throes of vicious guerrilla warfare by EOKA[18] terrorists against the British occupation, and that last year, Chief Superintendent Elizabeth Bather of the Met went to Cyprus to see if the time was right to send a contingent of women police. She'd decided that the situation out on Nicosia's "Murder Mile" was far too fraught, and it wasn't safe to send us out there.

"Last year was a no-no," continued Commander Legge, "but I hear on the grapevine that they do want more British policemen sent out, and if that's the case, it's only a matter of time before Miss de Vitré wants to send some of her gals out too. I think you'd be ideal."

Fear tingled in the base of my spine.

"W-would we get to choose whether we go or not?" I asked. I wasn't sure I wanted to do beat patrol far from

---

18 EOKA (Ethnikí Orgánosis Kipriakoú Agónos – the National Organisation of Cypriot Struggle), was an underground movement of Greek Cypriot nationalists whose aims were to end British colonial rule in Cyprus, and to achieve union (*enosis*) for Cyprus with Greece.

home on somewhere called Murder Mile with armed anti-British terrorists round every corner.

"Who knows?" said Commander Legge. "It would be up to Miss de V. She certainly wouldn't put her gals in any danger, and you can bet your life she'd go out there first and do a proper recce. Marvellous lady, she is."

I caught up with Miss Robertshaw, who was chatting with Henry and DI Dankworth. Henry and I studiously ignored each other, as we did in work situations, which probably made it even more obvious that we were an item. It was easier to ignore him than usual, and he wandered off to fuss the police dogs.

"Have you heard anything about Miss De Vitré organising a contingent of policewomen to go to Cyprus?" I asked her.

"I thought they'd shelved that idea after Miss Bather's visit last year," she said.

"Although if they did send Miss de V out, she'd make those raggle-taggle EOKA terrorists look pussy," I replied.

"Miss de V could make the whole British Army look pussy," said Miss Robertshaw, her eyes glistening and a big smile on her face. I sensed she might have a bit of a girl crush on Miss de Vitré, and to be honest, who wouldn't?

Barbara Denis de Vitré, our boss, was indeed a marvellous lady, renowned for her unfailing charm, warmth and humour. A 1920s career policewoman in Sheffield from the age of 22, she'd been sent to work for the Colonial Police Service in Cairo, supervising and registering the city's brothels so that "the ladies of the night" weren't exploited or unfairly treated. She had also spent time undercover as an armed agent for the Narcotics Bureau.

Coming back to the UK in the early 1930s, Miss de V worked with Leicester CID, once pretending to be pregnant by stuffing a pillow up her jumper to catch a backstreet abortionist, who'd then beaten her up. During the war, she served tea and sandwiches from a mobile canteen among Coventry's smoking ruins, then transferred to the Kent Constabulary to set up an enviable policewomen's department there. Appointed staff officer to HM Inspectors of Constabulary, she promoted and organised the women police UK-wide. And she could even ride a motorcycle without blistering her ankles.

"So you don't think we'll get sent to Cyprus?" I asked.

"Not in the immediate future. But what an opportunity if we did, eh?" Miss Robertshaw smiled.

A couple of weeks later, Henry and I were on our regular cinema date at the Rialto in Maidenhead. We could be a little more incognito there than in Wokingham where everybody knew everybody else and eyes were everywhere. You only had to walk past the town hall with a member of the opposite sex and 10 minutes later it would be the day's hottest gossip in the queue at Timothy White's.

Henry enjoyed Westerns, and I rather liked Stewart Grainger, so we'd decided on *The Last Hunt* as our date film and settled into the red velvet seats with a bar of Fry's chocolate to share. My lingering cold had moved into my sinuses, and despite chain-munching Hall's Mentho-Lyptus sweets to try and clear the stuffiness, my nose blocked up even more in the smoky auditorium.

The red curtains parted, and the Pathé newsreel delivered the pre-film world news of the day. Some unnecessarily dramatic orchestral music struck up and the screen filled with CYPRUS CATASTROPHE in huge letters.

"Aye aye, what's going on there now?" muttered Henry, as we watched footage of the British Army combing mountain forest looking for EOKA terrorists.

"Bloody hell, those are mortars they're using," he said, as the on-screen squaddies dropped bombs down drainpipe-sized barrels, arcing them into the air across the Mediterranean greenery. Further scenes showed a soldier firing a machine gun at some pine trees, a wrecked army truck at the foot of a ravine, and captured terrorists with hoods over their heads being driven around in Land Rovers. Cut to a field hospital where a medic was smothering burns casualties in something waxy, as the voiceover explained that the terrorists were now weaponising forest fires as a new guerrilla tactic. Nineteen British soldiers were now dead; apparently, the heaviest losses since the anti-terrorist campaign in Cyprus had begun.

"Is all this bloody worth it?" said Henry, dragging furiously on his cigarette. "We're fighting all over the world in other people's countries, against people who don't want us there. It's costing us a fortune in lives and armaments. I say we just pull out and leave the buggers to it."

I could see his point of view, but I couldn't agree with him, and I didn't feel up to arguing. Although I didn't know all the fine details, I understood that just pulling out of Cyprus and letting it unite with Greece wouldn't be a great outcome for the island's Turkish Cypriot inhabitants. With the traditional Greek/Turkish animosity, that could provoke civil war.

I'd also been worrying about what Commander Legge had said at the centenary parade; things were getting bad enough to send out an extra contingent of police, and now the newsreels were reporting that more British service personnel were being killed. If we pulled out of Cyprus, though, us policewomen wouldn't have to go there, and yet... I didn't know what to make of it, it was stressing me out, and I was getting even more of a headache just thinking about it.

Our film didn't help my stress levels either. Last date, we'd watched *The Feminine Touch*, a fluffy story of student nurses discovering life and love on the wards of a London hospital; it was a welcome escape. *The Last Hunt* featured a psychopathic cowboy with a bloodthirsty mania for slaughtering entire herds of bison. Much of the film depicted real, terrified American bison being chased around by mule carts, and an unpleasant sub-plot involving a kidnapped, abused Indian woman. Even the villain freezing to death at the end didn't cheer me up.

"Well, that was fun," I said to Henry, struggling to finish my glass of light ale in The Bear pub afterwards. "Did they really kill all those poor animals for a film?"

"No, they filmed the annual bison control cull in the American national parks. It was going to happen anyway."

We sat in silence for a few moments, until I broached the topic that was on my mind.

"To be honest, I'm now worried about the situation in Cyprus after seeing that newsreel. It seems as if it's getting worse..."

"Especially as they're bringing in mortars and Bren guns," Henry replied. "I don't trust that bloody Anthony Eden not to lead us into another war. He's got to accept that the glory days of the British Empire are over and focus on home policy, such as the shortage of police officers a bit more."

"So do you think we could be conscripted out there?"

"Who knows? Anything could happen. Did last time."

As we drove home in suffocating silence, an unexplained and unwanted panic rose in my chest, and I breathed through my mouth trying to quell it. Troubling thoughts swirled around in my head. *Will I find myself being sent out to my death on the dusty streets of Nicosia? Will all my detective training, enthusiasm and ambition be wasted, and I remain a WPC all my life? Why does Henry get so angry at the newsreels? Why did they have to kill all those poor bison and show it in such graphic detail? Am I ever going to shake off this wretched cold?*

Henry dropped me outside Mrs Cunningham's.

"I won't kiss you with that cold," he said. "I hope you get rid of it soon."

CHAPTER 8

Friends in high places

Wokingham
Summer 1956

Even outside in Rectory Road, I could hear the ruckus going on inside the police station lobby as I returned from yet another uneventful evening patrol.

"We weren't doing NUFFINK!" shouted one youthful voice.

"It was him what asked for it, not us!" shouted another.

"I did no such thing, officers, these ruffians are making it all up," wheedled an adult male voice.

I squeezed through the front door, into a sweaty mêlée around the front desk of PC Higgs, PC Sansom, PC Jones, two scruffy boys around 14 years old, and a thin, middle-aged man whose comb-over hair had come free of his scalp and was flapping around above his ear. I did a double take. Basil Gill again! That Wokingham "do-gooder", with a finger in every local pie, and a nasty attitude towards Commonwealth nurses. What on earth was he doing in the station? I trotted past, up the stairs, but then loitered out of sight, my interest piqued, listening.

"I demand to see Superintendent Barker!" cried Gill.

"PC Sansom, take these two to the cells, then go and inform their parents," monotoned Sgt Willoughby from behind the desk, "and PC Jones, please take Mr Gill into the interview room."

"Call the superintendent down, won't you?" insisted an exasperated Gill as Jones led him away.

I collected a couple of letters from the CID office and came down into the lobby on the pretext of putting them in the post tray. Higgs looked me up and down, grinning.

"What was all that about?" I asked.

"It's all kicking off tonight," said Higgs. "Jonesie was on his beat when a member of the public came up to him and complained there were two young lads hanging around the public conveniences offering..." he glanced at Sgt Willoughby "...should we say in front of the lady, Sarge? ...indecent services."

Oh for goodness' sake, cut the coy nonsense, Higgs. I've dealt with more indecency than you ever have.

"Right. Honestly PC Higgs, you're not going to tell me anything I haven't heard before. I'm a big girl now," I snapped, instantly regretting my choice of phrase.

He leered at my bustline. "I know you are."

"So," I asked. "Is it buggery, blowing or bestiality?"

Higgs reddened, right up to the roots of his wiry hair, while Sgt Willoughby betrayed the slightest twitch of a smile.

"Oh... well... um..." Higgs stammered. "I'm not sure. All the member of the public said was that the two lads were allegedly offering sexual favours in return for sweets and cigarettes. When Jonesie went into the lavs to investigate, there was Gill with his back to the urinal fiddling with his open fly buttons and the two boys standing round him. He swears he had just gone in

105

there for a pee, but they all jumped back looking pretty guilty, apparently."

"I don't understand how he would have been able to urinate while being accosted by the boys, and surely, he wouldn't want to lay himself open to any accusations by undoing his trouser buttons," I mused. "Unless…"

"Us blokes can pee in any situation," interrupted Higgs. "Doesn't bother us. Why do you think urinals are designed the way they are?"

It was my turn to redden. I'd never actually been into a gents' lavatory before, so I'd only heard about urinals. But I wasn't going to tell Higgs that.

We heard footsteps coming down the stairs. The EF – our superintendent – trotted into the lobby and we stood to attention.

"Where's Mr Gill?" he demanded.

"In the interview room, sir," replied Higgs.

"Right, we'll see about this," he said, and disappeared into the bowels of the station.

With nothing more to see, I wandered back upstairs to finish off my shift typing up some minor crime reports. Checking no one was around, I pushed open the door of the gents, and raised my eyebrows at the row of ceramic urinals; there really would be no privacy there. For once, I felt us women got the better deal.

At one minute to 10, I walked down to the front desk to sign out. Basil Gill and The EF stood on the station doorstep, shaking hands. I caught a few of the EF's words:

"Apologies… terrible misunderstanding… it won't happen again… but you would be willing to give evidence as a witness?… absolutely… see you on Thursday…"

Sgt Willoughby and I looked at each other.

"Scot-free," he murmured. "And guilty as hell."

Guilty (but presumed innocent until proved otherwise) and with no friends in high places to get them off, were the two youths, Frankie Anderson and Reggie Dyer. Hilda's male probation colleague Terry Fulford would be dealing with them. I popped into the probation office to see how Hilda was getting on with Marcia Lucas, my sweary shoplifter. Terry was at his desk too.

"I got Marcia two years' probation, a very small fine, and she just has to pay back the value of what she stole," said Hilda, poring over Marcia's file. "I haven't seen her name reported in the newspaper, so she hasn't had to answer any awkward questions and lose her job at the ironmonger's. She's promised to keep out of trouble, and you know what? I think she will."

"That's great, Hilda. She's a bit volatile, but in a funny sort of way I kind of like her spirit – she certainly saw through the shop manager Byrne for the ridiculous little man he is."

I turned to Terry. "You're dealing with the two boys who got caught importuning last night, aren't you?"

"Yes. We had their records checked and turns out they're habitual importuners, selling sexual favours all over the county. And they swear blind that this Gill character had prearranged to meet them at the public conveniences – not for the first time. 'Sweeties for sweeties', they called it. But then, it's only their word against his, no witnesses – even your PC couldn't be absolutely certain what had happened."

"And it looks like Gill is going to be called as a prosecution witness now, rather than being charged with any sort of offence," I said.

Terry huffed. "Yet another homosexual crime. I'm seeing them more often. Men interfering with young boys, youngsters prostituting themselves around public lavatories, gross indecency in public parks... If that Wolfenden gets his way and we start approving of this sort of behaviour, where will it all end, Hilda?"

Hilda looked over the top of her glasses.

"Oh Terry, my friend – you know my views on this. Men who sexually take advantage of children are criminals, end of," she said. "But adult men who are that way inclined and want to be with each other in the privacy of their own homes, I see no problem with it. *That* is what the Wolfenden committee is looking into."

"Well, they don't tend to keep it in private, do they?" spluttered Terry. "You let them have their liaisons at home, but that's never enough, is it? Then they want to go out and pick up their type in pubs and clubs, then, for some reason that I can't fathom, hang around the public toilets and go off into the bushes. Do we really want to see more of that coming to Wokingham?"

Terry's face had turned an alarming pink colour.

"And they're a security risk!" he continued. "Look at Burgess and McLean[19], spilling our secrets to the Russians, then running off to Moscow. Communists, most of them."

---

19 Guy Burgess and Donald McLean were two MI5 agents who happened to be homosexual. They passed British secrets to the Russians and defected to Moscow in 1951.

"I don't disagree with you about the security risk, Terry," replied Hilda, "but that's only because our current law is a blackmailer's charter. Think about it; when being homosexual is a crime, the Russians will elicit liaisons with civil servants or the military, then blackmail them into passing secrets to the Soviet Union, saying, 'If you don't give me these secrets, I'll expose our affair and you'll be in prison.'"

"It needn't even be as major as state secrets," I chipped in, loving the discussion. "A blackmailer could simply extort money by threatening to expose someone who's homosexual."

Terry didn't say anything, but stood up, grabbed his rolled-up *Daily Mail* from the desk and yanked his jacket off the coat stand.

"Much as I'd love to chit-chat all day, ladies, I've got work to do. Frankie and Reggie's home visits. I'll be off now."

As the door slammed, Hilda chuckled. "I love it when Terry doesn't have an answer. Cigarette?" She offered me one.

"So do you think there'll come a time when being homosexual won't be a crime, Hilda?" I asked.

"It should never have been a crime in the first place! Blame Henry VIII[20] for that."

"And the Criminal Law Amendment Act, 1885, Section 11," I recited, remembering a long evening in

---

20 The Buggery Act of 1533, passed by Parliament during the reign of Henry VIII, is the first time in law that male homosexuality was targeted for persecution in the UK. Sex between men was punishable by death until 1861.

my tiny room at Hendon trying to learn by rote all the 13 tedious sections about sex crimes.

"They used that particular Act to send Oscar Wilde to prison," continued Hilda, 'for committing acts of gross indecency with male persons'."

Oh no, not lovely Oscar Wilde. It was 1956, yet I was still supposed to uphold a law that had persecuted him in 1895.

"My opinion isn't popular in some quarters, Gwen," continued Hilda. "But when I hear from my father about the flourishing gay bars, cabarets and nightclubs in Berlin before the war, where the police turned a blind eye – they sounded so fun! We viewed what you view as a crime with a certain respect and regard – call it a subculture. But then of course along came Hitler and his pink triangles[21]."

"I can't imagine Wokingham embracing a Berlin-style cabaret culture anytime soon," I said. "Drag acts at the Galleon Tea Rooms – I can't see it happening." Hilda roared with laughter. "But it will be interesting to see what the Wolfenden Committee recommend, certainly."

Hilda got up from her desk and went to the bookshelf. She took down a hardback and handed it to me: *Against the Law* by Peter Wildeblood.

"This was published last year. Read it – it's very good. I think, with your natural sense of justice, it will make you as angry as it made me. You remember the Montagu case?"

---

21 Persecuted homosexuals in the Nazi concentration camps were identified by pink triangles sewn onto their clothing.

I vaguely did. In 1954, Lord Montagu of Beaulieu, Michael Pitt-Rivers and Peter Wildeblood had been convicted and imprisoned for "conspiring together to incite two RAF men to 'commit unnatural offences and gross indecency'". Lord Montagu received 12 months in prison; Wildebloode and Pitt-Rivers 18 months each.

"The way those three men were treated! And we call ourselves a civilized society. We'll discuss when you've read it."

"OK, I will, thanks. I need a good book right now. What was that word you used for homosexuals in Berlin?"

"Gay," replied Hilda. "It's a word that's increasingly being used in that community, and I rather like it."

"Really? Never heard that before," I said. "It certainly gives a new slant on that rhyme, 'And the child who is born on the Sabbath Day, is bonny and blithe and good and gay."

Hilda chuckled. "Oh, I do hope Terry was born on a Sunday."

One of our WPC duties was to escort female trial witnesses at court and into the witness box. It was one of those essential but dull jobs that involved hours of hanging around courtrooms, and it was usually given to a junior WPC.

As good as her word, Miss Robertshaw involved me in the upcoming trial of the alleged paedophile general. "His hearing is coming up before a special sitting of Wokingham Magistrates' Court this week," said Miss Robertshaw. "I'm escorting the complainant in the morning while she gives evidence – could you escort her friend Marlene?"

"Of course," I said, although I had mixed feelings about it. On the one hand, it felt like a step back, considering my years of experience and specialist training; but on the other it was such a high-profile case – those didn't come along often in Wokingham – that even mighty Miss Robertshaw was on escort duty. I was also interested to see if the general registered on my creep radar in the flesh.

On the morning of the trial, I met a scared-looking 14-year-old Marlene and her stony-faced mother outside the court. With her plaits and her school uniform kilt, Marlene looked younger.

We sat outside the courtroom on a hard wooden bench as I ran through the forthcoming procedure with her: what the oath was and how to take it, who would ask her questions, and how to answer them truthfully. Marlene nodded at me, saucer-eyed, but I could tell she wasn't really taking it in. We'd have to see how she got on when she was called.

We sat on that bench for hours, her mother wringing her hands and looking at the floor, not wanting to chat. Marlene apparently absorbed herself in Enid Blyton's *Five Have Plenty of Fun,* but I noticed she was still on page 10 two hours later.

I looked at my watch. It was 1 p.m., and time the court usually adjourned for lunch. It didn't help that the window was open, and a tempting smell of freshly baked pastries wafted through. My stomach rumbled and Marlene giggled.

"How long do we have to sit here for?" she whispered to her mother. "I'm hungry. All I can think about are sausage rolls."

Now all *I* could think about was sausage rolls until, eventually, the court usher came out.

"I'm afraid we're running over lunchtime recess," he said. "Miss Marlene? Come this way, please."

"Remember what I told you," I whispered to her. She was trembling, wide-eyed and pale, and I desperately wanted to give her a hug to try and make this whole sordid scenario better, because I knew what was coming.

I helped Marlene into the witness box. She held a Bible in her little hand and, barely audibly, whispered, "I swear by Almighty God that the evidence I shall give will be the truth, the whole truth, and nothing but the truth."

"So, what did you see when you came back to your friend after collecting some big sticks for the walls of your den?" began the prosecuting solicitor.

"I saw her standing there with a tall, old man."

"And did you notice anything untoward about her?"

"Unto-what?"

"Did you notice anything strange?"

Marlene hesitated and mumbled something at her shoes.

"You're going to have to speak up as the court cannot hear you."

"Yes – her knickers were round her knees," she declared.

"And the man?"

Marlene hesitated again, choosing her words and mustering her volume. "His trousers were undone and pulled down at the front."

Every pair of eyes in the silent courtroom bore into the poor girl and I cringed at the public nature of these intimate details. *Why do we have to put children through this process?*

"And did your friend give you anything at any point?"

"Yes, she gave me 1s. She said it was from the man."

The defence solicitor then stood up to cross-examine her. He put his glasses on the end of his nose and stared at her for a full 20 seconds, but she held his gaze. *Good girl.*

"Have you talked about the incident with your friend since it happened?"

"Yes, we've talked about it twice since," murmured Marlene.

"Speak up, girl, we can barely hear you!"

Please just make this stop, I thought. But I had underestimated Marlene.

"Yes, we've talked about it twice since," she almost shouted at the defence. Her knuckles were white as she gripped the edge of the witness box.

"So, you will have had ample opportunity to get together and make up a story about what happened with this gentleman." The defence gestured towards the gaunt, pasty general who stared, emotionless, into the middle distance, propped up by his blue-rinsed wife. *Yep, definitely a creep.*

"He..." Marlene jabbed a finger in his direction. "*He* ain't no gentleman, that's for sure." She was ready for a fight now, her eyes flashing. "And we're not making this up! I know what I saw."

"That will be all – no further questions."

And with that, Marlene's evidence was over. She looked almost disappointed as I escorted her and her mother from the courtroom.

"He bloody did do it, you know!" she implored outside.

"Language, Marlene, for goodness' sake," said her mother, shaking her head.

"You did really well," I replied. "Thank you for telling the truth."

I was about to come off shift when Miss Robertshaw waltzed through the door, flopped down in her chair, and triumphantly spun it round a few times, her arms in the air.

"They're committing him for trial at the Old Bailey," she said.

"Really?" I said. "That's a result! Too serious even for the Berkshire Assizes[22]?"

"They wouldn't touch this with a bargepole. But it's for a lesser charge of indecent assault, not carnal knowledge. With Dr Wickes's evidence that she was still a virgin, no jury would convict him of that, but the chairman did feel there was sufficient evidence to support trying him for a different offence."

"Well, that's great news. How did the victim bear up under questioning?"

---

22 Assize courts were held in the main county towns for more serious crimes, with judges from higher courts in London visiting to preside over them.

"Oh, don't get me started. That poor girl was in the witness box for nearly two hours. The defence, as we expected, tried to rip her to pieces. He suggested that her friend wasn't even there, then that she'd claimed to have 'done it' several times before, and even that the general was so tall and she was so small that what she accused him of was physically impossible. He'd even got her to admit that she'd made an indecent suggestion to the general and disarranged her own clothing. I feel he wound her up to such a state she didn't know what she was saying."

"That's dreadful," I said. "Why do we have to make children go through this combative process in open court?"

"And of course, when he'd exhausted all his usual trickery, he just shouted at her, 'Why have you come to this court today and told us a pack of lies?' And by that point, the poor lass was in floods of tears."

"That makes me so angry!" I replied. "But give him his due, the chairman made the right decision to send him up to a higher court."

Some weeks later, Miss Robertshaw stomped into the office with a newspaper, folded round a small column headlined *WAR HERO BOUND OVER*. She threw it down on my desk.

"It's a travesty!" she fumed. "At least he had the decency to plead guilty, but he's only been bound over[23] for three years with £50 costs."

---

23 Told not to do anything like this again for three years.

"The general? That offence could have got him up to two years imprisonment?"

"Yes, but look at who wrote in giving glowing character references."

I scanned the article. It read like a who's who of eminent war heroes, all making saccharine excuses and saying what a jolly good chap he was.

"There would not be a single man under his wartime command who would have considered him a liar... He was captured by the Germans but bravely escaped... I have never regarded him as anything less than a soldier of the highest calibre and military ability... He's only just had a serious operation, which undermined his self-control and exhibitionist urges... He has only three loves in his life: his wife, his family and Jesus... He only committed indecent exposure in 1950 because he was overworked..."

I was speechless.

"It gets worse! Have you seen what the prosecution – the prosecution, mind – said about the victim?" asked Miss Robertshaw.

I re-read the first paragraph and gasped. *"An untruthful girl of subnormal intelligence, dishonest, and clearly demonstrating abnormal sexual tendencies."*

"But she's 13! And if this is to be believed, vulnerable!" I ranted. "He's not a stupid man; he would never have got to his lofty official positions if he wasn't bright."

"Oh, he's clever enough to know what he can get away with, all right, with friends in high places," replied Miss Robertshaw.

"And surely if this were the case, he would have fought to clear his name, pleaded not guilty and it would have gone in front of a jury?"

"It stinks of the old boy network, doesn't it?"

The real sting in the tale was the judge's final comment: *"For at least six years, the General successfully resisted the temptation to repeat the offence he had committed in 1950. I am satisfied that he was NOT the instigator of this indecency."*

I marched home to Murdoch Road, my head spinning with frustration and outrage, desperate to be at the sharp end of investigating criminals like the foul general, rather than the victim support act. That's what the constabulary had trained me for, after all, and they weren't making use of me.

The lights in the house were off, so Mrs Cunningham was probably out at a drinks party and Suzette was working. As I opened the door, I noticed on the mat a small brown envelope addressed to me, with BERKSHIRE CONSTABULARY stamped on the front. My tummy turned over as I picked it up. Could this at last be notice of a detective constable position becoming vacant, or was I going to be sent to Cyprus?

CHAPTER 9

Newbury

October 1956

"Newbury?" asked Henry, shaking his head. "Why *there* of all places?"

Henry and I huddled on a secluded bench beside the river in Cookham as the first yellowing leaves of approaching autumn fluttered down. He'd hugged me for a good hour while I'd raged and cried hot tears of disappointment, soaking his tartan handkerchief.

"And as a WPC still, n-not a detective." My voice shuddered, and I blinked miserably at the transfer letter clutched in my hand. "They've already got two really good policewomen there – Eileen and Beryl – why do they even need a third? Newbury is hardly West End Central[24] for vice and larceny."

"The police station in Pelican Lane is pretty grotty," said Henry, "more like a tatty detached house stuck in the middle of a housing estate."

I snuffled. "Well, that's made me feel a whole lot better."

I'd been to Newbury a few times, and found it even more provincial than Wokingham, lacking a magnificent Arts and Crafts police station. The rest of the town was quite pretty, and historic enough to have seen three

---

24 One of the busiest Metropolitan Police stations, in the heart of London's West End.

unfortunate Protestant chaps burned at the stake in 1556, experienced a couple of English Civil War battles in the 1640s, and in 1772 had a stone bridge built over the canal that was slightly reminiscent of Venice if you half closed your eyes on a hot sunny day.

"Newbury's where your brother's stationed, isn't it?" asked Henry.

"Oh yes, perfect Ron's there. Mum's going to have no end of pleasure comparing us now."

We sat in silence as I dried my eyes and pulled myself together. I peered in my powder compact mirror and a pink-nosed, puffy-eyed mole creature stared back at me. Just a few more minutes on this bench until I looked normal.

"You're going to have to move to Newbury, aren't you?" asked Henry.

"I really don't want the upheaval, just to do exactly the same job in the same kind of provincial Berkshire market town. Wokingham's my home: I've got friends and family, colleagues – and you – all on the same easy patch."

It was probably *too* easy, if I was honest with myself. But, looking on the bright side, it did offer me the excuse to buy something I'd hankered after for rather a long time.

"How long do you reckon it would take me to drive from Wokingham to Newbury?"

"About an hour along the Bath Road," replied Henry.

"You know what, I think I'll stay in Wokingham and drive to Newbury. One advantage of being a WPC is my set shifts, so I'll know what times I start and finish."

"Sure you'll be OK with that?"

"I think so. A drive will set me up for a shift, and I'll be able to wind back down on the drive home afterwards."

I could feel my mood lifting.

"In that case, let's go and have a coffee and we can look through the newspaper small ads for a car for you," suggested Henry.

I chose a corner seat in the Cookham tearooms, while Henry went up to the counter to order. I left him the seat facing the door as he insisted; he couldn't stand people moving around behind him and always needed the full view of a room.

From the radio came the sound of two rapid, tinny drumbeats and Bill Haley's energetic vocals on "Rock Around The Clock". I couldn't stop my shoulders twitching in time to the infectious rhythm, and as I looked over at my handsome Henry, I longed to be on a dance floor, joyfully jiving with him. The music really lifted my spirits, and I had a big smile on my face.

"You look happier," Henry said as he returned with two coffees.

"I love this song," I said, all but dancing in my chair.

"Bloody rubbish," he replied. "This rock and roll nonsense from America ought to be banned, along with that stupid film that's inciting the youth to criminal damage."

Berkshire County Council, after consultation with our "fun sponge" Chief Constable, had just banned the film *Rock Around The Clock* from our cinemas, claiming it had incited youths to hooliganism in other towns. "We don't want that sort of thing here," they'd said. "Pandemonium" had broken out in a Burnley picture house, where jiving teenagers had ripped the arms off seats and turned a fire hydrant on, and overexcited Teddy boys in Croydon had squirted a cinema manager with a fire extinguisher as they danced out into the streets after the film.

"Ach, what a load of moral panic[25]." Hilda had sniffed at the ban. "I don't believe the members of the General Purposes Committee even bothered to watch the film. Most of them probably still think the magic lantern[26] is a novelty."

Deflated somewhat, I sipped my steaming coffee as Henry got a visceral dislike of Bill Haley & His Comets out of his system. "I didn't fight for six years against the Nazis for these hooligans to smash up whatever they like to *this* racket," he ranted.

I waited for him to finish venting, then turned my attention to scouring the small ads in the *Maidenhead Advertiser* for a second-hand car.

"She's a lovely little runaround. Gave my late wife many hours of motoring pleasure," said Professor Pickering, handing me the keys to a shiny 1952 Clarendon Grey Morris Minor a week later.

My first car! I spun the wheels on his gravel driveway as I got used to the clutch and accelerator, then drove out onto the main road.

I put my foot down along the A4 Bath Road to Newbury, relishing the speed and my first taste of

---

25 A widespread fear – usually irrational, and often media-fuelled, that someone or something is threatening the safety, interests or values of a community, or society generally.

26 An early form of slide projector, dating back to the 1600s.

independence. I hadn't seen my sister-in-law, Gladys – Ron's wife – and my toddler nephew, Brian, for a while, so, on the off-chance, I called in on them.

Sweet, warm Gladys hugged me, and we took our cups of tea into their police-house back garden to join in with Brian's game of throw-the-conkers-into-the-cups. This would be a bonus of working in Newbury: I could be Auntie Gwen more, spending time with this little man, who, with his dark hair, chocolate eyes, rosy cheeks and freckles, was the spitting image of his mum.

Gladys and I chatted easily, mostly about how ridiculous my mother/her mother-in-law was, but around 1.50 p.m. she kept looking at her watch.

"I mustn't keep you, chatting away," she said. "Gwen, you've probably got lots to be getting on with, what with your move to Newbury and all."

"Oh, I'm fairly easy today, Gladys, it's nice to see you and Brian."

"It's just… Ron is going to be home soon – he's on six-twos today – and I haven't done the washing up or ironed his shirts yet. He hates the ironing board being up…"

Brian managed to throw a conker in his eye, and he started screaming blue murder. It took an age to calm him down and check there was no damage done, and he cuddled snottily into my shoulder as Gladys walked me out to my car parked on their drive.

"Aye aye, what's all this then?" said a familiar voice. It was Ron, wheeling his bicycle home.

"Hello, Ron," I said. "I've just had a lovely time with your gorgeous son and wife."

"Have you now? We haven't seen you for ages. Sure you haven't just come round to show off this shiny new car of yours?" He roared with laughter at his own comment.

"We'll be seeing a lot more of Gwen," said Gladys. "She's being transferred to Newbury."

"Oh right. CID then?" he said, his face falling.

"No, still a WPC – for the moment," I replied through gritted teeth, stroking Brian's hair.

"Haven't we got enough of those here already?" Ron cackled. "After all that la-di-dah detective training up London and you still end up in the ranks with me. Mum always said you'd have trouble getting a proper detective posting."

Brian had begun grizzling again and it was time to go. I peeled him off my shoulder and handed him to Gladys, and then he really started to scream.

"He's very tired," Gladys said. "I'd better get him indoors for his nap. See you again soon, Gwen."

"Is my lunch ready, Glad?" asked Ron. "I'm ravenous. Yeah, ta ra, Gwen."

They trooped into the house. I reversed too quickly off the drive, narrowly missing the gatepost. Taking several deep breaths, I headed back to Wokingham.

DRRRRRRRRRIIIIIIINNNNNGGGGG! My alarm clock blasted through my deep, cosy November dreams. I slapped my bedside light on and gazed blearily at the clock face: 4.30 a.m. and pitch-black outside. I braced myself to throw off my eiderdown and get up. I hated winter earlies, and these had become even earlier with the drive to Newbury. My breath condensed in the room's freezing air as I gingerly eased myself into my clammy uniform.

Oh bugger. My car windows were frosted, and I wasted a precious 10 minutes scraping the windscreen. Fingers and nose frozen, I offered up a prayer of gratitude to Professor Pickering's late wife for choosing the optional extra of a heater in her car. I was soon toastily tearing along the empty Bath Road towards Newbury as fast as I liked – there were no speed limits outside built-up areas.

The other WPCs and I took it in turns to cover the foot patrols around town, and we seemed to spend an inordinate amount of time in the tea shops. And guess what I spent most of my time investigating? That's right – shoplifting.

"Woolworths is increasingly being targeted by those Teddy boys and girls," said our superintendent, Dick Baker. "As you're a new face, WPC Crockford, I'm going to put you in plain clothes with a PC there on Saturday morning. See if we can catch the little sods who are nicking their records."

I was no stranger to plain clothes, and had been known to scrub down into an all-too-convincing pensioner. I'd heard one of my previous shoplifters say you could always spot an undercover policewoman because they never wore nail polish. So, I went all out on my hair, make-up and nails.

"Miss Crockford!" said Miss Robertshaw on her Newbury WPC inspection before I changed into plain clothes. "It's very unlike you to be wearing nail varnish?

I hope it's for a sound reason; otherwise our uniform standards have really slipped."

Without my police cap flattening my hair, and in full make-up, I could pass as a well-to-do housewife, so I busied myself in character, studying Woolworths' kitchen equipment while keeping an eye on the shop entrance. PC Rose, disguised in some decorators' overalls, loitered by the Pick 'n' Mix, munching sweets he'd surreptitiously helped himself to.

And sure enough, in sauntered a group of four Teds – two Brylcreemed boys in crepe-soled shoes, and two big-haired girls in their uniform of rolled-up pedal pusher jeans, flat pumps, oversized velvet-collared dogtooth jackets and old lady lace blouses with cameo brooches and bootlaces at the throat. The girls made a beeline for the record section next to the mats and floor coverings, while the boys split up and wandered round the paints and tools. They'd clearly got their strategy to dilute a single store detective off pat, but hadn't bargained on two plain-clothes police officers.

PC Rose gave me the wink that he would keep tabs on the boys, and I winked back that I would watch the girls. And before long, the smaller girl picked an LP off the display and tucked it under her jacket. *Game on*. The girls pretended to show some interest in the knitting wool, then gravitated towards the door. Like sharks scenting blood, the boys approached, circling the girls, and together they walked out into the street and outside the law.

"Police! Stop!" I yelled, and the four Teds split in different directions.

The small girl with the record inside her jacket turned right and tore down Northbrook Street, knocking trolley-pushing grannies out of the way and leaping onto a stationary bus at the bus stop. I raced after her, apologising to the grannies as I went, congratulating myself for wearing flat shoes.

"Police! Hold the doors!" I cried to the bus driver.

"Are you all right, madam?" he asked. "You want me to call the police for you?"

"I am the police!" I panted.

"I'm sure you are, dearie. Are you getting on or what?"

I rummaged in my handbag and produced my warrant card.

"I'm a plain-clothes police officer! You've got a shoplifter on your bus."

PC Rose appeared, panting, at my side. "Lost 'em! But no matter, as the only one who stole something was yours."

"Hello, Alan!" said the bus driver. "Either you're in plain clothes too or you've been kicked off the force and working in the trades!"

"Afternoon, George. I do a lovely line of pebble-dash texturing if you want me to give you a quote?"

Er, can we get a sense of urgency round here?

"Gentlemen!" I interrupted. "Haven't we got a shoplifter to arrest?"

"Our new WPC," said PC Rose to George, rolling his eyes.

The shoplifter had squeezed herself under the seats, and it took two of us and the bus conductor to extract her. She still had the LP tucked under her jacket as we accompanied her to the police station. In the grubby interview room, Polly, as she was called, started sobbing, rivers of mascara running down her cheeks.

"I know this is upsetting, when you've done something wrong and got caught," I said, "but your mum's on her way and once I've taken your statement, you'll be able to go home. We won't be putting you in any cell."

"It ain't that," replied Polly, looking forlornly at the LP sitting as evidence on the table in front of her. "I wanted Bill Haley and The Comets' 'Rock Around the Clock' and instead I've picked up the crappy Embassy[27] version by some bleedin' band called The Canadians. It weren't worth all that effort."

Driving to and from Newbury soon lost its appeal as winter began to bite and the roads became treacherously icy. A couple of times I skidded on bends – incredibly, nothing was coming the other way – and thanked my lucky stars I'd had practice controlling a car on police skid pans. Another day, I burst a tyre in a pothole and had to change the wheel on a deserted stretch of road in the pouring rain. Where was a chivalrous lorry driver when you needed one?

It was also tiring.

"You've got big dark circles under your eyes, hon," said Suzette at supper one December evening. "Are you sure driving to Newbury all the time is good for you?"

---

27 Embassy records were Woolworths' own cut-price record label with cover versions of popular songs. They were just as disappointing as those *Top of The Pops* cover compilations we had in the 1970s and '80s.

"It's a lot of effort, Suz," I replied, "but something's holding me back from moving there just yet. I have this strange feeling that I *will* somehow end up in Newbury in the future, but not just now."

"Are you worrying about something? You know you can tell your Auntie Suzette?"

I pushed my plate away.

"I don't know. I'm not sure whether I'm simply afraid of change, whether I don't feel the Newbury job is worth making that change, or whether something's about to happen with Henry."

"Henry? What do you mean?"

"Well, we've been courting for nearly a year now, and it's usually around that time, or sooner, that men pop the question, isn't it?"

"You mean marriage? Weren't you the first one to say it was a shame that Pattie gave up all her police training and experience to get married?"

"Well, yes, but Pattie, bless her, was never particularly ambitious. She loved being in a relationship, and that's not really compatible with being a policewoman. Last time I spoke to her she was blissfully happy being a Met PC's wife, and that's right for her."

"But you *are* ambitious, Gwen," said Suzette, her brown eyes wide and encouraging. "You're frustrated that you can't get on."

"Yep, you're right – Newbury was a shock, and I'm still reeling from it if I'm honest. I'm trained in surveillance and observation techniques, I can analyse white collar fraud, I can stomach a post-mortem and offer hypotheses on cause of death, yet the most exciting detective work I'm doing is catching whoever's got their fingers in the Woolies Pick 'n' Mix. Is this what my life will be? I'm nearly 27 – getting on a bit for marriage and children, and stuck in an undemanding job."

Suzette sat back in her chair.

"One thing I would say, Gwen, don't be like me and rush into marriage. As the saying goes, 'Marry in haste, repent at leisure.' I've been repenting for a looooong time marrying my useless husband back in Barbados."

"But at least you have your lovely son, Colin." I usually refrained from talking about Colin as mention of him made Suzette teary.

She wasn't this time. "I'm seeing him soon."

"Are you bringing him over?"

"No. Actually, I've been putting off telling you this…"

"Oh?"

"…I'm thinking of going back home. Barbados is rolling out an NHS-style healthcare system and they're going to need trained nurses to help staff it. I've had experience here which will make me very valuable. My mother, who has so far done a brilliant job of looking after him, isn't getting any younger. I miss her, and my sisters, but most of all, I miss my boy."

Well, that was a blow, but completely understandable. Suzette was one of the people keeping me here in Wokingham. And thinking about it, I wouldn't miss my mother at all, my sisters were busy with their own lives, and I could pop over to see Dad whenever. Henry wouldn't be at Wokingham forever – he could be transferred anywhere in Berkshire. What was I thinking, putting myself through this mad commute?

The final nail in the coffin of living in Wokingham came courtesy of Henry's favourite politician.

"That bloody idiot Prime Minister Antony Eden!" he moaned. "By cantering into this end-of-Empire skirmish with Egypt for nationalising the Suez Canal, petrol supplies from the Middle East are all but cut off and we're back to rationing." He shook his paper ration book with a blue triangle on the front.

Rationing was back as a result of the Suez crisis[28]. We were technically allowed 200 miles worth of petrol per month, but this was pretty useless as (a) I was doing a 52-mile round trip every day, and (b) people panic-buying petrol emptied out all the stations, so if you weren't quick enough, you couldn't get fuel even if you had enough coupons.

So, it was with a heavy heart that I went to view a dismal olive-green spare room in a doggy-smelling house in Newbury, owned by an elderly widow who had two yappy off-white poodles with that brown crud running from their eyes to their jowls. Alone, on a painfully slow day in the women's office, I typed an acceptance letter to Poodle Lady for her doggy room. I shed tears as I wrote my notice to Mrs Cunningham, thanking her for sharing her rambling house with me and Suzette for the past four years, and for all the beige-but-comforting

---

28 In a nutshell, the Egyptian president, Gamal Abdel Nasser, supported by the Soviet Union, nationalised the British/French-owned Suez Canal (the gateway for petroleum shipments to western Europe) and seized it. Diplomatic efforts to settle the crisis failed: Israel invaded Egypt, then French and British forces occupied part of the canal zone. Britain and France were eventually forced to withdraw and lost much of their influence in the Middle East.

meals she had prepared day in, day out, in between her cocktail parties and bridge afternoons.

I was just licking the envelopes when I heard Miss Robertshaw's distinctive footsteps approaching, and hurriedly slid them under the blotter.

"Miss Crockford? Have you got a moment?" she asked, closing the door.

Oh, what petty thievery are you sending me to investigate now?

"Yes, Miss Robertshaw."

"To let you know, a detective constable position has come up. Interested?"

A bolt of lightning couldn't have made me sit up faster.

"May I ask where, miss?"

"Maidenhead and Windsor."

Christmas was coming, and it felt like all mine were about to come at once.

CHAPTER 10

Double trouble:
Maidenhead & Windsor

Maidenhead with Le Mercier
Spring 1957

"Behind every successful woman is a surprised mother, eh, Aggie?" said Dad as he carved our roast chicken Christmas dinner. He glanced at Mum, who glared back at him over the boiled cabbage, her lips barely visible.

"Here's to our very clever daughter who's just become Berkshire's first-ever woman detective constable! And in posh Maidenhead to boot!" He raised his schooner of Harvey's Bristol Cream in a toast, and the rest of the family chorused, "Here's to Gwen... in posh Maidenhead!"

"It took long enough," said Mum, stabbing a parsnip. "Ron – why don't you put in for detective training? It can't be that difficult if Gwen can do it."

"My Ron's not very good with blood." Gladys giggled. "Brian knocked his toenail off under the bathroom door and Ron nearly fainted."

"Shut up, Glad! I'm better with blood than most of the damn detectives I know," snapped Ron, pointing his fork at her like a weapon. "*They're* not the ones first on the scene at a multiple fatality road traffic accident when a family of four have gone under the back of a coal lorry and decapitated themselves. *They're* not the first to arrive when someone's put a shotgun in their mouth..."

Gladys shut up and fiddled with her napkin. We all shut up.

Another lovely Christmas dinner in the Crockford household.

"Anyway," Ron continued. "What special qualities do you need to be a detective?"

I opened my mouth to answer, but Dad got in first.

"A suspicious mind – you never believe anybody. Always alert to the first signs of trouble, and ready to get stuck in. Excellent hearing, eyes in the back of your head. Completely ruthless and prepared to kill if necessary... I think your mother ought to apply."

Everybody roared with laughter except Mum, who took herself off to bed before the plum pudding, complaining of one of her "heads".

Maidenhead was to be my base, but I would divide my time between there and Windsor police station. Petrol rationing due to the Suez Crisis seemed never-ending, some sources saying it would go on well into the spring of 1957. CID didn't do shifts, just unpredictable days that could be very long. It was time to grow up and move to Maidenhead, away from the bosom of Mrs Cunningham's lodging house.

"I'm going to miss you so much, my darling girlie," trilled a wet-eyed Mrs C, as I stood in her panelled hall with my packed suitcases, "and I'd like you to accept this gift from me as a little memento of your time here."

She handed me a pink tissue-paper parcel tied with

yellow ribbon. I pulled the bow and opened it. Beatific Jesus from my bedroom wall!

"Your job might get dangerous, so I wanted Him to look after you," she said.

Suzette gave me a cake tin. "To be eaten when you've come back from a long hard night, and you need a warm Caribbean hug."

I prised off the lid and out wafted a familiar rich, sticky scent of fruit and rum that set my mouth watering.

"Your black cake![29]" I said. "Who needs a drop of the hard stuff when I can have a slice of this?"

"It'll last for months in a cool place."

We loaded the suitcases into my car. I hugged Suzette and Mrs Cunningham swiftly, and jumped in before I let the tears come. Henry had managed to siphon enough petrol out of a police car to get me the 15 miles to Maidenhead, and I headed off there, blinking.

My new home, more compact than Mrs Cunningham's rambling mock Tudor lodging house, was in Sperling Road; a three-bed semi on a newish housing estate to the north of Maidenhead town centre. It had a small concrete driveway, perfect for my car. My new landlady, Mrs Foskett, a youngish widow who worked at the telephone exchange, greeted me as I huddled under the brick porch from the rain.

"Come in out of the rain, Miss Crockford. I'll show you your room."

---

29 Black Cake is a Barbadian speciality, made with finely chopped prunes, currants, raisins and glace cherries that are soaked in rum and red wine or Guinness for months.

The house smelled of the new, swirly, multicoloured carpet fitted throughout, and fresh gloss paint. Mrs Foskett accompanied me upstairs to the back bedroom overlooking a neat little garden. It had mint-green walls and curtains, brand new Schreiber furniture and that fashionably garish carpet. This would do nicely.

"I've only recently done up the house, and you're my first-ever lodger," she said. "I hope you like it. After my husband died it was such a relief to sell all that dark old furniture from his mother's house and get something that I liked for a change."

"It's lovely, Mrs Foskett," I replied.

"And I haven't got round to knocking the bedroom fireplaces out yet – that's a future project, but do let me know if yours makes your room draughty."

I was so used to sleeping in draughts all my life that I was sure they would help me feel right at home. And Beatific Jesus could sit on the mantelpiece.

"I've put a small ad in the *Advertiser* for the box room next to yours, so we'll see who turns up," said Mrs Foskett.

I wondered who my fellow lodger would be too.

At last, my smart grey suits would get worn for work. As I fastened the skirt button, I was relieved it fitted after all the cakes I had eaten in Newbury. On my first day, I cycled the five minutes from Sperling Road to Broadway where the police station towered over Maidenhead town centre. I loved a characterful police station, and Maidenhead's was another rather wonderful red-brick Edwardian edifice. With its bow-fronted corner, pointy roofs, arched windows and magnificent-but-pointless Norman-style bell tower, it looked like a wizard's castle, as drawn by an imaginative child. I loved it.

A row of blurry felons glowered at me from their WANTED posters just inside the door, but a friendly reception by senior officers greeted me as I arrived for my first duty – a contrast to the cursory nod given to me and Pattie by The EF on our first day as WPCs in Wokingham. Over coffee with top brass Chief Inspector Clegge, Inspector Morton and Detective Inspector Cockerill, I instantly felt part of the team and that I would be taken seriously.

"You'll be working with DS Ernie Le Mercier, Miss Crockford," said DI Cockerill. "He's out on a job, but as soon as he's back, I'll introduce you. Let's get you settled into the CID office."

Le Mercier? I wonder if he's French.

Cockerill accompanied me to the CID office on the first floor. Some desks, filing cabinets, shelves and pinboards were scattered throughout a long, airy room with tall windows.

"This room used to be the dormitory where the unmarried policemen would sleep," said Cockerill.

"And still is, on a slow day," said a voice behind us.

I turned round. A neat man, no taller than the regulation 5 feet 8 inches minimum height, with a greased quiff of black hair, dark brown eyes, slightly buck teeth, and deep cheek dimples leant against the door jamb, arms crossed.

"Ernie! Come and meet your new DC, Gwen Crockford," said Cockerill.

Ernie strode forward, hand outstretched.

"Delighted to meet you, Gwen, I've heard all about you. Welcome to the wonderful world of Maidenhead CID."

"All good things, I hope? How do you do, Ernie, good to meet you too." Ernie's handshake was strong and sincere.

"I'm going to leave you two to get acquainted," said Cockerill as he left the room. "Be gentle with him, won't you, Gwen?"

"I'll try my best, boss," I replied.

"This is where you'll be sitting, Gwen." Ernie indicated a rickety school desk, propped up on a paperback copy of *Scotland Yard* by Sir Harold Scott, and piled high with box files, wire baskets of yellowing paperwork, and an ancient Imperial typewriter. A mop in a tin bucket leaned against it.

Ah well, it's enough that I've got into CID with any kind of desk, I thought, hanging my handbag on the stark metal chair in front of it.

"Gotcha!" cackled Ernie. He pointed to the large leather-topped kneehole desk opposite his, with a leather-upholstered swivel chair. On it was an empty wire basket, a relatively new Olivetti typewriter and a black Bakelite telephone.

"*That's* your desk. We use this little one for dumping stuff we don't know what to do with."

"Very good – I almost believed you for a second there." I sat down and swivelled the chair from side to side, pinching my hand under the desk. *This is more like it.*

Ernie's telephone rang.

"Excuse me while I take this." Ernie tapped a packet of Kensitas cigarettes on his desk and offered me one of the two that popped up.

That's my brand. The man has taste.

"DS Le Mercier…"

Cradling the receiver under his chin, Ernie struck a match and lit my cigarette first, then his. We puffed away in companionable silence as a shrill voice wittered away in his ear. Not appearing to want to listen in, and hearing the buzz of a motorcycle and some shrieks of laughter outside, I wandered over to the open window and looked down on the station's back yard.

I couldn't believe what I was seeing. A motorcycle officer whizzed round the courtyard with what was obviously his mate on the pillion. His mate was in turn giving a piggyback to a large Alsatian with its paws over his shoulders, ears up, tongue flying, and what could only be described as a huge doggy grin on its face. They circled a short, stocky WPC who hopped up and down in fits of hysterical laughter, photographing this extraordinary trio with a Box Brownie camera.

Then, the chief inspector marched out of the back door towards the WPC. *Oh dear, this lot are going to be on report.* But he was laughing too.

The motorcyclist drew alongside the chief inspector, and the Alsatian hopped off, bounding up to him wagging his tail and leaning on him. The chief scratched the dog's ears and the officers chatted away cheerfully.

I'm going to like working here.

Ernie, his call finished, joined me at the window.

"Who are these then, Ernie? They've been having a jolly old time while you've been on the phone."

"Matt Wagstaffe been doing his circus act again? OK, he's the motorcyclist – a real joker, and a great backup uniform man to have with you on a difficult investigation. His mate is Reg Plomley, our dog handler, with PD Rex, our police dog. If there's any sort of disturbance, they get sent in to disperse it – 'The Scourge of the Teddy Boys', we call Rex. He's also a great tracker dog and an unstoppable land shark if we need him to take down a felon. And that's WPC Ursula Meeke, our pocket rocket. She's solid muscle, sportier than all the men and – can you believe it – a judo expert. Nobody messes with her."

"How well do you know Maidenhead?" asked Ernie as late afternoon approached, and we'd been through most of the current case files.

I wasn't going to tell him that Henry and I used it for our courtship outings. And, thinking about it, we would have to find somewhere else for our dates as I'd now be a familiar face in Wokingham *and* here.

"I've been here a few times, mainly Cookham and the town centre, but I can't say I know it *that* well."

"It's a bigger manor[30] than you'd think. Encompasses some very wealthy areas like Boulters Lock and Pinkneys Green, and some rough bits with caravans on. Probably the best way for you to get a feel for it, and what we're

---

30 Police term for "patch"

often up against, is to go out with one of our vehicle patrols. Up for that? Might mean a late evening tonight, though."

"Yes please!" I jumped at the opportunity. I was so pumped with adrenaline on my first day that I'd happily have done a full ten-six night duty as well. The plan was that I catch the tail end of a two-ten patrol, and Ernie and I grabbed a teatime pork pie in The Star pub next door.

"So, 'Le Mercier'?" I asked. "That sounds a bit French to me, Ernie."

"I guess it was French long ago, but I'm originally from Guernsey. Came over with my quick-thinking mother when we were evacuated in June 1940. Didn't see any reason to go back. So here I am."

We wandered back into the station yard where two flat-capped traffic PCs were about to head back out on vehicle patrol.

"Lads! Got a VIP for you to take out on the town this evening," called Ernie. The policemen looked me up and down. "You know we were getting a new detective constable…" he continued.

"Yeah, when's he supposed to be starting?" asked one.

"*She*… started today. Meet WDC Gwen Crockford from Newbury. WDC Crockford, meet PC Ingham and PC Letts."

I shook hands with two surprised men.

"They kept that quiet!" said Letts. "I wasn't expecting a w—"

"Well, she's going to be doing the same job as the rest of us in CID," Ernie interrupted, "with additional women and children stuff that I try to avoid like the plague. So don't put her off, whatever you do."

"After you, Miss Crockford," said Ingham, holding a door open for me.

I slid into the rear passenger seat, and Ingham and Letts took their seats up front.

Letts flicked a switch on the dashboard to activate the radio. Only our patrol cars had radios; no beat officers did.

"Just connecting us with Sulhamstead HQ," he said.

"HA 13 mobile, over," he said into the receiver, as we pulled out of the yard then stopped in a line of traffic in King Street where the radio crackled its first message.

"All patrol cars, calling all patrol cars. Be on the lookout for a green Commer Karrier three-and-half-ton truck, used in a theft of tyres from a garage in Wokingham."

"Get that? All eyes peeled for a Commer Karrier."

"In that case, I'll head out on the Bath Road, up round to Pinkney's Green, then swing by the Thicket," said Ingham. "You'll never guess whose house is on the unoccupied list this week. One for you, Miss Crockford."

"Oh, who?"

"Richard Todd! Wayside House!"

"You're kidding me!"

Aah, Richard Todd. One of my favourite heart-throb film actors. I couldn't believe we were going to drive right up to his house! Maidenhead was a hub of the British film industry, with Bray Studios, home of the Hammer Horror films, on the doorstep, and Pinewood Studios also close by. I would eventually become blasé about seeing Hollywood A-listers out and about in the town, but for the moment I was somewhat starstruck.

"He was bloody brilliant in *The Dam Busters* last year," said Letts.

"Daa da da da dada daa…" We all sang the "Dam Busters March" as we purred along the Bath Road.

Ingham pulled up outside a sprawling, partially timbered old coaching inn on Pinkneys Green.

Letts handed me a torch as we squeaked open the wrought iron gate. "I figured you'd probably want to look through the front windows, just to check everything's in order."

Of course I want to peek into the house of someone rich and famous! Who wouldn't?

"I'll check the garden, the doors and the back windows," he said.

Peering into the living room, my torch beam illuminated oil paintings of Regency dukes and duchesses, Baroque gilded mirrors, oriental vases and highly polished antique furniture. I wouldn't expect anything less of a Hollywood superstar.

"Packet sticking out of the letterbox," said Letts. "Perfect advertisement that the occupiers are away. I pushed it through."

We got back into the patrol car and accelerated along Pinkneys Drive. An unexpected odour of faeces filled the vehicle.

"What the hell's that smell, Les?" asked Ingham, wrinkling his nose.

"I must have got sh— I mean something, on my shoes," replied Letts.

"I think I have too!" I said. "Of course! The Todds have seven dogs! I read it in *Picturegoer* magazine. I'm not surprised we've trodden in mess."

"Oh bloody hell, Les," said Ingham, pulling over to let us wipe our shoes on the grass verge.

So with the faint odour of Richard Todd's dogs' excrement lingering in the patrol car, and a lame claim to fame I could regale friends with, we swung by Maidenhead Thicket, a large area of ancient wooded common. A notorious haunt of vicious highwaymen in the seventeenth and eighteenth centuries, and with alleged sightings of a phantom horseman galloping through in the dead of night, the place always gave me the shivers, particularly as us police knew of all the assaults, indecencies and suicides that happened there. The stark, leafless trees silhouetted against tonight's bright half-moon made it even more sinister. I was glad I wasn't out here on my own.

"I'm going to cut the lights. Keep 'em peeled for flashers and nancy boys[31]." Ingham chuckled.

Nobody was about at 9 p.m. on this semi-moonlit night, and the radio crackled into life again. "Calling HA 13, over."

"HA 13, over."

"Please proceed to Maidenhead railway station... lady in the ticket office... very upset... alleges a prowler followed her along Shoppenhangers..."

Ingham hit the accelerator, flinging me back in my

---

31 Derogatory, old-fashioned term for effeminate or homosexual males.

144

seat. We sped back along the Bath Road, screeching a sharp right into Grenfell Road, and tearing round the streets to the front of the railway station.

"Female complainant," said Letts. "We need to radio for a WPC to come out."

"Er, hello, I'm still here," I called from the back seat. "I may be CID now, but I've got five years of WPC experience!" *How good did that sound?*

"Of course! Forgot about that, miss."

"Two for the price of one."

A smartly dressed lady of about 30 sat in the waiting room with a ticket inspector, pale and trembling.

"What's your name, madam?" I asked.

"B-Betty Gibbs."

"What happened?"

"I got off the train around 8.30 and came out of the station into Shoppenhangers Road – I live along there, see, and a man followed me out. I'm scared of being followed, so I turned round and he stopped walking. So I carried on, a bit faster, and I could still hear footsteps, but every time I turned round, I swore he'd jumped into some bushes or a driveway. Now, I know if you think you're being followed, you should cross the road, so I did that, and he crossed too! I was getting scared by then, and there were no cars about, so I ran back to the station where there were streetlights and people, rather than home."

"Did he follow you back to the station?" I asked.

"I don't know," she replied. "I was running and didn't look back."

"Can you give us a description?" asked Letts. "We can have a spin round and see if we can spot any likely-looking characters."

"Obviously it was dark, and with the town lights behind us he was in silhouette, but he wasn't wearing a hat and he didn't have a beard. He was wearing a mackintosh and not carrying anything."

Letts shot Ingham a look. *Great, not much to go on.*

"We'll go and see what we can find."

They set off to search the area for what could be any man in Maidenhead. I sat in the chilly waiting room with Betty Gibbs, taking her full statement as she gnawed at fingernails that were already bitten down to the flesh. The man hadn't tried to hurt or touch her. As a one-off incident, it would be hard to say it was even an offence.

Letts and Ingham returned.

"Unless we're going to arrest the entire mackintosh-wearing population of Maidenhead, there was nobody we could find out there acting suspiciously," said Ingham. "But what we *can* do is run this lady home safely."

"And I'll file this report," I said. If anything like this happens again, Mrs Gibbs, you must get in touch with us immediately."

As we walked to the parked patrol car, I noticed a group of Teddy boys hanging around the Jubilee Clock Tower opposite the station, smoking cigarettes and horsing around with each other. One looked familiar – John Carroll. A little older, a little taller, but still with the glowering veneer of self-preservation that came from a tough childhood.

"Couldn't have been one of those?" I asked Betty.

"Ooh no – the man who followed me didn't have a quiff."

"Who are those then?" I asked Letts.

"They're the Teds who hang around at the Strande Castle caravan site. They don't seem to be getting up to mischief at the moment, so I won't move them on, but I'll let nights know they're in town. It's only when the Pinkneys and the Woodlands Park Teds turn up that it all kicks off."

After dropping Betty Gibbs at her house down the end of Shoppenhangers Road, Letts and Ingham ran me home.

"Bit of a more exciting manor than Newbury, eh, Miss Crockford?" asked Letts.

I started saying, "Anywhere's more exciting than Newbury," when the radio spat:

"Calling HA 13, over."

Letts groaned and reached for the receiver.

"This had better not be something major at the end of a shift. HA 13, over."

"Green Commer Karrier spotted abandoned in Egypt … please attend…"

"Egypt? Goodness, he must have been driving fast," I quipped.

"Egypt, to the mysterious east of Burnham Beeches, unfortunately," groaned Ingham. "Let's go, Les, get this bugger sorted ASAP. Nice meeting you, Miss Crockford."

And they roared off into the night. I really was going to enjoy working in Maidenhead.

CHAPTER 11

Petermen

Maidenhead with Le Mercier
Spring 1957

"Betty Gibbs, eh? This is a non-investigation," Ernie said to me the next morning, reading my report. "Just following someone isn't a crime."

"She seemed pretty shaken up by it," I replied.

"I can appreciate she was. But you need to understand that Betty Gibbs is, shall we say, one of our premier customers."

"Meaning?"

"There's rarely a week goes by she doesn't ring us fretting about someone in her back garden, or peering in her front windows, or tailing her when she's driving or following her round the shops. We send an officer out, but they never find a trace of a perpetrator. Being followed from the station is a new one, it seems. Mrs Gibbs is something of a worrier."

"To be fair," I replied, "we had Mrs Falmer in Cranborne who was always reporting people who 'looked funny', and vehicles she was convinced belonged to Soviet spies. She rang in one day to say she had a 'strange horse' in her garden. That turned out to be an escaped zebra from Billy Smart's circus!"

"I remember that!" Ernie chuckled. "Mrs Gibbs probably is wasting police time, but the one time we don't send someone out is the time she gets murdered in her bed. I'll ask one of our WPCs to pop by and suggest she gets her husband to meet her at the station from now on. I'll file this in the usual place."

Ernie put my report on the rickety desk's teetering "things we don't know what to do with" paperwork pile. The phone on his desk jangled.

"DS Le Mercier…"

He made a double-fingered gesture in front of his lips as he listened to the call, and I threw one of my cigarettes to him. He lit it and squinted through the first curl of smoke as he scribbled notes.

"Right," said Ernie, replacing the receiver and standing up. "We've got a proper crime to investigate over on the industrial estate. The Petermen have been at it overnight again."

"Petermen – who are they?" I asked.

"Safeblowers[32]. Pretty incompetent ones this time who are lucky to be alive. Apparently, they used so much explosive that they blew the safe door clean off, up through the asbestos roof, and into the yard outside.

"You're kidding me? Why didn't that wake half of Maidenhead?"

"It did apparently – place swarming with uniform. They've only just rung it through to us now they've identified it as a crime, not a gas explosion. Grab the fingerprint field kit, would you? Let's go!"

---

32 Thieves who used explosives to blow open safes and steal the cash and valuables inside.

In the unmarked CID car, we drove towards the engineering firm where the bungled raid took place.

"Where do they get all these explosives from, Ernie? Barely a week goes by without a safe-blowing being reported."

"They use gelignite for mine and quarry blasting, so it gets stolen from those sites. Sometimes shipments of the stuff to these places never arrive, or only some of it does, or it gets stolen en route. And don't forget there are loads of ex-servicemen in the criminal fraternity who know about explosives and detonators, and which wires to connect to what. Although with this level of incompetence, our lot were probably Pioneer Corps[33]."

"And why Petermen? I've not heard that expression before."

"Probably something to do with the saltpetre element of dynamite, but..." Ernie started giggling "...I've also heard it comes from the French word péter which means 'to break wind'."

"Bet there was a lot of that when the door went through the roof," I replied.

"Jet-propelled exit from the crime scene."

We blew raspberries like schoolchildren and giggled so much that Ernie nearly swerved into a ditch.

---

33 The Pioneer Corps was an army company that carried out most of the really dirty manual work, such as repairing roads and railways, clearing bomb debris, unloading supplies and labouring. The unskilled nature of the Pioneer Corps' work made them (often unfairly) the butt of contemporary jokes.

Arriving at Wallis Yates Tubing Ltd, on the outskirts of Maidenhead, uniform appeared to have everything well in hand, managing witnesses and preserving the scene. The safe door had come down corner first into the yard's asphalt and was sticking out of the ground, roped off so beautifully it looked like a piece of DO NOT TOUCH abstract art in a sculpture garden rather than a crime exhibit.

"I heard a tremendous bang during the night, but thought it was a car backfiring," one resident was saying to PC Wagstaffe as he took their statement.

Rex, the police dog, bounded over to greet us, with Reg Plomley stumbling up behind, his trouser bottoms spattered with mud and leaves.

"Hello, Rex, have you caught those nasty burglar men?" I cooed, scratching him behind his ears.

"He picked up a scent and followed it through the housing estate, but then lost it on the flooded waste ground unfortunately, miss," said Reg.

"That's a shame," said Ernie.

"The foreman's inside the office waiting to speak to you," Reg continued. "He'll tell you all about it."

We went through the open door of the unit, weaving past all the vicious-looking industrial machinery and tools in the workshop to the office in the back. The sun had come out by now. A shaft of sunlight swirling with dust and particles shone through a gaping 4-foot hole in the ceiling, illuminating a weary-looking foreman standing by the blasted, doorless safe. He was puffing fine white powder and sawdust off the purchase ledgers into the air.

"Please don't disturb anything, sir," said Ernie as we approached. "DS Le Mercier and WDC Crockford, Maidenhead CID."

"Roger Vickery, foreman." We shook hands.

"Well, they've made a right mess of your office, haven't they?" said Ernie.

"Didn't even get away with anything." Roger gestured at six crumpled white £5 notes sitting on the accounts desk. "There was only £30 in the safe and I've gathered it all up."

"That all?" asked Ernie. "They're even thicker than we thought if they didn't target the last Thursday of the month – the day before pay day when the safe is full of wages."

"Going to have to get a new asbestos cement roof though." Roger looked glumly at the ceiling. "Would have been less hassle for me if they'd done a decent safe job and just taken the money."

"All right if I come in?" a familiar voice called through the workshop. It was PC Bennett, our clues officer who now worked out of the photographic department at Sulhamstead.

"Hello, PC Bennett!" I said. "I'd better get dusting for fingerprints, hadn't I? Where did they gain entry?"

"Hello, Gwen!" said Bennett. "Nice to see you 'in the field' as they say. They jemmied the unit door."

"That's where I'll start dusting then – point of entry, then the door handle into the office, desk drawers, the safe itself lying on its back, then the safe door, I guess."

I took the soft round hair brush out of the fingerprint field kit and dipped it lightly in a jar of aluminium powder, tapping off the excess. Using curved strokes, just as I was taught at Hendon, I lightly brushed the powder over the door and desk handles.

"Nothing brilliantly distinctive, one or two partial prints, but those may be Mr Vickery's or other employees'," said Bennett. "I'll photograph them anyway for elimination, but it looks as if they wore gloves to break in."

I was inclined to agree with him.

I turned my attention to the safe door decorating the yard. As I dusted on the powder, some beautiful textbook finger and thumb prints showed up on its hard, dry surface. Definitely amateurs who couldn't resist taking their gloves off to do the fine work.

"Look," said Bennett, "they've removed the lock escutcheon, then packed the keyhole with gelignite – it probably kept disappearing inside and they couldn't see they were putting too much in. When they detonated it … Boom! It's funny stuff because it behaves like putty and smells like marzipan, so you can get a bit blasé with it."

"So they were only supposed to blow the bloody lock off?" said Ernie.

Fingerprints photographed, we returned to the accounts office.

"Can you take some samples of the sawdust packing that's come out of the safe walls, Gwen? We may need to send those up to Scotland Yard for analysis."

"Of course, Ernie. Why are we doing that?"

"Safes have got their own identifying markers. The older ones, perhaps pre-1900 had only sawdust, but after that they started mixing chemicals with the sawdust to make them fireproof – the chemicals would melt and create a heat barrier to protect the contents. Scotland Yard can analyse the composition. Then if we find matching sawdust residue on any suspects – and there's no way they didn't get showered with it when the safe went up – that's some pretty strong evidence."

We bagged as much evidence as we could: the sawdust, the six £5 notes – much to Mr Vickery's chagrin: "How am I going to pay for the repairs?" – the safe door and some scattered fragments of detonator wire, and took them all back to the CID office.

We returned to join uniform doing house-to-house enquiries, spending the rest of the day taking the same witness statements over and over again.

"…Really? The safe door went through the roof? … *Laughter*… Anything taken? … Nobody hurt? Hell of a bang from somewhere in the direction of the industrial estate… thought it was a car backfiring…"

"If I have to read another statement about backfiring cars, I think I'm going to backfire," said Ernie, blinking at a pile of paper. "Pint and a therapeutic game of snooker?"

"Sounds good to me," I said, rubbing my eyes, even though I'd never picked up a snooker cue in my life before.

Maidenhead station had a smoky police club on the ground floor with a bar and a snooker table where we could go to decompress and catch up with gossip. Ingham and Letts, just off their ten-six mobile shift, sat at a corner table with their pints and nodded in acknowledgement as we walked in.

Ernie brought me over a glass of light ale. "You've never played snooker before? I'm in for an easy win here, aren't I?"

"If I don't rip the green baize, I'll consider that a win, frankly," I replied.

As it turned out, I was a natural at snooker. I quickly mastered holding the cue steady on my thumb, and even potted a few reds and colours on my first game, despite feeling male eyes of off-duty PCs boring into my backside as I leaned over the table in my tight skirt to take the shots.

Ernie cleared the table so we wouldn't be there all night, although I'm sure he deliberately missed the black so I could pot that and end my first game on a high.

I could get quite into snooker.

Returning to the CID office, we surveyed the piles of papers pertaining to the safe-blowing with waning enthusiasm.

"There's nothing new here that can't wait till the morning," said Ernie. "Go home and get some sleep and we'll do it all over again tomorrow."

"Even the snooker?"

"Especially the snooker."

I cycled back to Sperling Road, a big smile on my face. My first proper CID investigation and I'd done a lot and learned so much from Ernie. I'd worked with Bennett, who I considered the best clues officer ever, and not made a complete idiot of myself at the police club snooker table. It had been a good day.

An enviably shiny, maroon-and-cream Ford Consul saloon with glinting chrome trim sat outside the house.

Nice car. The front door was open, and piled up in the hallway were some cardboard boxes, a wooden Singer sewing machine case and a battered but stylish WW1 officer's leather suitcase. Upstairs, the light was on in the box room next to my bedroom.

I glanced at the hall telephone table where there was a note in Mrs Foskett's handwriting left for me.

GWEN

5.30 PC Falconer called. Please call him back.

6.20 PC Falconer called again, please call him back.

7.35 PC Falconer called YET AGAIN, please call him back, it must be something important.

I looked at my watch. It was gone 8 p.m. and I was hungry, and ready to make myself some soup and a sandwich, but I didn't want to risk annoying my new landlady if Henry rang again. I dialled his number and made a note of the time for payment purposes.

"Wokingham 2490," said the voice.

"Hello, Henry, it's me. How are you? Everything OK?"

"Yes fine. Where have you been?"

"At work. We had ever such an interesting case today. Some safeblowers – Ernie calls them Petermen – broke into an engineering firm and blew the door off the safe…"

"And the door went through the roof and ended up in the yard, I know." Henry sighed.

News of crimes travels fast in the police fraternity.

156

"Well, yes, that's what we've been investigating all day."

"That's a long day," said Henry.

"We did go to the police club for a break, and I played my first-ever game of snooker with Ernie. I didn't win though."

"Did you now? I hope you didn't make too much of a spectacle of yourself. You've got to remember as the only woman detective eyes will be on you all the time, judging you."

"I wasn't drunk, and I didn't poke the superintendent with the snooker cue, if that's the sort of thing you mean?"

"No, it's fine. And at least you were in the police club, not The Star next door."

Henry had a strange relationship with pubs. Some bobbies were a fixture in their local, considered one of the regulars. Henry maintained that it was all too easy to get friendly and familiar with the types who frequented public houses, which could result in being expected to turn a blind eye to things, and he wouldn't risk being compromised. "A man is known by the company he keeps," he would say. He would have a light ale with me in a saloon bar, but wouldn't be seen in a public bar.

"What were you ringing me about anyway?" I asked. "It sounded urgent?"

"No, not really. I'm on nights for the next week and just wondering when you wanted to go out for an early dinner one night and where."

As Henry rattled off the options, a pair of feet in polished brogues appeared at the top of the stairs, followed downstairs by some long slender legs and an equally slender torso in a fitted white shirt, and finally a chiselled face with strong cheekbones and a floppy blond fringe appeared.

Henry's voice faded into the background as this svelte Adonis gave me a broad smile and a wave before sweeping up the Singer sewing machine and going back up the stairs two at a time.

"Gwen?... Gwen?... You there?" I tuned back in to Henry's voice.

"Oh yes, sorry. Somebody was just moving stuff about in the hallway."

"So, dinner at The Steak House on Wednesday?"

"Yes, absolutely, as long as I don't get stuck at work. You know what it's like with CID. Look, I've got to go – see you on Wednesday."

Mr Adonis was at my side again, this time collecting the leather suitcase.

"So sorry to disturb your phone call," he said. "Let me introduce myself. I'm Victor Cartwright, and I'm the new lodger." Victor held out a long, elegant hand and I shook it.

"Gwen Crockford." I could feel myself blushing. "I'm in the room next to you." *Oh, why did I have to say something as banal as that?*

"Well, I'm delighted to meet you, my dear, and what is it you do?" asked Victor.

"I'm a detective," I replied. *Gosh, that sounded good.*

"So which stores do you work in? Just so I can be on the lookout when I'm shoplifting... Just kidding!"

"Not a store detective – a real detective! In CID. I'm with Maidenhead and Windsor police."

Victor's smile faded and a serious look momentarily crossed his face.

"But you're a..."

"Woman? Yes, we're starting to get everywhere, aren't we? But don't worry – when I'm here I'm off duty. Just make sure you fence those stolen goods before you come back home, eh?"

Victor's smile returned.

"And what do you do?" I asked.

In Mrs Foskett's kitchen over a cup of tea and a cigarette – a pipe in Victor's case – I learned that he was a costumier for the film studios dotted around the area, and that he would be a most interesting source of showbiz gossip.

"So Errol Flynn really did that?" I asked, aghast at the blue anecdote Victor had just told me.

"As I live and breathe. Never seen anything like it."

"The closest I've got to the local celebrities is stepping in Richard Todd's dogs' faeces," I regaled.

"Oh, those bloody things! He lets them crap everywhere. I've probably trodden in it myself, darling."

I was going to enjoy sharing a house with Victor.

"I think we've got 'em!" said Ernie the next morning as I hung my coat on the stand.

"That was quick."

"Local gamekeeper found a couple of likely lads hiding in a makeshift shelter in the woods. One with burns to his hands and face – really needs a doctor. I'm going to interview them with DI Cockerill later, but could you have a look through their belongings and

159

see if you can find something that links them with the safe-blowing at Wallace Yates? At the moment, the burnt one, John Moffat, is claiming he got drunk and fell on their campfire, and his mate, Donald Digby, says he can't remember."

I collected what looked like two army kit bags from the front desk and took them upstairs to the CID office. We had a spare desk that I decided to commandeer and keep clean for forensic purposes, as long as Ernie's "stuff we don't know what to do with" didn't creep onto it.

Working on each kit bag separately, it was clear which belonged to whom. The first bag contained cleanish, neatly folded trousers, a sweater and a jacket, with a pair of pliers in the pocket and a roll of wire that looked as if it would match the detonator wire we found at the scene – that must be Digby's.

The second bag – Moffat's – contained a jacket peppered with tiny holes, as was a jumper no doubt worn underneath it, and a pair of filthy trousers, ripped at the knees. Apart from a packet of Woodbines and a box of matches, there was nothing in the pockets. There were, however, some tiny, dust-like fragments of sawdust on the jacket. Very proud of myself for noticing, I spent an hour painstakingly picking them off with tweezers and making the tiniest sample of sawdust in a glass tube.

My eyes smarting from the close effort, I then held up the trousers to look for holes, noting with distaste the organic-smelling brown stains that had seeped through the seat. As I looked down, I saw that the turn ups were full of sawdust – enough to fill three glass tubes, in fact.

Damn. I made a mental note to look for the bigger things first in future and then scale back for the smaller stuff.

I went down to the interview room with an empty glass tube and knocked on the door. Ernie opened it and peered out.

"You got Digby in there?" I asked.

"Yes," he replied. "He's not being particularly forthcoming."

"Ask to have a look in his trouser turn-ups, and if you can, put what you find in here."

"Can you believe he said the sawdust in his turn-ups came from a visit to the circus?" chuckled Ernie, as we made up a package of evidence and posted it off to Scotland Yard's Forensic Science Laboratory.

Within a few days, we received it back with a report: the detonator wires found at the scene matched the wire found in Digby's pocket. Both suspects' turn-ups contained identical spruce sawdust with fragments of iron and brass turnings and matched the ballast sample from the Wallace Yates safe. Our Fingerprint Department found that my dusted prints matched Moffat's and Digby's exactly.

In court, Digby pleaded guilty to breaking into Wallace Yates and attempting to steal £30; causing an explosion likely to endanger life and property and being in unlawful control of explosives. He got five years.

Moffat stood in the dock, his face still red and scarred, and pleaded not guilty. It didn't take long, however, for a jury to deliver a guilty verdict, and for the judge to pass sentence on him.

"Safe-blowings are, regrettably, becoming increasingly common," said the judge. "You deliberately broke into an engineering firm, armed with all the burglarious tools of the Peterman's trade, and blew up a safe with gelignite, damaging the building in the process. At least Mr Digby was decent enough to plead guilty. But you, Mr Moffat, in the face of evidence that was so plain, went into the witness box and committed perjury[34], showing not the slightest trace of remorse. I sentence you to eight years."

"Good job, you two." DI Cockerill raised a glass to us in the police club bar. "That's two felons behind bars, not particularly smart ones, granted, but off the streets all the same."

My final task was to drop the £5 notes back to Mr Vickery, as they had done their job as evidence, so he could get his asbestos roof mended.

---

34 Telling lies under oath – punishable by up to seven years' imprisonment.

CHAPTER 12

Filth!

Windsor with Kinch
Spring 1957

"Enjoying Maidenhead CID, Gwen?" asked Ernie one
Friday morning.

"Yes, I am," I said, brightly.

"So – nicely settled, you know what you're doing, and
who you're working with?"

"I do, and it's a good feeling," I replied. *Why are you
asking me these things?*

"Hate to break it to you, but Windsor want to borrow
you."

"What, now?"

"Yes, afraid so. If you could go over there and meet
DS Kinch, he'll fill you in on their investigation."

"All right," I sighed. "Although to be fair, Ernie, that was
the deal when I signed up – based at Maidenhead, but
covering Windsor as well. How big a job is it, d'you know?"

"Something to do with indecent publications. I've
said I'll lend you out, but I want you returned to me in
the same condition, if not better." Ernie grinned.

Where Maidenhead had a general air of affluence and
gentility, sprinkled with some louche showbiz glitz and

glamour, Windsor's atmosphere was tangibly tougher and more militaristic, a product of centuries of tradition. Not surprising really when the Queen's imposing second home, Windsor Castle, sat plonked right in the middle of the town, policed by the Met (not us) and guarded by barracks full of soldiers tramping the cobblestones day and night. Outside its walls stood a bronze statue of Queen Victoria moodily poking at something with her sceptre, and even the police station was square, squat and red brick, like an angry colour sergeant.

I stood stock-still just inside Windsor police station lobby, unsure what was about to kick off in front of me.

"I KNOW MY FAAAKKKIN' RIGHTS AND YOU GAVVERS AIN'T GOT NUFFIN' ON ME!" roared a beefy, flat-capped character, jabbing a finger at the desk sergeant and at a tall, moustachioed man in a suit. The tall man, noticing me, grabbed my elbow and bundled me through a door into an office behind the front desk.

"Just discharging a difficult prisoner, bear with," he said, in a strong Birmingham accent.

"AND I WANT MY FAAAAAKKIN' STUFF BACK!" yelled the voice from the lobby.

"DS Stanley Kinch. How do you do, WDC Crockford," he barked breathlessly, and pumped my hand in greeting, before squatting down and taking a tray of belongings out of a locker.

"Let me just get rid of this bastard – I think he's as guilty as hell but his alibi stacks up, so we've got to let him go."

I peered into the tray. In it was a filthy handkerchief, a wristwatch with a cracked glass, a box of matches, a flattened packet of Players cigarettes and a single condom. Kinch pulled a drawing pin off the noticeboard, picked up the condom and punctured it twice.

"That'll teach him," he snarled, disappearing through the door with the tray.

The roaring man gone, and peace restored, DS Kinch led me up to the CID office. At once I missed Maidenhead's airy space, as every surface looked as if it was piled with "stuff we don't know what to do with". I perched on the edge of a chair.

"Now, will you be my wife?" was Kinch's opening question, his ice-blue eyes gazing into mine.

I felt my cheeks burning, and whatever answer I gave, yes or no, would only make them burn more.

"Well, I..."

Kinch laughed and leaned back in his chair.

"We've had reports that there's a stall in Charles Street Saturday market openly selling obscene books and cine films. We need to go along, undercover, posing as a husband and wife looking to... shall we say... spice up our marriage, so we get an idea of the full range of 'goods' on offer."

I wasn't sure how a wife looking to spice up her marriage would dress in public, so the next day, Saturday, I put on my dowdiest skirt, white blouse, green woollen overcoat and a felt beret. I dabbed on some pale pink lipstick; I avoided scarlet as I felt it would make my undercover wife persona seem too sexually confident and less needing of marital aids to be convincing.

Kinch, wearing a long dark overcoat, tie and a flat cap met me on the corner of Peascod Street and William Street.

"May I say you are looking particularly fine this morning, Mrs Kinch," he said, offering me his arm.

"As do you, Mr Kinch," I replied, cursing the blush creeping up my neck.

Trying to look married, we made our way to thronging Charles Street. The market was crammed with basket-carrying housewives, Silver Cross prams with babies sitting up in them, and stallholders yelling their wares.

"Pahndapearspahndapearspahndapearsthruppence[35]."

I loved a good outdoor market, the handcarts stacked with pyramids of tinned goods, rolls of itchy wool blankets, pegged lines of towels, tea towels and tablecloths, and wooden crates of muddy vegetables fresh from the farm. The sight of hanging bunches of bananas always gave me a little dopamine hit of pleasure; as bananas could only be imported after the war, I associated them with dark times coming to an end, and sweet times ahead.

One stall, in particular, stopped me in my tracks: an island of colour in an otherwise beige-neutral mid-fifties landscape. *Munshi's Indian Silks*, it said on a wooden placard. I felt intoxicated just looking at the shiny dresses, scarves, bags and rolls of fabric in peacock blues, kingfisher teals, scarlets, golds, purples, emeralds and

---

35 "I am selling a pound of pears for three pence."

saffrons that decked the stall. I wanted to buy everything, wrap myself in yards of printed silks, or at least dig out my sewing machine and make a cheerful bedspread.

"Cheap, very cheap," said Mr Munshi, a dapper, bearded gentleman in a sheepskin jerkin and a pointed astrakhan hat, gesturing expansively at his rainbow stock. "Cheaper than Woolworths."

"It's all so lovely!" I enthused. "Don't worry, I'll be back."

"You'll be very welcome, ma'am," replied Mr Munshi.

I wonder if Victor knows about this stall for his costumes.

"When you've quite finished fantasising about what you're going to be wearing for our Saturday night dance, we've got a book stall to visit... dear," said Kinch.

Towards the end of the market, we found the book stall. A dumpy, rosy-faced woman with straw-like long hair, fingerless gloves and a stained fisherman's sweater sat on a stool puffing a roll-up cigarette.

"Take yer time, me loves, and 'ave a good browse," she said.

"Thank you," said Kinch.

We began to scrutinise the spines of the books neatly laid out on the stall top and in upright bookcases at the front. Lots of hardback Dickens, Trollope, Brontë sisters; enough Bibles and Books of Common Prayer to stock a Sunday School; gold-embossed memoirs of Victorian generals; *Ingoldsby Legends*, Bunyan's *Pilgrim's Progress*, *Clans and Tartans of Scotland*, *Cassell's Natural History*, *Peoples of the World in Pictures*, Lady Trowbridge's *Book of Etiquette*, 10 volumes of *The Children's Encyclopaedia*... so far, so respectable.

We started on the rows of Penguin and Pelican paperbacks, squinting at the spines. Right in the middle were three books with their spines positioned downwards. I reached for one, and out of the corner of my eye I noticed the bookseller watching me. I pulled it out. On the cover was an etching of a young man peeping through a keyhole and the title *Within Temptation's Reach*.

I passed it to Kinch. "That might be suitable... for us."

"Hmm-mm," Kinch murmured.

I reached for another. Titled *Enslavement*, the cover illustration depicted a stereotypical Arabian prince leering above a blonde woman writhing on a Persian carpet. The third book, *Seven Lonely Nights*, showed a woman swooning against a horse as a hunky blacksmith nailed a shoe onto its hoof.

"We'd like to take these two, please," I said to the woman, proffering *Within Temptation's Reach* and *Enslavement*. I deliberately left *Seven Lonely Nights*; if indeed these books were obscene, and we had to get a warrant under the Obscene Publications Act 1857[36], we needed to leave something to seize.

"Are these for your private use?" asked the woman, giggling.

Time for some acting.

---

36 A magistrate would need to agree that these materials were obscene according to the law of the time, which was the Obscene Publications Act 1857, before they could issue a warrant to seize the materials.

"We like to be a bit adventurous... don't we... er... Marmaduke?"

Kinch's eyebrows shot up. *Marmaduke? Why the hell did I call him that?*

"Well, yes, we do... er... Hepzibah," he blurted.

I sniggered at his ridiculous cover name for me and had to hope the bookseller thought I was embarrassed about the books.

"Would you like some films?" she whispered.

"Films?"

"Yeah, films... like your books... if you've got a projector..."

"I don't think we own a pro..." I began.

"Yes, we've got a projector, dear" cut in Kinch, nudging me hard in the ribs.

The stallholder rummaged about in a cardboard box under the table and pulled out a metal film canister labelled *The Mislaid Necklace*.

"Sorry, I only seem to 'ave one of these left, but if you like it, I can get some more."

"Where do you get them from?" I asked, casually.

"Oh, a studio somewhere in Slough..." She hesitated. "But I can get you whatever you want."

"How much is the film?"

"Two pounds special price to you, my loves."

"And the books?"

"Two bob each."

"We'll take them," said Kinch.

"That'll be two pounds four bob in total, please, darlin'."

The woman wrapped the books and canister in brown paper and tied the parcel with string. Kinch handed her the money.

"Can I have a receipt, please?" he asked.

"You can, but I ain't writing what it's for," she said, scribbling something illegible on a scrap of paper and handing it to him.

"Thank you very much," we said.

"See you, loves. I'm 'ere every Saturday in case you need summat for the weekend." She gave us a saucy wink as we wandered away.

"Bugger – I'm not going to get my two quid four bob reimbursed on my detective duty allowance with that dodgy receipt, am I?" moaned Kinch.

"I'll vouch for you," I replied. "It's all evidence anyway, if we discover these things are obscene."

We started on the books. I would have been perfectly happy to read them quietly, but Kinch, feet up on the desk and lounging in his chair, couldn't help himself.

"Listen to this… Hepzibah."

He started reading. *"Penelope had been languishing on the harem's damask chez [sic] longue all the long, lonely after-noon. The Arabian heat stirred her loins and animal urges had consumed her late in the afternoon. She tried to resist the feeling, but her hand was drawn inexorably down to the warm, soft Venusian [sic] mountain atop her thighs, her fingers desperate to explore once more. Crash! went the opening door to the harem, and there stood Sheikh Abdul, arrogant and panting with desire. He advanced upon Penelope, pulling aside his robes to expose a member that stood as proud as Cleopatra's Needle on the Victoria Embankment, and it, Penelope thought, was not a lot smaller..."*

"Oh, stop it now... Marmaduke!" I cried. "I think we've heard enough to ascertain that these books are filthy enough to count as obscene under the 1857 Act. The quality of writing is a crime in itself."

"What's yours about?" asked Kinch.

"A peeping Tom and what he sees the chambermaids getting up to together, then he goes and joins in," I replied, not wanting to read any of it out.

"Considering the subject matter of the books, I think we'd better have a look at the film, don't you?" asked Kinch. "I'll set the projector and screen up, and we'll watch it."

Well, funny how many police officers suddenly needed to get stuff out of the CID office or show Kinch something while we were running *The Mislaid Necklace*. A small, uniformed crowd gathered, spilling out into the corridor, as we watched a woman in a nightie playing a piano, except there was no sound, and a couple of wags hummed "Für Elise" as a makeshift soundtrack.

Another woman came in and started dancing, but before long, her nightie fell off to cheers from the assembled PCs, leaving her wearing only a large heart-shaped necklace. She danced more and more frantically, our crowd now dah-dah-dum-ing "Night on the Bare Mountain", before her necklace flew off and out of a conveniently open window. Cut to the naked dancer bending over rummaging about in a shrubbery, when presumably the gardener, naked from the waist down, appeared out of a bush and approached her from behind. The PCs burst into a rendition of "Bobbing Up and Down Like This".

Then the film snapped and flapped, the screen went white, and to boos of disappointment, the show was over. The PCs trooped out of the CID office, with files and paperwork held firmly in front of themselves.

While everyone's attentions were elsewhere, I'd opened the film canister. Stuck to the inside of the lid was a small, faded label.

> *Richard Pike*
> *Wedding Photography*
> *Waterbeach Road*
> *Slough*

I showed Kinch.

"C'mon, Hepzibah, we're going on a vice raid."

A nondescript man with thinning hair and wire-rimmed glasses opened the door to a nondescript suburban semi in Waterbeach Road, Slough. Showing him our search warrant, we soon found a neat pile of films with titles such as *Florence and Fanny*, *Freedom of Youth* and *Fields of Joy*, with some catalogues.

"I don't *produce* the films, officers," said Pike. "I just sell them for a few pounds as a sideline to my wedding photography business, along with comedies and travelogues. I sell them quite openly, there's nothing underhand about it – my name is on all the canisters."

"But you do know what's on the films, don't you?" growled Kinch.

"Nothing that bad, surely?" Pike replied. "Nobody gives you any guidance about how far you can go with these art films…"

Richard Pike appeared before Windsor magistrates charged with publishing obscene "super-glamour" films. The magistrates had insisted on watching all the films so they could be absolutely sure of the nature of the material. Pike pleaded guilty, and was fined £100 with £6 16s costs.

We returned to the bookstall in Charles Street Market to find the stallholder had replenished her stock of dodgy paperbacks with 10 more. She beamed when she saw us.

"Back for more, my lovies? Enjoy the last two?"

Kinch flashed a warrant at her, and her face fell.

"Oh. You're rozzers."

"DS Kinch and WDC Crockford, Windsor CID," he said.

"So you ain't married to each other after all, then?" She huffed.

"We're here to seize a quantity of books and films under the Obscene Publications Act of 1857," said Kinch.

"Obscene, my love?" she replied. "I 'ad no idea my books could be thought of as obscene. Romantic, maybe. Couples like reading 'em to each other at bedtime, they tell me. Nobody's complained to me they're obscene before…"

The stallholder looked on, arms folded and puffing on a roll-up, as we located all the likely spine-down paperbacks and stuffed them into a carrier bag. We didn't find any more films.

"Don't take all my bleedin' stock! That's my livelihood!" she pleaded. "If I lose my pitch, I'll have no alternative but to go and sell my body on the streets!"

"You won't get much for that…" scoffed Kinch.

"Well, charming," said the woman.

"…unless you sell it by the pound."

Peggy Fish, from Staines, as we discovered she was called when we arrested her, also appeared before Windsor magistrates. She maintained she was unaware that any of her books could be classed as obscene.

"But, madam, I have read each and every one of them," the chairman of the magistrates retorted, "and I can assure you that they are utter filth and must be taken out of circulation."

Peggy Fish was trying hard to keep a straight face, even as the magistrate fined her £20 with £10 10s costs.

I think we were supposed to take the films and books away and destroy them, but Kinch put them in a filing cabinet drawer in the CID office, meaning to get round to doing it later. Over the next year, the contents of the drawer gradually diminished until eventually there was nothing in there at all.

CHAPTER 13

Snout

Maidenhead with Le Mercier
Spring 1957

Back at Maidenhead late one Wednesday afternoon, Ernie wiped tears of laughter from his eyes as I regaled our exploits with Peggy Fish, Richard Pike and *The Mislaid Necklace's* impromptu screening.

"Don't get too good at these undercover obscenity stings, Gwen, otherwise the Met will be poaching you for Clubs and Vice[37]." He chuckled. "Kinch is a brute, but he gets the job done."

I couldn't disagree.

One of our civilian secretaries tapped on the door.

"There's a journalist from the *Express* downstairs, Miss Crockford," she said. "Wants to interview you, apparently."

A sweaty, florid-faced man in a trilby and mackintosh with a camera slung round his neck crunched my knuckles with a bear-like paw.

"George Porter, *Windsor Express*," he wheezed, taking out a notebook and pencil. "I'd like to get the lowdown

---

37 The Metropolitan Police's Clubs and Vice Unit was an operational command unit that dealt with policing nightclubs, vice and obscene publications.

on Berkshire's first woman detective, if you don't mind giving me a few moments of your time?"

"Yes, that's fine, I'm happy to talk to you."

"And might I say that you are looking particularly trim and efficient."

"Er, thanks."

"How old are you?"

"27," I replied.

"Really? You look young for your age. And you took up your duties a few days ago?"

"No, I've been here a few mon—"

"And you'll be dealing mainly with women?"

"No, my work as a member of the CID is the same as the male detectives, so I'll be dealing with housebreaking, larceny, shoplifting... But no doubt I'll be working on cases involving women too."

"So how did you get to where you are today?"

I reeled off my journey to CID: six years as a shorthand typist in a solicitors' office, on the uniform beat for five years in Wokingham and Newbury, detective training, and now my current role between Windsor and Maidenhead CIDs while in digs in Sperling Road.

"Any men in your family in the police force?"

"Yes, my father, Walter Crockford, is a special constable in Wokingham and my brother Ron is a PC at Newbury."

"And finally, be honest here, how many people have you arrested?"

"Quite a few actually." I wasn't prepared to go into details.

"Can I get a picture outside with the station in the background?"

I stood under the blue lamp in the late afternoon gloom, and George Porter's flashbulb didn't go off.

"Not sure that will come out – too dark." He sniffed. "Look out for the interview in next week's *Express*. Toodle-pip."

I skimmed the resulting article when it came out.

Berkshire's first woman detective, 27-year-old Miss Gwendoline Crockford has been appointed to the East Berkshire (Windsor and Maidenhead) Police Division… Miss Crockford will deal not only with the usual cases involving women but with any type of crime that turns up, whether it is housebreaking, larceny or shoplifting. With fair, curly hair, Miss Crockford, looking trim and efficient in a grey suit and red jumper, told us she had been a shorthand typist for six years before becoming a policewoman five years ago… Miss Crockford admits that she has arrested "quite a few people" while she has been a police officer. Her father, Mr W.M. Crockford, is a special constable at Wokingham and her brother Ronald is in the police force at Newbury.

And my next job did indeed involve larceny.

Every police officer deals with many sorts of "breaking in" during their career. According to the complex, rambling, loathed-by-trainees Larceny Act of 1916, burglaries had to be night-time (between 9 p.m. and 6 a.m.) break-ins at "dwelling houses[38]" *only*, while housebreaking could be any building: shop, warehouse,

---

[38] According to *Moriarty's Police Law*: "some permanent structure in which some person or persons habitually sleep as member or members of the household that occupies and dwells in it".

office, school, factory, garage, pavilion, dwelling house and the like, at any time. So, your house could be "broken into" during the day, but "burgled" at night, and your office "broken into" night or day.

As a WPC, I had generally been sent to break-ins where women were present. Pattie and I had had great fun attending a burglary at the mansion of glamorous Hollywood actress Gloria Gilmour, where we'd joked that the burglars probably had to tidy up all her mess before they could find anything to steal. I'd also been first on the scene at a break-in at a Wokingham butcher's shop, and an opportunist burglary through a kitchen window that had been left open. After attending, we would then leave CID to get on with investigating it and hope that DI Dankworth wouldn't upset or patronise the victims too much.

Now I was in CID, I was one of the ones investigating it after uniform had left, and my WPC experience informed my victim aftercare. Being broken into could be an incredibly upsetting experience; it was a violation of personal space, disregard for the victim's order of things, and unsettling that one's security could be penetrable.

Ernie and I were called to a break-in at a tiny, dusty lingerie shop run by the Prings, an elderly couple who probably should have retired from shopkeeping long ago. Dingy and dark, oak panelled, with creaky wooden floorboards and smelling of beeswax polish and mothballs, it was probably the last place in Maidenhead where you could buy "intimates" such as big satin camiknickers, boned corsets and elasticated Victorian bloomers – in plus sizes too.

Was this where some of our shoplifters bought their tools of the trade? I wondered.

Oasis of the Roaring Twenties' opulent fashions as this little shop was, it couldn't compete with the light, bright, lingerie department in Woolworths or the bigger stores filled with modern, floaty nighties, undies and dressing gowns in fashionable nylon.

As we arrived, WPC Ursula Meeke was comforting a tearful Mrs Pring inside the shop with a cup of steaming tea she'd acquired from somewhere.

Good girl – that's a really important part of your job.

PC Matt Wagstaffe was doing his best to stop Mr Pring picking up the sea of silks and violated semi-naked lingerie-clad mannequins flung all over the floor.

"I know they look as if they need rescuing, sir, but you really mustn't touch anything until CID arrive," we could hear him pleading.

"Don't worry, we're here," called Ernie, tiptoeing round the strewn lingerie and over to Mr and Mrs Pring. He shook hands with them and patted Mrs Pring's shoulder.

"Ah, no, I wish they wouldn't do this," he said. "So unnecessary to make a mess of all your stock."

Mrs Pring started sobbing again.

"Maybe somebody saw the thief?" asked Mr Pring.

"I think there's a good chance that they had stockings over their heads – probably not on the way in, but certainly on the way out," said Ernie.

There was a silence. *Oh no, Ernie, was that really appropriate?* Then both Mr and Mrs Pring burst out laughing, and so did we, and the mood lifted.

"What have we got?" Ernie asked Ursula.

"They went round to the back kitchen window, punched a small hole through a pane of glass, lifted the catch and climbed through," she said.

"Classic breaking and entering," said Ernie.

"They jemmied open the cash register, which had about £40 in it, and threw that on the floor."

Some neighbours arrived and scooped up Mr and Mrs Pring for sympathy and no doubt more tea, as we got to work.

"Could you two go and do some door to doors, see if anyone saw or heard anything?" Ernie asked Ursula and Matt, who headed out to make wider inquiries.

Our findings were as follows:

- Fingerprints: No – definitely wore gloves and kept them on
- Footprint: Partial and indistinct
- Witnesses: Nobody saw or heard anything
- Equipment: none found

"Pretty clean break in – not a lot to go on," said Ernie, rubbing his chin.

The next major break-in happened not long after. Ernie and I were just getting the day going with our first coffee and cigarette when the phone rang.

"DS Le Mercier... yes, good morning to you, guv... where's that, Windsor? ... Kinch away, is he? ... Mmm... hmm... yes, sounds remarkably like the one at Prings' lingerie shop... we'll be right over."

We drew up outside Boots the Chemists in Thames Street to be met by Cockerill and the Boots manager, Mr Elisha.

"What have we got, guv?" I asked.

"Mr Elisha opened up at 9 a.m. and discovered that the display cases had been raided and their contents thrown around on both upper and lower shop floors."

"Much stolen?"

"Mainly fountain pen and propelling pencil sets, electric razors, perfume, aftershave, jewellery... Mr Elisha reckons about £150 worth of goods."

"How did they get in?"

"Not sure, that's what we're about to find out..."

Nothing was obvious around the front of the building, so we went round the back to where a metal fire escape led up to a small, seemingly intact window.

"Mind where you're treading, guv!" cried Ernie.

"Oh good God, I'd forgotten about this at break-ins," said Cockerill, lifting his beautifully polished Italian leather shoe off a large, soft turd.

"They don't have a guard dog here, do they?" I asked.

"I'm afraid this is very much human," said Cockerill, wiping his shoe on a discarded cardboard box, "and you'll find it at nine out of 10 break ins. Just before they break in is a tense time for criminals. They're anxious that they're going to be seen or caught, the adrenaline's flowing to get the job done, so they'll often have the urge to defaecate near the scene."

"This one certainly got a job done," quipped Ernie.

Revolting as it was, I couldn't help seeing a forensic opportunity here.

"But guv, what if we gathered that, er, deposit, as evidence and analysed its contents? I can see pea skins in it from here. We could question a suspect about what they've been eating, then try to match that with what we find in the excreta?"

Ernie and Cockerill stared at me, noses wrinkling.

"Well, if *you* want to do that, WDC Crockford, absolutely be my guest," said Cockerill, "but Scotland Yard wouldn't thank you for sending it up there. Perhaps if we were looking at a murder and we had no other clues."

I looked again at the squashed turd, and my forensic fervour evaporated. Ernie was by now at the top of the fire escape.

"I can see how they've got in," he called. "They've punched a little hole through the window, lifted the latch and climbed in that way. Just like at the Prings'."

I searched the yard below, and we'd been so fixated on the faeces that we'd missed a length of discarded string with a piece of a Boots paper carrier bag handle still attached to it.

"They must have lowered the stolen items down out of the window on a string, or strings, and come out the way they went in," said Cockerill.

I picked up the string and dropped it into an evidence bag.

Well, this break-in had only a little more evidence than the last one:

- Fingerprints: Definitely wore gloves and kept them on.

- Footprints: None discernible
- Witnesses: Nobody saw or heard anything
- Equipment: A piece of string and a carrier
  bag handle fragment

"It's definitely the same bloke," said Ernie. "Same MO[39]."

We filled the CID office with smoke and empty coffee cups trying to make some sort of breakthrough on the two cases. Then Ernie opened his desk drawer, took something out and put it in his coat pocket.

"I've got a headache," he said. "But I've also got an idea. Let's go for a walk."

Sometimes there's no point sitting staring at a problem; you've just got to get out into some fresh air for a new perspective. We walked through leafy Kidwell's Park, admiring the crocuses and budding trees, and chatting amiably about the cases before heading North along Cookham Road. Ernie stopped outside the double doors of the Catholic church, and turned the handle.

"Just need to pop in here for a while, Gwen," he said, and we walked into the cool, red brick peace of its nave, the clacks of our heels on the stone floor amplified by the high arched ceiling.

Taught from a young age to maintain a reverential silence in church, I refrained from asking Ernie what on earth he was doing. *Perhaps he's praying for some divine guidance?*

He walked up to the altar and nodded at it, then seemed to disappear behind a wooden cupboard.

---

39 Modus operandi – way of doing things.

He's probably lighting a candle; that's what these Roman Catholics do, isn't it? I slid into one of the wooden pews, looked around, and contemplated how this church was really no different from All Saints C of E Church in Wokingham, despite what my mother would have us believe about "those funny Papists with their bells and smells".

Ernie re-emerged from the cupboard and trotted towards me with some urgency.

"Ray Street, now," he murmured.

"What was all that about?" I asked as we quick-marched over the Strand Water bridge towards Ray Street.

"When in doubt, ask your friendly neighbourhood priest what they hear in the confession box," replied Ernie.

"Are they supposed to do that?" I asked, aghast. "I thought whatever you told a man of the cloth would remain completely confidential?"

"Father Geoghegan doesn't exactly come into the station with a weekly list of crimes and misdemeanours, you know – we have to ask," said Ernie. "But he's as unhappy about the rise in crime as we are. And 'do not steal' is one of the Ten Commandments, so he's not very happy when one of his parishioners gets away with that. Plus, he likes the whiskey I slip him when he gives us a tip-off."

Well, fancy that. I always thought the grasses, snouts and coppers' narks[40] would be dodgy geezers down the

---

40 Police informants.

pub willing to sell out their fellow felons for monetary reward or lighter sentences.

We knocked on the door of a terraced house in Ray Street and a young, buxom, raven-haired woman opened it.

"Good afternoon, madam, DS Le Mercier and WDC Crockford of Maidenhead police. We're looking for a Mr Aron Walsh. Have we got the right address?"

"Er, yes, he's my husband. He's OK, is he? He hasn't done nothin' wrong, has he?"

"We're not bringing any bad news. We'd just like to ask him a few questions if that's all right."

"I'm just getting his tea ready. He'll be home very soon. Do you want to come in and wait?"

We stood in the small double-aspect living room, as Mrs Walsh – Rosie – busied herself in the kitchen, making us cups of tea and boiling potatoes that steamed the windows up. Through the mist, I noticed several satin camiknickers and slips hanging on the washing line in the little garden. While Ernie peered into a wastepaper bin that contained some screwed-up paper carrier bags, I went into the kitchen.

"I must say, that's some very pretty lingerie you've got on the line – where did you get that from?"

"Ooh, I don't know," said Rosie, blushing. "Aron buys it for me."

I could see Ernie silently sliding open a sideboard door and peering inside, so I felt I had to keep the underwear conversation going in the kitchen for as long as possible.

"I find I just don't have time to go underwear shopping – nobody sees it, so why should it matter if it goes grey, saggy and the elastic perishes?" *Why on earth am I telling a suspect's wife all this?*

"I'm guessing you're not married then." Rosie giggled.

"Haven't got time for that either," I told her. *Too much information. Keep it together, Gwen…*

Over Rosie's shoulder, Ernie was maniacally giving me silent thumbs up gestures at the open sideboard, which was stacked with rows of similar-looking items that looked, from where I was standing, like fountain pen and pencil sets, electric razors, perfume and aftershave.

The front door opened, and a male voice called, "Hello, me darlin', I'm home!" as Aron Walsh walked in.

"Here's Aron now," said Rosie.

"And who the hell are you?" he barked at Ernie.

"DS Le Mercier of Maidenhead CID," announced Ernie, flashing his warrant card. "Aron Walsh, you're under arrest for shopbreaking at Prings' lingerie shop and Boots the Chemist in Windsor. You do not have to say anything, but anything you do say may be taken down in writing and may be given in evidence."

The sheer horror on Rosie's face was enough to tell me that this sweet girl had no idea that her husband was involved in criminal activities.

"What have you done, Aron love?" she cried. "Are you saying that he didn't buy my knickers and slips; he stole them?"

"I'm afraid we are, and this lot as well." Ernie gestured at the contents of the sideboard.

"I never even knew that was in there!" wailed Rosie.

I would love to say that Aron Walsh shoved us aside

screaming, "You'll never catch me!" before running into the garden and leaping over the back fence with us in hot pursuit, until Ernie rugby-tackled him to the ground and I slapped handcuffs on him. But he didn't. He simply sat down heavily on the settee and said, "Sorry, love."

Rosie's eyes filled with tears.

"You're not even going to be able to have your tea now. And it's your favourite: fish fingers, mashed potatoes... and peas."

We recovered most of the stolen items - although not the money, as Aron Walsh must have hidden that carefully – along with a jemmy, a ball of string, some gloves and a Boots paper carrier bag that was missing part of its handle. The evidence was overwhelming. I doubt he ever found out it was his own priest who dobbed him in to us, and we weren't going to say anything.

The judge at the Quarter Sessions accepted that the evidence for his arrest came from a police informant, and a priest was not required to give evidence of a confession made to him in that capacity anyway. Walsh went to prison for seven years, and I often wondered what became of Rosie, who had a happy life snatched away from her that afternoon.

"That was such a good result, I'm going to suggest you take the rest of the afternoon off to go shopping," said Ernie as we left the court.

"Oh, that's not necessary, Ernie, I'm really busy."

"It is. No WDC of mine fights crime in grey saggy knickers with failing elastic."

CHAPTER 14

Affluent neglect

Maidenhead with Le Mercier
Summer 1957

One of the things I hadn't factored in when I achieved my ambition to be a detective was the lack of day-to-day female company in Maidenhead and Windsor. I dated a policeman, I shared a house with a man who wasn't often in, and I worked alongside Ernie, Kinch and Cockerill. With the CID chaps, to their credit, I never felt treated as anything less than one of the boys, although having me around probably moderated the really filthy jokes in the police club. This pleased Ernie: while he was funny, he was never intentionally crude.

"Sorry to do this to you, Gwen," said Ernie one morning as he rummaged in a filing cabinet. "There's some teenage girl stuff come in that you'd be so much better suited to than me. Looks like it might end up as a care or protection. Would you be able to work with WPC Newman on it?"

"Of course, Ernie. CID would be missing a trick if they didn't use their female detective for women and children cases, wouldn't they? I've been expecting to."

"Pop over to the women's office and she'll give you the lowdown."

"Promise me you'll call me back if there's a juicy murder though, won't you?"

"If there's a post-mortem in the offing, you can bet your life I'll be elbowing you off the teenage girl case and taking it over as my own."

I liked WPC Heather Newman. She'd been the only one to notice when I had been limping round HQ's sports field for the centenary parade and make sure I was OK. I knew from general canteen chat she had been married to a policeman, who'd sadly died, and she had then joined the police herself – a radical decision for a widow.

She often joked that she was a reluctant copper because she was naturally shy, but her calm, empathetic reticence was just what was needed in her job. She could be stern when she needed to be, and children talked for years about the scary red-haired police lady who'd told them off for cycling on the pavement or for mucking about in Timothy White's.

Walking to the women's office, I felt a warm glow of familiarity. The predictable shifts, the regular patrols, the gentle interactions with the public who hadn't always had something horrible happen to them were in contrast with CID's always-on culture. Through the open door, I saw Heather standing there, looking pensively out of the window, her striking auburn hair a fiery red in the morning sunshine.

"Penny for your thoughts, WPC Newman?" I asked, tapping on the door.

"Well, if it isn't WDC Crockford. Sometimes I stare out of the window and think, and sometimes I just stare. You've caught me just staring."

"You don't want to be doing too much of that thinking nonsense," I replied, and we chuckled.

"So, Heather, Ernie tells me you need some CID input into something involving a teenage girl?"

"Yes. Pepita Cantley-Davis." Heather sighed.

"Some name," I said, and it seemed to ring a bell.

"She's some girl," replied Heather. "To say she's 'a bit of a handful' would be an understatement. Take a seat and I'll tell you."

I sat down and lit a cigarette, as Heather opened a file and spun it round to show me the contents.

"Pepita has been on my radar for a while now," she continued. "She's 15, an only child and something of a wild child, staying out well beyond the curfew set by her parents. They want her in by 9.30; they're lucky if she comes back in at 10.30. They even got in touch with the police to ask if we could do anything, as her mother suspected she was hanging about with unsuitable boys. I went round there and gave her a talking to – I laid it on a bit thick that there could be men out there capable of abducting and strangling a young girl out on her own at night – and she toed the line for a while."

"So what's happened now?"

"OK. One of the ticket inspectors at the train station phoned in to report that on his way home last night he saw who he thought was Pepita and a man doing indecent things in Bridge Gardens. They ran off before he could say anything, apparently. He recognised Pepita as she gets the train to school each day, and the man, because he's a railway maintenance worker. I've taken a statement off the inspector."

"I need to interview Pepita and this railway chap, then," I replied. "See if they know anything about it."

Borrowing the CID car, I pulled up outside an expensive-looking property in Boulters Lane at 5 p.m. when I hoped Pepita would be back from school.

I rang the doorbell and an impeccably groomed woman in a pastel blue twinset and pearls opened it.

"Mrs Cantley-Davis?"

"Yes?"

"WDC Crockford from Maidenhead CID. I wonder if I could come in and chat to your daughter Pepita?"

"Oh lawks, what has she done now?" she tutted.

"I just need to speak to her about an incident last night that was reported to us."

"Incident? What sort of incident?"

"Well, I'm not sure. That's what I need to ask Pepita."

"You'd better come in."

She showed me through an opulent hallway, tastefully decorated in lemon yellows and creams, into a similarly elegant sitting room, all Chinese rugs and comfy settees.

"PEPS!" called her mother up the stairs. "There's someone here to see you."

I heard footsteps clumping down the stairs, and some urgent whispering. A tall girl with long blonde hair, her school skirt rolled up from the waist to reveal legs like a racehorse, sauntered into the sitting room chewing gum and flumped onto the sofa opposite me. If I had to guess her age without the school uniform, I would put her anywhere between 16 and 21.

"You're police, yeah?" she said. "Whatcha come to see me about?"

"Hello, Pepita. I'm WDC Crockford. May I ask you where you were last night?"

"I was out, wasn't I?"

"Were you with anyone?"

Pepita shot a look towards her mother who was hovering about in the hallway.

"Yeah. I was out with Bobby."

"And who is Bobby?"

"Guy I see from time to time. He works on the railways and was always pestering me to go out with him."

This is ringing true.

"And were you in the Bridge Gardens last night?"

"Yeah."

"May I ask what you were doing there?"

"We were shagging." She shot another look at her mother. "Yes that's right, Mother – shagging."

I wasn't expecting that.

The telephone rang in the hallway, and Mrs Cantley-Davis dithered between answering it or listening in, before choosing to answer it.

"And how old is this Bobby?" I asked Pepita.

"Oh, I don't know. 20? 21?"

"And you're 15?"

"Yep."

"You know you're underage, and Bobby is going to get into a lot of trouble. He didn't force you to do anything against your will, did he?"

"Nah. I know what I'm doing."

"So that wasn't the first time something like this has happened?"

Pepita stamped both feet on the rug and sat forward on the settee, glaring at me with wide, challenging eyes. Pointing a sassy finger at me, she said, "Lady – I've shagged three men in and around Maidenhead, and I'm sure that's three more than you ever have."

Lordy. Heather wasn't wrong when she said Pepita Cantley-Davis was "a bit of a handful".

"Right. Can you give me their names?"

"I'm not going to press charges, so I don't see why I have to."

"Look, Pepita, it's not up to you whether you press charges or not. You're 15, under the age of consent, and they've committed an offence. Technically, you've committed the offence of outraging public decency by, er, what you were doing in Bridge Gardens." *I'm not going to push that one though.*

"It's in our hands now," I continued. "And I'm afraid you're going to have to have a medical examination to back up what you're saying."

Some of Pepita's sass evaporated, and a worried scowl crossed her face.

"What, you're saying some old doctor is going to look at my fanny and see if I'm a virgin or not?"

"Well, bluntly speaking, yes, and to check you haven't picked up any venereal disease... or that you might be pregnant. Have any of the men you've had sexual intercourse with used a French letter[41]?"

Pepita's face froze, her eyes widened, and she stared into the middle distance. I was expecting the answer no, and got it.

"W-what disease? W-what are you talking about?" she stammered, her remaining bravado now giving way to fear.

"There are particular kinds of diseases you can catch from having sexual intercourse, such as gonorrhoea and syphilis. They're pretty unpleasant if you don't treat them early with penicillin. And genital warts that you can't get rid of."

"Warts? On your...? Oh God. Yuck."

And even if you don't catch venereal disease, you might get yourself pregnant."

"Oh no, I won't. Bobby says you can't get in the family way if you do it standing up."

Oh, Pepita. How many unscrupulous men have spun that lie to young girls over the centuries, taking advantage of their ignorance?

There was precious little in the way of sex education in schools; studying plant pollination or the reproductive system of rabbits in biology was as good as it got for the girls, who were then meant to make their own connections to real life. No wonder Pepita found out the reality of sex with the men she'd been seeing, and they wouldn't have been exactly forthcoming with the downsides.

---

41 1950s expression for condom.

My face must have had scepticism written all over it as Pepita bit her lip, dropped her gaze and picked furiously at her thumbnail. The only sound in the room was the gentle tocking of the mantel clock for what seemed like minutes, but was probably only 30 seconds.

"All right. I'll see the doctor then," she said finally. "And if I've got to do all that, I'm not going to protect the blokes I've done it with."

Good girl. I don't think you're as irresponsible as you're made out to be. Just naïve, maybe, and a product of our unenlightened education system.

"They're Bobby Wiseman, he lives in Larchfield Road, Jack Chesterfield, he's from Cookham, and Ivan Tully from Holyport village."

I wrote down the names and addresses.

While Mrs Cantley-Davis blithely chatted away to someone on the phone in the hall, I got Pepita to repeat everything so I could get it all down as a statement. She added some eyebrow-raising sexual details that I was certain she wouldn't have told me if her mother was in earshot.

"Can I go now?" Pepita asked, standing up.

"Yes – I need to have a word with your mum if you could ask her to come in."

Mrs Cantley-Davis finished her phone call and sat on the settee opposite me.

"You're going to need to bring Pepita into the surgery in the morning to see the GP, Dr Malachi – I'll make an appointment for you," I said.

"Dash it – I'm supposed to be going for morning coffee with my cousin down from London tomorrow. We haven't seen each other for yonks, and this was the only date she could do. Does Peps really need me to be there with her?"

"I think this is a situation where she's going to need her mum, so yes."

"I'll have to call her and postpone, then."

"Please do."

Mrs Cantley-Davis rubbed her forehead between her thumb and forefinger, and I thought she was about to cry. She took a deep breath and looked at me, dry-eyed.

"Miss Crockford, I can't deal with Pepita any more. She's running completely out of control. Since last summer, she's been stopping out later and later – now I know why; she's some sort of nymphomaniac. Lord knows, Laurence, my husband, and I tried our hardest to encourage her to stay in at night – we bought a television set, we bought a piano…" she gestured towards a baby grand in the corner of the sitting room "…music lessons, even a pony. She isn't interested in any of them. Your lovely WPC even came and had a chat to her, but did that make any difference? No. I've heard there's somewhere that tearaway girls can be sent to when parents can't cope any more – do you know?"

Goodness, that escalated quickly.

"An Approved School, but Pepita will have to go through a probation officer and the juvenile court as a care or protection case before that could be considered."

"What are they like?"

"Well, they're run on boarding-school principles, with a headmaster and houses and tuck shops – strict but fair. They're nothing like Borstal – that's a juvenile prison, and that's not what these are. The girls are not locked in, and they can go into town and attend community events such as church. They're taught lessons at their level of education, which in Pepita's case would probably be quite advanced, and they'll learn practical skills as well to keep them busy."

"They don't hit them, do they?" asked Mrs Cantley-Davis. "I've heard horrible stories of boys getting caned."

"I can assure you that the only corporal punishment allowed in girls' Approved Schools is being caned on the hand. And once a girl is 15, there's no caning at all. So Pepita, and you, wouldn't have to worry about that."

"I see. It sounds just the sort of place that might be the making of Pepita. Can we get her into one?"

"I'll have to see what happens after her medical examination tomorrow. You'll really need to be there."

Mrs Cantley-Davis let me out of the front door, and I walked to the car. As I reached for the doorhandle, I suddenly remembered where I'd heard her name before. She was Miss Robertshaw's "bored" shoplifter wife of an investment banker who had stolen a raincoat in 1956.

I can't say I enjoyed interviewing the three men that Pepita named. All undeniably handsome, but rough, with unsettling sexual edges, I imagined they were a far cry from the type of suitors the Cantley-Davises wanted for their daughter. Bobby Wiseman, the railway worker, denied that sexual intercourse had taken place, yet insisted he thought she was 18 or 19.

I'm not sure why her age would be an issue if he didn't have sex with her.

Jack Chesterfield, a lorry driver who didn't strike me as particularly bright, admitted he did have sexual intercourse with her, but "no other funny business". Ivan Tully, a coalman, said, "That's news to me," when I told him Pepita was 15; apparently he'd never asked her age, and had no idea she was a schoolgirl.

Heather accompanied Pepita and her mother to her medical examination the next day. I caught up with her afterwards.

"Pepita wasn't virgo intacta – no surprise there – and the medical evidence is consistent with her statement to you. Because of it, they've sent her to a remand home while they prepare probation reports. She'll go to the juvenile court 'deemed to be in need of care or protection' as her parents are claiming she's beyond their control."

"You're liaising with the probation officer, aren't you?"

"Yes I am."

"Who is she?"

"Kerry Rance?"

I didn't know her. I couldn't imagine working with another probation officer, and it gave me an excuse to phone Hilda.

"What an interesting case!" she said. "We don't often hear about young girls being quite *that* promiscuous, but it happens. It sounds to me like 'affluent neglect'."

"What's that then, Hilda?"

"Children from wealthy families can be as emotionally neglected as those from the poorest ones. Fathers working long hours, mothers wrapped up in their social life, nannies and housekeepers, private schools, boarding schools – the children miss out on loving emotional connection with their parents, and try to find it elsewhere, as this girl clearly did. Some parents throw extravagant gifts at their children thinking that will compensate…"

"Like pianos, televisions and ponies?"

"Exactly that. But really, children need parents to spend time with them."

"That explains a lot, Hilda, thank you. And do you know Kerry Rance by any chance?"

"Kerry? Yes, I do. She's a good probation officer. She'll do what's right for this girl, don't you worry. Now, Gwen, have you read *Against the Law* yet?"

I hadn't, but I needed to because I wanted to meet up with Hilda in a social capacity. I was craving challenging conversation: Henry wasn't keen on talking police shop, preferring to tell me about motorcycles and how things weren't the same since the war. With Hilda, there was no fluffy small talk; our opening conversations would always be straight into the salient social issue of the day. No doubt she'd want a lively debate about the upcoming Wolfenden Report, and I needed to be on top of the issues.

"How did Pepita get on at the juvenile court?" I asked Heather when it was all over.

"Approved School for a year," she replied. "Miss Rance recommended that she needed strict supervision to stop her running wild again – she thought leaving her at home would be too risky."

"Just what her mother wanted, it seems," I replied.

"The parents refused to read the statement you took from her when it was given to them in court, and the chairman wouldn't let it be read out."

"I'm not surprised. It was pretty X-rated stuff."

"And the chief inspector says that it's likely proceedings will be taken against the three men Pepita named."

"Good. Why should they get off scot-free?"

And eventually, the three men were indeed committed to the Berkshire Assizes to be tried under the relatively new Sexual Offences Act, 1956. It was an offence for a man to have sexual intercourse with a girl aged between 13[42] and 16, but he could be found not guilty if he was (1) under 24, (2) had no previous convictions for a similar offence, and (3) had reasonable cause to believe the girl was over 16.

Chesterfield, the lorry driver, (25) pleaded guilty to two charges of having sexual intercourse with a 15-year-old girl, and not guilty to two charges of buggery, which the prosecution accepted. With previous convictions for a similar offence, he received nine months in prison.

Tully the coalman (20) was acquitted after claiming he didn't know she was 15. "This girl looks much older than she actually is, and she actively encouraged what happened. It would be wrong to suggest she was not a willing participant," agreed the prosecution.

In the case of railway worker Wiseman (22), the judge stopped the trial after the prosecution's case, which

---

42 It was always a felony for a man to have sexual intercourse with a girl under 13.

featured my statement from him denying he'd had sex with Pepita, and insisting he believed she was 18 or 19. Without any corroborative evidence, said the judge, he could not allow this case to go in front of the jury. Wiseman was found not guilty, and acquitted.

"I think I'm always going to feel some guilt about Pepita Cantley-Davis," said Heather over a light ale in the police club one evening. "Being taken away from home must be a terrible thing for a teenager. I wish I could have been able to help more."

"No, she was on a fast track to doing something very stupid, or getting in with someone who could really do her some harm," I replied. "Fifteen-year-olds think they know everything and can make some disastrous decisions. I think we saved her from herself."

I told Heather about a time in 1953 when Hilda had the opportunity to recommend shop thief Bernie Carroll be sent to an Approved School, but then didn't. Bernie's life took a turn for the worse at the hands of her abusive father, and arguably, she'd have been better off at an Approved School.

"But hindsight's a wonderful thing," I said. "We can only do what we think is right at the time. And what we did for Pepita is right."

CHAPTER 15

Observations

Maidenhead with Le Mercier
Summer 1957

My next job was going to be classic detective work: observation and surveillance. Being able to observe is an essential skill for any police officer, uniform or CID. Every day, we'd meet many people in different places – victims, onlookers, suspects – and we had to be able to remember their faces, descriptions and information about them. Police are highly trained in observation. You can guarantee if you see a police friend in the street as you drive past, they will notice you and wave, whereas most other people won't.

Surveillance is slightly different: it's still observing, but this time it's closely watching a person or persons who are under suspicion of wrongdoing. It's an essential part of being a detective, and sometimes called a 90-10: 90 per cent boredom, 10 per cent panic. No wonder none of us enjoyed it very much.

Ernie and I were listlessly playing a game of throw-a-paper-pellet-into-the-wastepaper-basket when Cockerill opened the CID office door and we hurriedly rustled the files on our desks, pretending to be busy.

"Fancy doing some undercover dance hall surveillance?" he asked. "I've had a complaint from the Drill Hall's manager that dance takings are dropping, although the numbers coming through the doors are staying constant."

"So he's thinking that the cashier might be fiddling the takings," I said.

"Exactly. Could you two pop round there and have a chat to him?"

"We're on it, guv," said Ernie.

As Cockerill went to leave the office, he picked up one of the paper pellets, threw it into the air and kicked it with his heel straight into the wastepaper bin.

"You're a bloody showoff, guv," Ernie called to his retreating back.

Ernie and I walked round to the Drill Hall, one of Maidenhead's bigger dance venues, and met Mr Hughes, the manager, in the lobby. After explaining about the shortfall in takings, he showed us a small glass-fronted ticket office by the front door where the alleged offence was taking place.

"With the best will in the world, I'm not sure we'd be able to observe your cashier, Mr Fry, without him noticing," I said. "Sure, I could dress up in my Saturday night best, but I'd look a bit obvious hanging round here all night."

"You'd have no end of blokes trying to pick you up," said Ernie, grinning.

"I guess you could say you were waiting for someone, then pretend to get stood up at the end of the night?" suggested Mr Hughes.

"Believe me, us girls won't wait all night for someone who isn't going to turn up. We either go home or accept a better offer. That's not going to work."

We scratched our heads for a few moments.

"In that case, the only other thing I can suggest is I drill a couple of holes in the ceiling above the cash desk and you two could watch him through the holes?"

"What's above it?" asked Ernie.

"It's just a storeroom. Want to take a look?"

We followed Mr Hughes up some backstairs to a tiny, windowless room crammed with banqueting rolls, paper serviettes, paper towels, toilet rolls and sundry cleaning equipment. Moving some boxes aside, he pointed to the old dusty floorboards.

"If I drill one hole here…" he pointed to one board "and one here…" he pointed to another, "that's roughly above the cash desk. You'll each be able to peer down at him and watch what he does."

"Seems a sensible solution," said Ernie. "Thank goodness the dances don't go on all night."

"So I'll get those holes drilled in time for Saturday's bop, and you can be in position from seven before Fry arrives, for open doors at eight?"

"We'll see you then," replied Ernie.

As we walked back to the police station, Ernie said, "Seeing as Saturday is going to be a long night, do you want to come and have an early dinner with me and my wife, Celia, beforehand? We only live five minutes' walk away, and she's dying to meet you."

Ernie didn't often talk about his wife, but then again I didn't often talk about Henry.

"That would be lovely. I'd like to meet her too."

"She's a great cook, and I'd like her to entertain more people. She sees the ladies from her church, but she hasn't yet got a circle of best friends. I'm hoping you'll hit it off and perhaps become good pals."

We'll see.

I was in a wardrobe quandary. Clearly the obs job was going to be a dirty one, laying on the floor of a storeroom, and I'd even contemplated wearing trousers for it. But now, I felt I needed to be smart to meet Celia. In the end I put on my grey suit. If it got filthy in the line of duty, I always had my detective's plain clothes allowance to buy another one.

Late afternoon on Saturday, I bought a box of Cadbury's Milk Tray and a bouquet of flowers from the posh florist, then walked to Ernie and Celia's neat little terraced house in Albert Street with its wooden gate and gravelled front garden. I rang the buzzer.

"That'll be her, I'll get it," I heard Ernie's voice call from within.

The door opened. Ernie, wearing an open-necked shirt, and freshly shaven with a fragment of toilet paper stuck to a cut on his chin, beckoned me into a cosy hallway with geometric Wilton carpet all the way up the stairs.

"She's even come bearing gifts, Ceel," he called.

Celia Le Mercier tripped out of the kitchen, wearing a floral dress and a lacy white cardie. She looked so much like Ernie that she could have been his twin sister rather than his wife.

People do say you marry someone who looks like you, I thought, trying not to stare.

She pressed her hands together and gave a little squeal.

"Gwen! It's so nice to meet you at last!" she said as she pecked me delicately on both cheeks.

"And lovely to meet you too, Celia," I replied, giving her the flowers and chocolates.

"Ooh! Are these for me? How lovely! Please go through to the dining room and I'll fix us all some drinks. Gin and tonic?"

"We're not allowed to drink if we're going on duty, you know that, my love," said Ernie.

"Ooh, yes, silly me! Tonic, ice and a slice instead, perhaps?"

"That will be perfect, thank you, Celia."

Ernie gestured me into the dining room, in the centre of which was a circular pale-wood table with four ultra-modern butterfly-backed chairs around it. There was no tablecloth, and the place settings, laid with trigonometric precision, sat on cork tablemats depicting various foxhunting scenes. Above the grey, square tiled fireplace, a large cross-stitch tapestry announced:

CHRIST is the HEAD
of this household
THE UNSEEN GUEST
at every meal
THE SILENT LISTENER
To every conversation

Ernie clocked me looking at it. "D'you think we could get Him to join CID? With skills like that He'd save us a hell of a lot of time."

I stifled a laugh as Celia walked in with a tray of drinks.

"I hope you're not taking the Lord God's name in vain, Ernest," she scolded. "It took me a very long time to stitch that tapestry."

"Take anything in vain?" replied Ernie. "Not me, dearest."

"Sit down and I'll bring the starter in," chirped Celia.

Starter? How big is this meal going to be? I usually had baked beans on toast before an evening shift.

Proudly, Celia placed in front of us a wobbling ring of prawns suspended in a greenish jelly, the centre filled with more prawns in salad cream, and garnished with chopped apple, cooked peas and watercress. For some reason every post-mortem I had attended flashed across my mind.

"Prawn aspic mould!" she announced. "I've just got the latest cookbook and it's full of recipes for these terrine-type hors d'oeuvres."

"Great. I just can't wait," said Ernie.

It took an awful lot of bread roll to get Celia's prawn aspic mould down, and I was feeling slightly nauseous before the main course even arrived.

Over vast helpings of beef stroganoff served on a bed of noodles, Celia quizzed me about my career choice.

"I was a shorthand typist too before I met Ernie, but I never thought about applying for the police force. I can't believe you worked your way up to being a detective. What's it like?"

"Well, it's pretty much exactly what Ernie does, except I might get more women and children cases, and Ernie gets more assaults and robberies."

"Children cases? What like finding missing toddlers or schoolkids playing truant?"

I didn't feel Celia would be up to hearing about Pepita Cantley-Davis or the Carroll family abuse case over dinner, so I simply said, "Yes, we sometimes deal with things like that."

"I keep saying to Ceel she ought to think about getting herself a little job. She got all distinctions in her School Certificate[43] so she's not daft, are you, dear?" said Ernie.

"But who's going to wash and iron your shirts, keep the house spick and span and have lovely meals ready for you at the end of your shifts if I'm out working too? And my church wardenship takes up a lot of my time."

"It might be nice if I'm not the only one forking out for new furniture and mod cons like food mixers and fridges," grumbled Ernie.

"You're not really *buying* them though, are you, love? With HP[44] we can pay for things over long a period of time, which makes them affordable, doesn't it?" She

---

43 The School Certificate was usually taken at age 16. Performance in each subject was graded as: Fail, Pass, Credit or Distinction. Students had to get six passes including English and Maths to obtain a certificate. It was abolished after the GCE O-Level was introduced in 1951.

44 Hire purchase or the "never-never" was a credit system that powered the post-war boom; goods were paid for in instalments, and were considered on hire until the final payment was made.

giggled. "I'll get the dessert. Talking of mod cons, come and have a look at my kitchen, Gwen."

I helped Celia gather up the plates and carry them into a thoroughly modern, mint-green kitchen space.

"Here's my all-electric cooker, and my fridge – it's got a freezer compartment, and my absolute pride and joy…" she gestured under a formica worktop "…my twin-tub washing machine! My mother is so envious. She's still using a tin bath and a mangle."

Celia produced a pineapple upside-down cake and took a tub of ice cream out of the freezer.

If I eat any more I'm going to explode.

"Oh good Lord, is that the time?" said Ernie, scraping his pudding bowl. "We need to be at the Drill Hall by seven."

"Thanks, love, smashing grub tonight," said Ernie, kissing the top of Celia's head. "Don't wait up, I'll be late back."

"Yes, thank you, Celia, that was delightful, and it was so nice to meet you," I said.

"I hope we can see each other again soon, Gwen," replied Celia. "There's a Bible study group on a Wednesday evening. With your enquiring mind, I think you'd really enjoy it, so if you'd like to come along…"

Before I could reply, Ernie whisked me out of the front door and we half-walked, half-trotted to the dance hall. By the time we arrived I'd got a stitch in my side from all that food.

Mr Hughes showed us back up into the storeroom. He'd drilled the two half-inch holes through the floor about two feet apart above the cash desk, and cleared a space three feet by six feet for us to lay down in.

"You'll need to be very quiet as the ticket office is well insulated from the music, and you can hear what's going on in the storeroom above," he explained. "And you won't be able to have the light on as it will show through the holes. But don't worry, light from the outside passageway comes under the door."

In the gloom, Ernie and I would each keep a tally of the tickets we saw sold using a pencil and paper, or at least make marks that we could tot up later. And we agreed that if we needed to communicate we would murmur; murmurs are less audible than whispers.

"Fry's just arrived!" whispered Mr Hughes. "Get into position!" He closed the door on us.

Ernie and I struggled down onto the dusty floor and laid flat on our stomachs. It was agony. I could feel Celia's prawn aspic mould, beef stroganoff and pineapple cake pressing upwards into my oesophagus.

Ernie burped. "Pardon me! So sorry, Gwen. I shouldn't have had that ice cream."

There wasn't much space and we had to crush up against each other as we peered down our respective peepholes. With any of my other male colleagues this would have felt awkward, but with Ernie it felt normal, and even quite nice – like when I used to hide in the understairs cupboard at Seaford Road with my brother Ron while we played hide-and-seek as children.

We watched Fry sitting behind the desk with his pile of dance tickets, waiting for the first punters to come through.

"Achoo!" Ernie sneezed, and Fry looked quizzically from side to side.

I nudged him.

"Dust," he mouthed, pinching his nose to stop another sneeze.

The trickle of punters through the doors for the night's bop became a rush, and Fry was doing such a swift trade that we were having difficulty keeping up with tallying the tickets. I noticed that some people were buying extra tickets and getting Fry to hold on to them, presumably for friends who were coming later. He made a separate pile of those. I murmured that observation into Ernie's ear, and he nodded.

As the evening wore on, the punters coming in slowed to a trickle again, and Fry got bored, swinging round in his chair and scratching his head. We heard a voice down the passageway call out, "Who's left that bloody light on upstairs? It's like Blackpool illuminations!" before switching off the light outside and plunging us into darkness.

My elbows had pins and needles, my face and eyes ached from pressing them against the peephole, and Ernie's innards were making alarming gurgling sounds. He wriggled about and the floorboard creaked, making Fry look upwards. We froze. Would he notice the holes? He seemed not to, but we felt we couldn't move a muscle now.

At around ten, there was a rush of more people through the doors. As we watched closely, Fry was taking some tickets off his "reserved for friends" pile. Some he handed straight over, others he was taking cash for, and I didn't see that cash go in the till.

With about half an hour to go before the dance ended, boredom and concentration began to turn into hysteria, and everything became funny. When Fry thought nobody was looking, he delved a finger deep into a nostril and examined what he extracted, then he stuck his hand down the back of his trousers and had a good scratch. I could feel Ernie shaking with mirth at this gross behaviour, and I caught the giggles too.

I'd only just managed to pull myself together when there was a loud "PPPPPPPPTHPPPPPTT" sound, like a small motorcycle going past.

"Oh Ernie, you haven't?" I murmured, probably more loudly than I should have.

"I'm... really... sorry... Gwen," he squeaked through tears of laughter. "I've been holding it in... all evening..."

Fry looked quizzically up at the ceiling, straight at the two holes, and I swore we made eye contact. As the tiny, cramped storeroom filled with a terrible smell, we had to call a halt to the surveillance operation, drag our stiff limbs upright and stagger out into the passageway, gasping for fresh air.

"We've got *some* evidence anyway," said Ernie as he rushed off to the gents.

We went to Mr Hughes's office at the end of the night to report our findings. Amazingly, we had both tallied that 226 people had paid for admission.

"Are you all right to hang around and see what Fry brings in?" asked Hughes.

We were more than happy to stand outside the back

door and inhale our first cigarettes in over four hours until Mr Hughes called us back in.

Fry was standing there, and Mr Hughes was red with fury.

"Here are the detectives who both calculated that 226 people came in, yet you've handed me takings from only 207. They watched you reselling tickets that had been set aside for latecomers who didn't show and presumably pocketing that money."

"I thought there was something funny going on upstairs. Enjoy your job spying on people, do you?" said Fry. "Those tickets you thought I resold were paid for by blokes and collected by their girls when they came in later."

"A few were, not all," said Ernie.

All right, Mr Hughes, if you really think I've been swindling you, I'll pay the shortfall out of my own pocket. Here."

Fry slammed £3 10s down on the desk.

"I haven't stolen anything now, have I?"

Arriving back home after midnight, I wearily checked the hall telephone table for messages. There were none. *Thank goodness for that.* As I tiptoed onto the landing, Mrs Foskett's bedroom door creaked open and a bleary face, blobbed with thick night cream and framed with a pink nylon hair net, peered out.

"Gwen!" she stage-whispered. "That PC Falconer of yours phoned at half past five, then half past six, then quarter to eight. He rang again at a quarter to 10, and quite frankly I've had enough! I've asked him not to tele-phone after 9 p.m., so please could you address what-ever it is he wants to speak to you about, so he doesn't keep calling?"

I groaned inwardly. Mrs Foskett sounded really cross.

"I'm so sorry, Mrs Foskett. I thought I'd told Henry I was out on a job and wouldn't be available until Sunday. I'll make that clear to him."

"Thank you. I'd be grateful."

Mrs Foskett's face disappeared behind her closing door.

Flopping on my bed, mortified, I thought about Celia. Was that what marriage to a police officer did to a woman? All those mod cons to save time, but save time for what? Baking more cakes and organising ruddy church jumble sales? Not for me, certainly not now.

"Sorry," I said to Beatific Jesus on my mantelpiece, "but since you are the unseen guest at every meal and the silent listener to every conversation, you'll get where I'm coming from."

"Well, all that was a bloody waste of time," grumped Ernie, coming into the CID office and throwing his hat on the desk. "Fry got the case against him dismissed."

"Oh no – why?" I asked.

"Apparently because the money wasn't checked in front of him, and he handed over the cash in his pocket, the chairman gave him the benefit of the doubt."

"Well, I think he was very lucky to get away with that," I said.

"It was fun though, the obs job, we had a laugh, didn't we?" said Ernie, grinning. "Sorry again about the... you know..."

"My Lord, I had forgot the fart![45]" I replied, "as Queen Elizabeth the First said to some earl or other," and we laughed like schoolchildren all over again.

"Maybe next time I can persuade Ceel to use her fancy blender to just make us some soup and a sarnie," replied Ernie. "No more prawn aspic moulds."

---

45 According to diarist John Aubrey, the Earl of Oxford broke wind while bowing to Queen Elizabeth I and was so embarrassed he left the country for seven years. When he finally returned, Her Majesty welcomed him back with "My Lord, I had forgot the fart!"

CHAPTER 16

Anything but Meeke

Maidenhead with Le Mercier
Summer 1957

"I *did* tell you I was going out on an obs job…" I explained down the phone to Henry, sitting on the stairs.

"I had no idea how long we were going to be there for… got back about 12.30… sometimes these things can go on all night, you know that… yes, I know I'm *supposed* to do only nine to five… the criminals don't, though, do they? …I was on obs with DS Le Mercier… yes… yes… it was pretty funny, actually… we… Ah, I see, you wanted to arrange a night out… you probably don't need to ring multiple times… OK… OK… I'll see you later…"

The phone clicked off, and I stared at the receiver, puffing my cheeks out. Some long legs edged past me on the staircase.

"Boyfriend trouble, darling?" asked Victor, taking his coat and hat off the hallway peg. "Mrs F was getting rather pissy about all the calls from your Mr Falconer."

"I know. I'll speak to him so he doesn't keep calling if I'm not here," I replied. "I don't understand. He's in the force himself, so you'd think he'd be familiar with what CID gets up to."

"Maybe it's not what CID gets up to – it's more what his girl gets up to in CID. He hasn't joined the dots up yet," said Victor.

I don't know whether I can be doing with this for much longer.

A few days later, I was in the front office catching up on uniform gossip with *Inspector* Robertshaw (that's right, she did get promoted – two pips[46] on her epaulettes now – as I'd had no doubt she would) when the front door crashed open, and we heard loud, excited voices in the lobby shouting over each other.

"I bloody nearly had him, you know! Boy, was he a slippery bastard, putting up resistance like that."

"You just couldn't keep hold of him, could you? You were that close…"

"If only I'd just been able to hook my foot round him like that… and do this…"

We heard a thud and the low-pitched "Ooof" of somebody being winded.

Miss Robertshaw opened the door to find PC Matt Wagstaffe in a heap on the lobby floor and WPC Ursula Meeke, her stockings torn to shreds, straddling his legs and holding his arm halfway up his back in a savage lock. The duty sergeant was peering over the desk at them, laughing.

"…we'd have been able to arrest him like this, Waggy!" cried Ursula triumphantly.

"Truce! Truce!" cried Wagstaffe, banging his free hand on the floor like a professional wrestler.

---

46 Silver Bath stars, also known as "pips".

"What on earth is going on, Miss Meeke?" demanded Miss Robertshaw.

"Oh hello, Inspector. Judo, actually," said Ursula releasing the armlock to a whimper from Wagstaffe kneeling back on his shins. "Waggy, I mean PC Wagstaffe and I, recognised a housebreaker we'd been told to look out for and gave chase, but we lost him."

"My DS, Ernie Le Mercier, recently investigated those break-ins at a tobacconists where a load of cigarettes, confectionery and money got stolen, and one at a posh house in Boulter's Lane where they stole loads of stuff, including a portable record player and a brown suitcase," I said.

"That's the one!" cried Ursula, her eyes lighting up.

"Well, I think I need to hear all about this," said Miss Robertshaw.

Rarely in my police career did I willingly make cups of tea for a group of officers, on principle, but it sounded like Ursula and Wagstaffe needed it, and we all wanted to hear more.

Over steaming cuppas in an interview room, Ursula regaled us with the story.

"Obviously we've been told on shift parade that these break ins had happened, what had been stolen, and what to look out for. Waggy and I just happened to be patrolling near the station when I spotted a youth with a suitcase and a record player. When I asked where he'd got the record player from, he replied, "From a mate who works in Castle Street – do you want to go and check with him?" but then he threw the record player at Waggy and the suitcase at me and ran for it. We chased him

218

along Shoppenhangers, and I managed to grab hold of his shirt collar just outside the golf club, but he shoved me off and went to kick me, then raced onto the golf course. I lost him in the wooded bits because all the brambles were tearing my stockings to pieces."

"She was amazing, like a terrier – I couldn't keep up with her," said Wagstaffe, his eyes glistening with admiration. "I blew my whistle, but by the time the other lads arrived, she had lost him. He could have gone anywhere – there are so many copses he could hide in and slip away from."

"That's my girl," said Miss Robertshaw with a twinkle in her eye. "And you've got a good description we can circulate?"

"Absolutely. Tall lanky youth, with thin mousy hair, pimply pale skin, prominent Adam's apple…"

"Can run like the clappers," added Wagstaffe.

So at least we could add a description to our housebreaker and keep our eyes peeled.

Although CID didn't patrol in the same way that uniform did out on their beats, we were encouraged to wander around the town and keep our eyes and ears peeled. We could patrol if we'd reached a work hiatus, if we needed a break, or on the pretext of looking for a suspect if a description came in. People would stop saying or doing things if a uniformed officer appeared, but not if that officer were in plain clothes. Because I was small, mousey and unassuming, with a forgettable face – and a woman – nobody expected me to be a police officer.

Thus it was on a sunny but slow Sunday morning that I fancied some fresh air, and wandered out with Ursula.

"I was thinking as it's such a lovely day, we could head up through the town centre to the gravel pit, loop round, then come back via The Moor – show a bit of police presence to the families out and about on a Sunday," she suggested.

"Good plan, I'm up for that," I replied.

We wandered up Queen Street, deserted because the 1950 Shops Act meant every shop had to close to customers on a Sunday. There were exceptions (and local authorities could make further exemptions): some pharmacies, newsagents and tobacconists could open, and you could buy a bale of hay to feed your horse, or a part for your aircraft, but if you fancied fish and chips from the chippie, you'd have to wait until Monday.

Ursula and I peered in all the shop windows.

"No evidence of anyone illicitly trading tinned milk or peaches that I can see," she said.

"Silly law, isn't it? If they're not in a tin, you can buy them on a Sunday."

From the dead town centre, we followed the footpath behind Father Geoghegan's church with its faint scent of incense on the breeze, and down a little alley that brought us out in Holly Drive. At the junction of Ray Mill Road West, we turned right to wander along a residential road. The meaty, parsnipy, cabbagey, apple-crumbly smells of a hundred Sunday roasts wafting through kitchen windows made our stomachs rumble.

Near the end of the road, a lone figure sat on a garden wall by the bus stop, engrossed in a newspaper. My observation training instinctively kicked in: male, long legs, blue trousers, brown sweater, young, sparse fair hair, pale, acned skin, prominent Adam's apple...

"Ursula, do you think that could be..."

"Well, bugger me! It is!"

We slowed our pace and hatched a plan to catch our thief.

I hung back while Ursula crossed to the opposite side of the road from the bus stop and walked with purpose, seemingly ignoring the youth. He clocked her and raised the newspaper to hide his face. I took out my cigarettes and put one in my mouth. When Ursula was well past him, I went up to him.

"Excuse me, love, have you got a light?"

I've never seen anyone jump and recover so quickly.

"No! No, I 'aven't, sorry," said the youth, engrossing himself back in the newspaper, eyes wide.

I could see Ursula in the distance crossing back over to our side of the road. I had to keep him distracted.

"Don't smoke, then, love? Don't blame you. If you believe some of these doctors on the television, smoking's bad for you."

He grunted and nodded.

"Do the buses run along here on a Sunday?" I continued. "I assume you're waiting for one?"

"Er, sorry, dunno."

Like a ninja, Ursula materialised by his side behind his newspaper.

"I think we've met before, sonny, haven't we?" she said.

The youth jumped up, ready to run once more, but we had the advantage and seized both his arms. In a blink, Ursula applied the same savage armlock that she did to Wagstaffe, and hooked her foot round his heel. Our youth was soon pleading that he would come quietly. A man with some garden shears came out of his gate and walked towards us, brandishing them like a weapon.

"Can I help you, officer?" he asked.

"If you've got a telephone, could you call Maidenhead police station for a patrol car please?" asked Ursula.

"I'll do that," called a woman coming out of another house, and soon a small crowd gathered round us, tutting about the youth of today and rising crime rates, as our patrol car rolled up.

"And you made a citizen's arrest, did you?" Shears Man asked me.

"No, I'm a police officer as well," I replied.

"Plain clothes?"

Much as I'd have loved to shout out, "I'm a detective!" I didn't, and just nodded.

"Looks like you could learn a lot from this brave little WPC here. Stick with her, and you'll be in uniform before you know it," he said.

I love the great British public, I thought, biting my tongue.

But he was right. There *was* a lot I could learn from Ursula. Whereas I was very much "feel the fear and do it somehow", Ursula was just "do it". She got stuck into every aspect of her job with good humour and gusto, and without hesitation. It helped that she was a sportswoman, particularly keen on rowing and swimming, neither of which I could do.

"I can't believe you didn't get taught swimming and lifesaving at Mill Meece training school, Gwen," she said.

"It was back in 1951," I replied. "We got taken to a morgue instead."

"Lifesaving was the best bit!" she exclaimed. "I got my bronze medallion at training school, and I loved the judo too. Less keen on the dead body thing, I must confess."

I don't think I was the only one who was happy to leave patrolling Maidenhead's many waterways to Ursula. She was the best police officer for that job, and 22-year-old Clarice Harvey-Leighton probably owed her life to her abilities.

"Could you go to Maidenhead hospital and take a statement from a young lady who got tipped out of a punt into the river by some ruffians?" asked Ernie, one summer morning.

"Goodness, that's my idea of a nightmare," I said.

"Mine too. Yes, the poor girl was actually knocked unconscious, and these yobboes swam off and ran away when they saw what they had done, just leaving her. Utter cowards."

"Miss Harvey-Leighton has only just woken up, so I don't want her upset or overexcited," said the brisk ward sister, trotting me to the side ward where Clarice was recovering, her head bandaged, accompanied by Ursula. Far from being upset, Ursula and Clarice seemed to be jovially comparing notes about how many times they had each fallen in the Thames.

"Here's our detective now," said Ursula. "I'm going to leave you in her capable hands while I find us some tea."

"So, Clarice. Nasty business. Can you tell me what happened?" I asked.

Clarice pulled herself up on her pillows.

"Well, I often hire a punt from along Ray Mill Lane on a warm evening and take myself down to Bray and back again. I'd just gone past Skindles Hotel and Guards Club Island when these five youths swam out to me and surrounded my punt, rocking it and saying they'd tip me in. A man in a motor launch chased them away, and I carried on under the railway bridge a bit further, but I wasn't in the mood any more and wanted to go back."

"I'm not surprised," I said.

"But when I came back round the other side of Guards Club Island, the boys were waiting for me and really rocked the boat and splashed me with water. The last thing I remember was two of them grabbing the punt pole, and me losing my balance, and I must have hit my head on the way down and blacked out – and I woke up in here. I'm told a young girl on the bank saw me fall into the water, swam over and pulled me out and WPC Ursula here helped give me artificial respiration until the ambulance arrived."

Ursula walked through the door with a tray of cups of tea.

"Well done, Ursula," I said.

"Oh, I wish I could say that was me, and I was more than ready to leap in and save Clarice, but the girl got in before me. She did the artificial respiration. I just did some first aid on Clarice's cut head and organised the ambulance. Team effort. Oh, and I got a statement from her too, so I'll drop that into your office."

"Brilliant, thanks, Ursula. Now, can you give me a description of these youths, Clarice?"

"They were wearing swimming trunks, so obviously I can't describe their clothes, but the funny thing was, they all had those greased Teddy boy haircuts that were water resistant, so I'm sure I would recognise them if I saw them again."

"And did they all attack you?"

"There were three who seemed determined to have me fall in, the two who grabbed the punt pole especially, and one who kept rocking the punt, but there were also two hanging back who were laughing, not getting involved."

I finished taking Clarice's statement, and Ursula walked me to the door of the hospital.

"Pretty appalling, cowardly attack, running off, leaving a young woman in the river unconscious with a head injury," I said. "If that girl hadn't been so quick thinking, and you hadn't been around, we could have been looking at something much more serious."

"I think I know who those blokes are," said Ursula. "They're often mucking about by the river when I go rowing, although I'm usually with my team so they don't bother me."

Anyone who tried to bother Ursula would come off worse, I thought.

"They're the Woodlands Park Teds who hang out in … Woodlands Park, funnily enough. A lot of them aren't schoolboys any more; they've got jobs and money, but still want to be part of the gang."

"Are they now? Is it me, Ursula, or are the Teddy boys getting nastier? Time was, they just did a bit of dance hall scrapping, or set off a fire extinguisher in the cinema, but to wantonly do this to a young woman who just wanted a relaxing punt down the river seems beyond the pale."

"There's definitely nasty rivalry between the local gangs of Teds, the Pinkneys, the Strande Castle lot and of course Woodlands Park," said Ursula." And that's just Maidenhead! Then you get the gangs in Windsor and Slough, and they'll travel to have a ruck with each other, like some sort of need to be top dog. Maybe that feeds the machismo and bravado that makes them do this sort of thing."

A sociological analysis worthy of Hilda, I thought, warmly.

"But my dad says a spell in the army would knock it out of them. And I agree with him."

A few days later, when Clarice was well enough, we pulled in a group of the Woodlands Park Teds we'd seen throwing stones at the swans by Boulter's Lock. I recognised one as John Carroll, but he didn't seem to recognise me.

We organised an identity parade at the station, pulling in some willing teenagers from a church youth group as volunteer "suspects". Bless them, they tried to embrace their brief to look street tough, but they were no substitute for the snarling, testosterone-fuelled swagger of the real gang members, who Clarice picked out immediately. She didn't point out John Carroll, though.

Ursula was spitting tacks when she came back from the magistrates' court where she had given evidence in Clarice's case.

"Bastards all pleaded not guilty to assault and bodily harm, and some wanky charge of 'occasioning nuisance to a person using the River Thames'!" she fumed.

I certainly hadn't heard of that last misdemeanour before.

"I really felt for Clarice having to go into the witness box and see their stupid sneering faces after what they did to her," she continued. "The blokes said it was just a bit of joking around and mickey-taking until she 'accidentally' fell in, then the defence said it was summer high jinks that went a bit too far."

"They would, wouldn't they?" I replied.

Ursula was at that early stage in her police career where she hadn't yet learned to take most defences with a pinch of salt. Or maybe I'd just become too cynical.

"The chairman fined them all £10, and he did commend the young girl who fished Clarice out, but I can't help feeling this was a lot more serious than it was made out to be."

And as for our lanky youth, he was sent to Berkshire Quarter Sessions where he pleaded guilty to breaking into a tobacconist and a private house, and stealing goods worth over £85. He asked for *15* other offences to be taken into consideration, and was sent to a detention centre for three months.

"So why do crims even ask for other offences to be taken into consideration?" Ursula asked me as she sipped a pint of brown ale in the police club. "Won't that just increase their sentences? Surely they'd be better off just keeping their mouths shut and hoping other offences would never be linked to them?"

"Well, it might, but a judge will see TICs[47] as a genuine effort to help the police and wipe the slate clean," I explained. "Any further sentencing would probably be less than if they got found out for other crimes and sentenced for those further down the line."

"So, it's really a trade off? 'Fess up, do your time, have peace of mind, or spend the rest of your life looking over your shoulder, wondering whether past misdemeanours will catch up with you?"

"Absolutely that," I said, "although you'll find many criminals have no conscience and don't ask for TICs.

Ursula sighed. "I'm beginning to realise that."

---

47 Offences Taken Into Consideration.

CHAPTER 17

Firestarter

Maidenhead with Le Mercier
Autumn 1957

Ernie sniffed. "Nice place she's got here."

An acrid smell of burnt plastic, wood and insulation mingled with the chill morning mist as Ernie and I stood among the puddles of mud and soot around a blackened caravan. A few scruffy children watched us from their own caravan windows, but for most the show was over and boring now. The caravan had gone up in flames the evening before, with all the attendant excitement of a fire engine arriving at the Strande Castle site, firemen hosing out the blaze, and police running about questioning witnesses. By comparison, two detectives in grey overcoats standing around the ruin smoking fags weren't a very interesting proposition.

"Here's a Scotland Yard Wolseley," said Ernie, throwing his cigarette butt in the direction of what looked like a giant black Morris Minor trundling through the churned-up mud towards us.

The back door opened and a jovial man in round spectacles and a black bowler hat stepped gingerly out into the mire, holding a briefcase.

"I forget how filthy the Home Counties can be," he chuckled, holding out his hand. "Dr Laurie Dixon, Scotland Yard Forensic Science Laboratory."

"DS Ernie Le Mercier and WDC Crockford, how do you do, sir?" said Ernie.

"Ah yes, Miss Crockford, it was you I spoke to, wasn't it? I'm seeing if this caravan has been set on fire deliberately?"

"That's right sir, we suspect malicious damage – arson."

"I'm not expecting to find any charred human remains, am I?"

"Not unless we've massively missed something," I said.

Dr Dixon looked almost disappointed.

"The caravan's sole occupant, Mrs Flint, was evicted for non-payment of rent, and as soon as she moved out, it burst into flames," I continued.

"I think you've got your perpetrator, motive and felony in that single sentence, Miss Crockford. Can I go home now?" said Dr Dixon.

We all laughed.

Dr Dixon clambered up into the caravan. Through the charred doorway we watched him tiptoe around it, observing, measuring, sniffing, taking photographs, and putting swabs into glass vials, while we chatted to his cheery police driver about how difficult the Strande Castle caravan site had been to find.

"What do you reckon?" asked Ernie, helping Dr Dixon down from the caravan.

"I'll need to get these samples properly analysed, but there are paraffin deposits in a box inside what was the wardrobe, and some round the stove in the middle of the caravan. They look independent of each other, so at first sight, the fire does appear to have been started deliberately. But I'll put that in a report and no doubt I'll be appearing in your witness box at some future juncture. Toodle pip."

As the Wolseley trundled back London-wards, Ernie said, "Mrs Flint left a forwarding address with a neighbour – she's staying at some holiday caravan park in Littlehampton now. Assuming she hasn't managed to torch that caravan as well, could you have a little seaside day trip down there and interview her? Although don't charge her yet until we've gathered all the evidence – we still need to do all this by the book."

"Yes, of course. I notice from some of the witness statements quite a few people think the fire was started deliberately, and with Dr Dixon's evidence too…"

"Cockerill and the chief inspector will be thrilled with this one, I'm sure," said Ernie. "I can't see it being anything other than a cut and dried conviction – great for our crime stats."

At last, a job perk. I spent a most pleasant train journey down to Littlehampton in a carriage all to myself, finally reading *Against The Law* that Hilda had lent me, and eating bloater paste sandwiches with my flask of tea. Arriving in Littlehampton, it was a short, brisk walk across the bridge over the river to a caravan park in Ferry Road where nothing was on fire.

I knocked on the door of the caravan number I'd been given, and a wide-eyed woman with straggly hair and several missing teeth opened it.

"Mrs Flint?"

"Yeah, who's asking?"

"WDC Crockford of Maidenhead CID. I wonder if I could ask you a few questions about…"

"The fire in the caravan it weren't me what done it I made a cup of tea before I left but I'm sure I turned the stove off it's the shitty stuff what that bastard owner puts in his crappy caravans dangerous it is just dangerous I weren't going to pay him the exorbitant rent what he charges for substandard accommodation when as you can see it bursts into flames at the drop of a hat and I'm happy to be away from all that just now…"

Mrs Flint took a breath.

"And now you police lady you gotta waste your time comin' all the way down here to ask me about the fire which was already an accident waiting to happen and I'm just glad it didn't explode and there weren't no kiddies what got hurt and it's all that bloody bastard owner's fault and I didn't do it."

Goodness, my head's spinning.

"Sorry, Mrs Flint, can you slow down and repeat all that, so I get this down in a statement?" I asked, taking out my notebook and pen.

"Yeah… The fire in the caravan it weren't me what done it I made a cup of tea before I left but I'm sure I turned the stove off…" And so on, again.

I read the statement back to Mrs Flint and got her to sign it.

"You ain't arresting me, are you?" she asked, her eyes wider than before.

"No, we're just at the investigation stage at the moment," I replied.

"It's that bloody bastard shitty owner you need to be arresting, not me…"

She doesn't seem to like the landlord very much.

I flumped down in the train carriage for the return journey from Littlehampton, wondering what just happened, and poured myself a reviving cup of tea from my Thermos flask. Dozing off to the rhythmic clickety-clack of the train wheels and the afternoon sun on my face, just past Winchester I suddenly felt a surge of adrenaline from deep in the pit of my stomach and I jerked awake, gasping.

"Oh God, I didn't caution her!"

A man with a military-style moustache sitting opposite me peered over his newspaper. "Are you all right, madam?"

"Oh yes, fine, thank you, just something I think I forgot to do."

And all the way back to Maidenhead, I envisaged the cut-and-dried case of Mrs Flint the Arsonist collapsing because I forgot to administer the caution before taking her statement – and it would all be my fault.

"How did you get on with our pyromaniac?" asked Ernie, throwing me a cigarette as I walked into the CID office.

"Mad as a hatter, and completely denying that she set fire to the caravan," I replied, sidling over to the bookcase and pulling off my copy of *Moriarty's Police*

Law. I turned to the Record of Evidence chapter on page 66.

Persons suspected of crime

(1) When a police officer is endeavouring to discover the author of a crime, there is no objection to his putting questions in respect thereof to any person or persons, whether suspected or not, from whom he thinks that useful information can be obtained.

(2) Whenever a police officer has made up his mind to charge a person with a crime, he should first caution such person asking any questions or any further questions, as the case may be.

I felt a wave of relief wash over me. We didn't have to caution if we were just questioning a suspect, only if we were about to charge them, and I'd been explicitly asked not to charge Mrs Flint yet. *I know all this stuff, why did I doubt myself?*

"You all right, Gwen?" asked Ernie. "You look a bit pale,"

"Just double-checking I didn't need to caution Mrs Flint before I started questioning her."

"You didn't charge her or arrest her, so no, you didn't need to caution her," he replied. "Stand down."

Phew.

Henry and I were on our regular dinner date night that evening I came back from Littlehampton, and I must

234

admit I was feeling tired and grumpy before I even met him in the little café in town. I listened patiently to a long-winded account of a problem he was having finding a certain part for his motorcycle, and I stifled a yawn.

"Sorry, am I boring you?" he asked.

"I'm just a bit tired, that's all. I've been to Little-hampton and back today."

"Littlehampton? Why on earth did you have to go all the way down there?"

I told him about the caravan fire, Dr Dixon from Scotland Yard, and the watertight evidence that we had against mad Mrs Flint. It was Henry's turn to glaze over and look bored.

"And you'll never guess what," I continued. "I even had a wobbly about whether I should have cautioned a suspect before I questioned her and took her statement."

"Of course you should have," he replied. "If there are grounds to suspect someone has committed an offence, you should caution them before you question them so that their answers are admissible in evidence in court."

"Now hold on. I checked *Moriarty*, and it's only when we've made up our minds to charge someone that we need to caution them,"

"So what happens when you're asking so many questions that you're getting to the bottom of that person's involvement and they've more or less admitted their guilt?"

"Well, that's the time to charge them, and that's when I would caution them," I replied.

"And I like to hedge my bets, so I always say, 'You are not obliged to say anything but anything you say may be given in evidence' *before* questioning a suspect."

"But you don't *need* to. That does make it very formal, and some people clam up because it all sounds so official. I find I can get a lot more out of people just by having a chat with them. Then when I'm absolutely certain we've got the right person, we go in with a charge or arrest and a caution."

"Bloody hell, Gwen, are you a copper or a social worker?"

It was at that moment I realised I'd had enough of Henry. For long enough, I'd tolerated his up-and-down moods, his lateness picking me up, his fixation with his motorcycle, his unwillingness to accept that society had moved on from a war footing to something freer and less militaristic, and his constantly wanting to know where I was and what I was doing. Being at Maidenhead and Windsor with the likes of Ernie, Kinch, Ursula, Heather and Wagstaffe had opened my eyes to how much fun being in the police could be, and I wanted to embrace it without having to justify my whereabouts all the time. I just wasn't finding Henry's company enjoyable any more; he was becoming hard work.

"Look, I think I'm going to go home," I said. "I'm tired and I've got a headache."

"I'll run you back."

"No, you're all right, I'll walk. It's a lovely evening and I could do with clearing my head."

"Is it something I said? I was only winding you up about the caution – you know what you're doing. You've probably questioned more people than I have, and…"

"Let's just leave it, shall we? I've had a long day of police procedure and I just wanted to get away from it."

"But you never do get away from police procedure, do you? CID is 24/7, and you're always either tired or full of the case you're working on at the time. You're not much fun at the moment if I'm honest, Gwen."

I'm not much fun? That's rich coming from him.

"Well, if that's the way you feel, let's just leave it there, shall we?" I picked up my coat and bag and headed for the door.

"Gwen…"

But he didn't follow me out.

Back at home, I made a cup of tea, took an aspirin, and flopped on my bed, exhausted but wide awake now. I could smell the scent of vanilla pipe tobacco and hear conversation and laughter in the room next door – Victor chatting about Dostoyevsky with one of his arty literary friends again, no doubt.

I had two letters to write. One was a reply to Suzette who'd sent me an airmail letter from Barbados brimming with excitement about being back home with her son Colin and her new job. She was working as a ward sister in a nearby hospital, and by her description it sounded as if the Caribbean healthcare system really was receiving an innovative and progressive NHS-inspired overhaul. I would tell her she was exactly what they needed.

The other was *the* letter to Henry. With tears that were more relief than sadness in my eyes, I took out my cream Basildon Bond writing paper and my fountain pen and started to write.

Dear Henry,
Although it makes me very sad to write this... I think
both you and I know that our relationship has come
to a natural end... We've had some wonderful times
together... we've grown apart... different people now...
I still maintain you only need to caution before charge
or arrest... I hope we can still be good friends and
colleagues...

A couple of months later, Mrs Flint was charged with maliciously damaging a caravan to the tune of £150 and brought before Maidenhead magistrates. The hearing was long, and several witnesses, me included, took the stand.

The caravan owner testified, "Apart from the first week's rent in November, Mrs Flint hadn't paid me a penny. That was the only reason I evicted her."

Mrs Flint's neighbour, a Mrs Renfrew, said, "I looked after all her possessions on the day she was evicted, then she returned to the caravan to make a final cup of tea before a friend came to drive her to Littlehampton. She could have accidentally left the stove on."

Dr Dixon testified that, "My forensic investigation concluded that this fire was started deliberately."

My palms sweating as they always did when I went into the witness box, I read out my rather breathless-sounding statement from Mrs Flint denying setting fire to the caravan.

"And did you caution Mrs Flint before she made the statement?" the chairman asked me.

My stomach flipped over. *Did I really get this wrong and Henry was right after all?*

"No, sir, I didn't caution her as at the time we had no intention of charging her, and indeed did not do so for another two months," I replied.

"As is quite correct, Miss Crockford."

In your face, Henry Falconer.

"I'd still like to have the statement put in as evidence, as Mrs Flint made it quite voluntarily," said the chairman.

At the end of the hearing, the chairman addressed the accused. "I believe that spite and revenge against the caravan's owner were your prime motives for setting fire to the caravan, Mrs Flint," he said, "and I am committing you to the Newbury Quarter Sessions for trial on two bail sureties totalling £100."

So, we had to give the same evidence all over again in Newbury a couple of weeks later.

"I'm sooooo bored with this case now," Ernie whispered in my ear as we sat at the back of the court after giving our evidence again. "A nice fat guilty verdict, and there'll be brownie points for us from the top brass."

"I would like to call Mrs Renfrew," said the prosecution.

"Yes, I was Mrs Flint's friend and neighbour," Mrs Renfrew said in the witness box. "I took in quite a lot of Mrs Flint's belongings before she left, but there were still a few bits she needed to collect before she left. She made a cup of tea when she collected them and I think because she was so upset at leaving, she forgot to turn the stove off."

"Convenient that, pop over to the caravan just before you leave, get the rest of your stuff and torch it," murmured Ernie in my ear.

"But what I would say," continued Mrs Renfrew, "is that there is another key to the caravan held somewhere on this site, and lots of children live here, as well as the band of youths calling themselves the Strande Castle Teds, who have been known to participate in all kinds of delinquency. It's a possibility that someone other than Mrs Flint gained access to the caravan and set it on fire."

There were some murmurings and whisperings around the court. This was new information, and a possible turning point.

"They're not going to buy that, surely?" murmured Ernie.

The prosecution's case concluded, the judge sent the jury out and mumbled something with the defence and prosecution counsels.

"Having heard the evidence, I do believe there is grave suspicion against Mrs Flint, but grave suspicion is not enough to convict. I do not feel it is safe to leave the matter in the hands of the jury," he said.

"What the…" said Ernie, open mouthed as the jury were brought back in and instructed to return a not guilty verdict, to whoops and cheers from Mrs Flint and Mrs Renfrew.

Ernie and I drove grumpily back to Maidenhead station – no brownie points for us.

"It was arson, I tell you," said Ernie.

"No question," I replied.

"A whole load of arson around."

"Ha bloody ha," I said, but at least he'd made us smile.

CHAPTER 18

Felo de Se

Windsor with Kinch
Summer 1958

Before you read this chapter, I must tell you that it contains details of attempted suicide that some of you may find upsetting.

I squeezed past the boxes and piles of paperwork, evidence and God-knows-what-else stacked in Windsor's CID office to get the briefing for my next investigation. Kinch was on the telephone, his feet on the desk and squinting from smoke curling up from a burned-down cigarette hanging from the corner of his mouth. He gestured to me to sit down as he wound up his call.

"Yeah... yeah... well I'm not too bothered *how* you get it, as long as you get it, if you understand my meaning ... Just bloody do it. Bye." He replaced the receiver and stubbed out his cigarette in the ashtray.

"Morning, Hepzibah." He grinned. "You can't keep away, can you?"

"However hard I try, I can't, Stan." I smiled. "DI Cockerill tells me you've got a situation you think would be better suited to the 'gentle arm of the law', i.e., me?"

"Oh bloody hell, yes. I can't be doing with hysterical females, and I've got a right one here. Twenty-year-old staying at the YWCA slashed her wrists and took pills over an argument with some boy or other, apparently. She's known to the woodentops, and they want her prosecuted as an attempted suicide. I'll need statements from the girl herself and her friend who patched her up."

I cast my mind back to Hendon detective training school and our class on suicide and attempted suicide. Our po-faced lecturer had stood in front of a blackboard that had the single word SUICIDE written on it, and solemnly pronounced four words that sounded like "fell in the sea". My fellow students Irene, Dick, Hedley and I looked at each other in puzzlement, then Dick exclaimed, "Oh I get it, he didn't commit suicide, he fell in the sea!" to titters from the other, equally puzzled recruits. Wordlessly, the lecturer turned to the blackboard and wrote FELO DE SE on it.

"Felo de se, gentlemen – and ladies – is a felony against oneself. Where a person is of sound mind, of the age of discretion, and voluntarily and deliberately kills himself, he is a felo de se. Suicide is the homicide of one of Her Majesty's subjects. It is a felony. But as the perpetrator is beyond earthly justice, there can be no criminal consequences. Attempted suicide is, however, classed as a common law misdemeanour – an attempt to commit a felony – and once the offender has recovered, he may be arrested and dealt with in a court of law."

Then, the lecturer showed us some sobering slides of people who had killed themselves. He pointed out the tell-tale marks of a self-inflicted ligature, and the hesitation cuts made before somebody sliced decisively into their wrist or neck with intent to take their own life. Nobody found felo de se funny after that.

"What's her name and the name of her friend?" I asked Kinch.

"Buggered if I can remember," he replied, rummaging through a pile of notes and pulling out a scrap of paper. "Marcia Lucas, and her friend is called Annie Sage," he read.

"I know that name, Stan. I think I came across her shoplifting in Wokingham Woolworths a couple of years ago – she got two years' probation."

"Sounds like she just can't keep herself out of trouble then. Go and see if it's the same person."

I walked to the Windsor YWCA and met the manager, Mrs Briley, a wiry middle-aged lady with hair scraped back in a bun.

"Hello, I'm WDC Crockford from Windsor CID. I believe one of your residents, Marcia Lucas, attempted to commit suicide last night?"

"Well, that might be putting it a bit strongly, dear, as she's something of a drama queen."

That's Marcia.

"But she told her friend she had swallowed some aspirins and there are cuts on her arms," she said. "I mentioned it to your officer who popped round, and he's insisting on treating it as attempted suicide."

Why did a male officer get to her first?

"Did she go to hospital at any point?"

The manager looked at me blankly.

"Well, there wasn't much blood, and she threw up most of the pills, so we didn't bother."

She led me along a corridor to a bedroom and knocked on the door.

"Who is it?" came a voice from within.

"It's a police lady come to talk to you, Marcia."

The door opened, and I immediately recognised the small pale girl I arrested for shoplifting in Woolworths two years previously. The stringy blonde hair was shorter, and she was thinner, but she had that same direct stare that told me a sweary outburst wasn't far off. Her forearms were loosely and amateurishly bandaged.

"I know you from somewhere," she said.

"Hello again, Marcia, I'm WDC Crockford. I used to be at Wokingham but I'm now with Windsor police."

"It was you what put me in touch with that Miss Bloom, wasn't you?"

"For your probation, yes."

"She was nice. Liked her."

"Hild— I mean Miss Bloom is nice."

And she would be upset about this current situation. "Can I come in?"

"S'pose."

"I'm going to leave you two to it," said the manager, moving off down the corridor. Marcia flumped down onto one of the three empty beds in the room.

"So, Marcia, can you tell me what's happened?" I asked.

"I cut my wrists with a razor blade and I swallowed 30 aspirins. It's the best way out for my boyfriend Johnnie and this other b— girl he's seeing."

"I can't believe it is for one moment, Marcia. How did it come to this, then?"

"Well, you see, me and Johnnie, we've been dating for a few months while I've been living here, but while I've been out working in the baker's, he's been seeing her behind my back. I got let out early yesterday evening, and I saw him with the bitch, holding hands."

"I can see that would be upsetting. What happened next?"

"Well, we just had this massive argument, and I ran out and stayed out wandering about town until the early hours. Two of your mates in a police car brought me home. I saw Johnnie again the next day and we just started arguing about her again and I started crying."

"What happened after that argument?"

"Johnnie went out for a walk with her again. It's clear he wants her rather than me. So I got a razor blade and cut my wrists with it. And I took the aspirins.

"And then what happened?"

"I felt sick, and the plasters I'd put on my cuts weren't really stopping the blood, so I knocked on my friend Annie's door…"

"Annie Sage?"

"Yeah, and I asked her if she could bandage my arms for me, then I was sick in her wastepaper basket, and then Mrs Briley the manager came over. I can remember her saying, "Don't do anything else stupid, you silly girl," and the next thing I remember was waking up back in my own bed with sore arms.

"So did you really intend to take your own life, Marcia,

or did you hurt yourself out of frustration, or as a cry for help?"

I really hope you say this was just a cry for help.

"I wanted to die. I wanted to kill myself. I can't see a future without Johnnie. I've really messed up my life."

I don't want to write these words down, but I have to.

Marcia gazed directly at me, eyes blazing. *Here we go.*

"Anyway, it's my sodding life, nobody else's, and I can do what the hell I like with it. It's none of your fuckin' business neither!"

...none of your effing business neither... I wrote, finishing Marcia's statement. I read it back to her and she scrawled a signature onto it.

I then took a statement from Annie Sage in the room opposite.

"Can you tell me what happened?"

"Marcia, she was screaming and crying and banging on my door, like, so I let her in. She said she had hurt her arm and could I put a bandage on it. Well, I saw the plasters across the insides of her wrists, and I asked her what had happened and she said she'd accidentally cut her wrists on some razor blades she had in her handbag. I said I ought to have a look at them. One cut was quite deep..."

"How deep?" I asked

"About quarter of an inch? The other one was really just a scratch."

Neither deep enough to sever an artery.

"And were there any other cuts besides these ones?"

"No – just the two."

Good – no hesitation cuts just before she went for the big one. These wounds are not screaming attempted suicide to me.

"And then what happened?"

"I put bigger plasters on and bandaged her wrists, then I made her a cup of tea. It was then she said she felt sick and was going to be sick because she had taken 25 aspirin tablets, so I got the wastepaper basket and she was sick in that. I could see several tablets in the sick. I got Mrs Briley and she said Marcia was just being hysterical and needed to calm down and get a good night's sleep. But one of the police officers who ran her home last night dropped in to see how she was, and Mrs Briley told him she thought she 'might have tried to do something silly', which is how you've got to hear about it."

"And did Marcia at any point say to you that she'd wanted to kill herself?" I asked.

"No. like I said, she said the razor blades were in her handbag, and I just assumed she'd taken the aspirins for the pain."

Poor feisty Marcia. From my inquiries, and knowing her background, I could see a troubled young woman who'd probably misguidedly tried to scare her wayward boyfriend into coming back to her, but events had spiralled out of control to the extent that the police were involved, and she was now looking at a serious charge of attempted suicide. All I could do was hand my statements in to the inspector who would prepare her prosecution case, and hope the magistrates would see what I could.

Marcia Lucas initially pleaded not guilty to a charge of attempted suicide at Windsor magistrates' court. *Good girl*. But then my statement, with its stark admissions, was read out, and she changed her plea to guilty. *Damn*.

Our inspector, prosecuting, outlined Marcia's short, but troubled past:

"Miss Lucas was in a Barnardo's home from the age of five until 18. She's had some shop, secretarial and telephonist jobs but was dismissed from all of them, and currently works in a bakery. Two years ago, she was put on probation for shoplifting items in Woolworths Wokingham…"

Marcia's defence solicitor stood up, and in mitigation said, "All that has happened here is Miss Lucas became somewhat hysterical following the altercation with her boyfriend, and, in her hysteria, caused some mild self-harm, not even worthy of a medical report. This was not a serious suicide attempt, but a bit of exhibitionism, that's all."

Marcia was put on probation for another two years, at a London probation hostel this time.

I went back to Wokingham that following weekend and met up with Hilda over coffee and toasted teacakes in the Galleon Tea Rooms.

"Ach, Marcia, that poor girl," sighed Hilda, her eyes a little moist. "She was a handful, and I put that down to her childhood in care, but she also has spirit. I hope she can find a new life in London."

"You know, Hilda, I can't help feeling partly to blame," I replied. "I had to question her and take down her statement, and of course there in black-and-white she's admitted attempting suicide. That's what the prosecution latches on to, and she can't deny it. Maybe if I'd asked the questions differently…"

"You cannot engineer a statement to fit your own sense of justice, Gwen," said Hilda. "You have to do your procedure to the letter, and unfortunately when the law of the land considers attempting to kill yourself a crime, *you* have to uphold it."

"You're right of course, Hilda." I sighed. "Sometimes though, particularly now I'm a detective dealing only with the aftermath of crime, I feel I'm an agent of the state, implementing laws I don't necessarily agree with. When I was in uniform, I could spot potential criminality and step in before it escalated. WPCs are so more much more preventative than WDCs."

"Is the gloss coming off CID, then?" asked Hilda.

"No. It's forensically fascinating in a way that uniform isn't. I just feel that some good WPC intervention could have helped Marcia rather than criminalise her. I don't understand why attempted suicide is a crime. When somebody is that desperately unhappy that they want to take their own life, surely they need help, not punishment through the courts?"

"It is inhuman and archaic!" said Hilda, "At least we no longer bury suicides at crossroads rather than in consecrated ground, or confiscate their property, but it is high time it was decriminalised[48]."

"Ooh, that reminds me," I said, reaching into my handbag for *Against The Law*. "Here's your book back."

---

48 Attempting to take one's own life wasn't decriminalised until the Suicide Act of 1961.

"What did you think?"

"It didn't help me feel any less of an agent of the state, that's for sure. Those young men really did nothing wrong, did they? They just fell in love with people the law says they shouldn't have fallen in love with, and got caught and punished. The Wolfenden Report was absolutely right: what goes on in private between consenting adults should be none of the law's business. A shame the government rejected its recommendations."

"It was, but all is not hopeless," replied Hilda. "A lot of influential people, including JB Priestley, have written to *The Times* calling for Wolfenden's recommendations to be implemented, and I believe there's a group called the Homosexual Law Reform Society campaigning for decriminalisation. There will be reform; it's just a question of when."

Hilda and I ordered another pot of coffee and carried on putting the world to rights, stretching our minds and challenging each other's preconceptions.

They say for every action, there is an equal and opposite reaction, so my soul-nourishing meet-up with Hilda had to be balanced with a visit to my parents in Seaford Road. The front door was open slightly so I pushed it and walked in. I heard their voices in the parlour:

"Ow, Wally, you're hurting me! Be a bit more gentle!"

"Just keep still, Aggie."

Grunting sounds.

"OW!"

"Keep still, I tell you, I can't get it in."

Sighing sounds.

"Well maybe if you pinch it and push it up higher?"

More grunting sounds.

"That's it! It's going up now."

"OOOOOH!"

Ripping sound.

"Wally, you idiot! You've torn it now!"

I gingerly knocked on the parlour door. Dad, red-faced and perspiring, opened it, tucking his dress shirt into his trousers.

"Hello, Gwennie!" he said, giving me a kiss. "This is a surprise!"

"Clearly. Are you two all right in there?" I asked, feeling a blush creeping up my neck.

"Not really," he said. He pushed the door open to reveal my mother standing there in her one and only evening gown, the zip broken and her bare, fleshy back spilling out of the torn material.

"We've got the Masonic Ladies' Night coming up soon and thought we ought to make sure our evening dress fits. Mine does, but Ag can't get into hers any more."

"I would have got into it if your father had been more careful doing the zip up. Now he's ripped the material," moaned Mum.

"There's no way on God's earth that zip was doing up round your back, Ag," said Dad. "The only good thing about rationing was it kept us all slim."

He was right. Now there was plenty of food in the shops and a little more money to buy tasty things, Mum especially had put on weight. No way was she going to fit into her admittedly lovely dark burgundy evening dress.

"I can't afford to buy a new one," she wailed. "And I don't want to miss the Ladies' Night."

I had an idea.

"I'll take your dress, Mum, and I can let a piece into the back and put in a new zip," I offered.

"You'll never be able to match this colour."

"I'm not going to match it. I'll let in some lovely contrasting material, and it'll look like a brand-new dress."

"Where are you getting this 'lovely contrasting material' from, anyway?"

"Mr Munshi's stall in Windsor market."

She sniffed. "Sounds a bit foreign."

"Oh, it is. Rolls of beautiful Indian silks and fabrics by the yard. I've been wanting an excuse to go and shop there for ages."

"Well, don't go and ruin it," said Mum, handing me her ruined dress.

Mr Munshi recognised me when I took Mum's dress along to his stall the next Saturday morning.

"You have come back, madam, you are very welcome," he said.

I showed him the dress and explained what I wanted to do with it.

"It is beautiful. Such a dark red," he said. "I think I have something very special for you to sew into the back." He squatted down and pulled out a roll of silky material from the bottom row. Its base colour was teal, and velvety swirls of exactly the same burgundy as Mum's dress ran through it. I gasped at how lovely it was.

"You will make your mother very beautiful, yes?"

"It's going to look fabulous, Mr Munshi. I'll have two yards, please. I'll use any extra to make myself some cushion covers."

I poured some shillings into Mr Munshi's hand, and after more cooing over his delicious fabrics, took my material home to make a start.

CHAPTER 19

Au revoir les debutantes

Maidenhead with Le Mercier
June 1958

Can you imagine picking up the phone to your local police and asking, "Could you send a couple of plain clothes detectives round to my daughter's 18th birthday party to mingle with the guests and check nobody steals anything? And while you're at it, a police car patrolling the nearby lanes looking out for potential troublemakers or gatecrashers would be nice too?"

Well, back in my day you could, although it helped if you were part of Berkshire high society, with a massive country house, and some minor royals on the guest list. I have no idea who paid for this service – the taxpayer, or some private arrangement between the police top brass and the socialites themselves, but what I do know is that I did undercover security for several posh functions.

"Get your glad rags ready, Gwen," said Ernie. "We're going plain clothes at the Guards Club Saturday week."

"You mean the ball at the end of Ascot Week? Won't we have to dress up to the nines?"

"I assume so. Evening gown, high heels, sequinned handbag... and that's just what I'm wearing."

I chuckled. "Very amusing, Ernie."

"I've told them to put us on the guest list as Lord and Lady Algernon Hardley-Therre."

"Have you really?" I was laughing now. "Dahling – we're doing The Season."

"Yeah, what's all that 'season' stuff about anyway?" asked Ernie. "I've only ever thought about it as events for a load of toffs that we have to police. Do you know much about it?"

I'd never made a big thing of it, but I was a bit of a secret Royal watcher, and I even used to keep a scrapbook of newspaper cuttings about the royal family. Now, with less time on my hands, I made do with reading the *Tatler* magazines in the dentist's waiting room to catch up with what the Queen, Princess Margaret and all their attendant aristocrats had been up to.

"Well," I replied, "The Season's for daughters of the nobility and gentry, once they reach marriageable age, to 'come out' into society – they're called debutantes. They go to events like Glyndebourne, Chelsea Flower Show, Royal Ascot, the Royal Windsor Horse Show, the Boat Race, Henley Regatta, etcetera, in the hope of meeting and marrying suitable young men who can 'keep them in the manner to which they have become accustomed'."

"Right, so it's really a posh meat market?"

"Ha! Sort of. But I do think the days of the debutante are coming to an end, and we might not see many more Guards Club Balls in the future."

"Why's that then?"

"The Queen stopped the presentation of debutantes at Buckingham Palace back in March after 200 years of doing it. Or rather, rumour has it, Prince Philip stopped it, calling the whole thing 'bloody daft'. So, the girls who made their curtsey in front of the Queen this year – and will be at the Guards' Club Ball – will be the last debutantes."

"Made their what?"

"Curtsey. So, the debutantes go to Buckingham Palace and queue in the freezing cold for their turn to go inside and curtsey in front of the Queen. That's it. That's all they do. And later in the spring there's a ball where they all dress in white ballgowns and this enormous birthday cake gets wheeled in on a trolley and they have to curtsey to that…"

"You know what?" replied Ernie. "I'm with Prince Philip on this one – bloody daft."

Now the next problem was finding something to wear. My detective's plain clothes allowance wouldn't cover a couture gown, not to mention the long satin gloves, evening bag and something warm to go round my shoulders that such an evening called for. There was a church jumble sale coming up, and the Maidenhead ladies always donated beautiful clothing, so I could look for some eveningwear there. Or I could perhaps make myself something? I was quite good at hand sewing (or so I thought), and it would give me another excuse to go and see Mr Munshi and buy more Indian fabric.

But before I did that, I needed to refresh my sewing skills on Mum's torn dress. I laid it out on Mrs Foskett's dining room table and snipped out the ripped fabric. Then I cut out and pinned two pieces of teal material into the back of the bodice and started to stitch them. But being such fine fabric, the stitches snagged and puckered it. Perhaps it would look better when I put the zip in? It didn't. Two hours and three unpickings later, I held my head in my hands surveying the wreckage of Mum's only evening dress and some ruined silk. I leaned back and my elbow knocked an open tin of 1000 dressmaking pins off the table and all over the linoleum.

"Oh, bloody sod this bloody sodding thing!" I wailed, ready to throw it across the room.

I heard two pairs of footsteps trotting down the stairs, the front door opening, and Victor's voice murmuring: "Bye darling... yes... bye... bye" to whatever erudite friend he had been entertaining in his room.

"Somebody's not having a good day," he said, peering round the dining room door.

"That would be me, Vic. I used to be able to sew but I've made a complete pig's ear of my mum's dress *and* this beautiful material."

"You can't expect to be a crime-fighting heroine by day and Cristóbal Balenciaga by night, darling," he said. "Something's got to give."

I laughed at last, my fury dissipating.

Victor took a magnet on a string out of his pocket, and in no time at all he'd gathered up all my scattered pins from the floor.

"Bloody pins," he continued. "As a costumier, this happens to me all the time at work. And I meant to thank you for tipping me off about Mr Munshi's. I've got some gorgeous fabrics and trimmings for costuming there. It's a treasure trove. Anyway, what are you trying to do?"

I explained about my mother's dress, the Guards' Club Ball, and my now rather misguided plan to make myself something to wear for that evening.

"The material is always going to bunch up as you're not putting a let into the skirt as well," explained Victor. "That silk needs a light touch and a small needle so it doesn't pucker. You've got enough material left, so why don't I put in a contrasting panel all the way down from collar to skirt hem and refit the zip?"

Goodbye cushion covers, I thought, but I didn't mind.

"Would you do that for me, Victor? Won't it take you ages?"

"Not when I've got trusty Mr Singer to help me. The job of minutes, rather than the hours you're making it."

"Ah! Your sewing machine, of course."

"And don't forget the years of tailoring expertise driving Mr Singer. By the way, I'm guessing you're five feet four inches and take a size 10?"

"Spot on! How do you know?"

"As a dresser, darling, I pride myself on being able to look at a woman and just know her dress size and vital statistics. Saves a lot of time on set when it comes to selecting costumes from Wardrobe. I can see from this dress that your mum was a size 12 on top and is now a 14?"

I wasn't going to disagree with Victor.

"So, what are we going to be doing at the Guards Club Ball, Ernie?" I asked as we had a planning meeting of sorts over cheese sandwiches in the CID office.

"Well, there was some Teddy boy trouble there last year when a whole gang of them were trying to get over the wall into the club, and even threatened the inspector and another PC he had with him. But then Reg and PD Rex turned up, all hunched shoulders, curled lip and bared fangs... that was just Reg... and they backed off. We'll be keeping an eye on the perimeter of the club, and that includes the riverfront, as they have been known to swim over from Guards Club Island and make a nuisance of themselves."

"OK. Promise me one thing, Ernie," I said. "If there's any going in the river, you'll do it, as I can't swim."

I was *supposed* to be able to swim, and even though I'd fallen in a river apprehending a felon a few years back, I still had no inclination to learn.

"What makes you think I can?" he replied.

"Weren't you supposed to learn at Sandgate Police Training College?"

"I still don't know to this day how my pathetic doggy paddle got me through the exam, but it did. I remain a great advocate of the first principle of lifesaving – run and get the lifebelt."

"I suggest we both keep well away from the river, then."

Ernie chuckled. "Bet you wish you were going to be on duty with that hunky PC Falconer boyfriend of yours, him with the bronze lifesaving medallion, rather than the pigeon-chested disappointment that is me, then."

I hesitated. I didn't usually talk about my personal life with my colleagues, but I'd got to know Ernie so well, working with him was like putting on your favourite old, warm, moth-eaten jumper – all cosy and safe.

"I'm not actually seeing Henry any more," I ventured.

"I'm sorry, I didn't realise," said Ernie.

"Oh don't worry, nothing to be sorry about. We're just different people now, going in different directions. As you know, CID hours aren't really conducive to nurturing external relationships…"

"Oh I know. Tell me about it. Celia's always saying—"

We were interrupted by a knock on the door and Beryl the typist came in with two gold-embossed invitation cards in her hand.

"Lord and Lady Algernon Hardley-Therre?" she asked.

"That's us – obviously," replied Ernie, mock-rolling his eyes.

She handed us our undercover passes, laughing. "You'd better be home by midnight or you'll turn into pumpkins."

I was half reading, half dozing on my bed when there were three portentous, theatrical knocks on the door.

"Gwen, darling, are you decent?" called Victor. "I'm at least giving him time to climb out of the window, here—"

"I'm completely decent, and alone – you can come in."

The door opened and Victor floated in with two suit bags and a large paper carrier.

"I've done your mum's dress," he said, unzipping one of the suit bags and holding it up for me to admire.

I gasped at what he had done. At the back, the teal material fanned at the neck, then flowed down, narrowing at the waist, before flaring out again below and cascading to the floor. The sleeves and the neck were edged with delicate bands of the same material, and Victor had made a teal cummerbund at the front. Mum's wrecked dress was like a new couture gown fresh off a Paris catwalk.

"Like it, darling?" he asked my incredulous face, "Or more importantly, will your ma like it?"

"Like it, Victor? I LOVE it! I'm sure she'll love it too!" I gushed. *And I'm ashamed to admit I am now utterly jealous of my own mother.*

"I'm glad," he said. "It was a slightly tricky material to work with, but once I'd got a feel for it, it didn't take long to do."

"You've done an amazing job, Victor, thank you!"

"And Cinders, you *shall* go to the Guards Club Ball!" he proclaimed, unzipping the second bag. He pulled out a cream gown dotted sparingly with large red and pink embroidered flowers. The fabric effortlessly crossed over at the bust and tied in a bow at the back, its two short sleeves creating a sweeping boat neck. My jaw dropped open for the second time in 10 minutes.

"It's a fine example of a Dior, darling," continued Victor, "with a deep V at the front, cut on the bias to create a beautiful wrap. The sleeves are grown on and short to keep the bodice small against the full skirt. Paulette Goddard[49] wore it for some American television films she was making a couple of years ago and it's been sitting on the rail ever since. She's the same size as you. Try it on!"

Victor nipped out of the room, and I eased myself into

---

[49] An American actress, best known for her roles in Charlie Chaplin's *Modern Times* and *The Great Dictator.*

it. Pouting in the mirror, I marvelled at how a dress had the potential to transform a mousy little Home Counties policewoman into a Hollywood starlet.

"You can come in now," I called.

Well, lucky, lucky Ernie if he's accompanying this Cinderella to the ball," said Victor, fastening the bow at the back. He rummaged in the paper carrier and brought out some raw silk evening shoes, cream velvet elbow gloves, a double necklace of large iridescent fake pearls, and a white mink stole edged with the unfortunate creatures' little tails. With the skill of the theatrical dresser, he arranged them on me.

"Oh my God! You're going to look a million dollars, darling!" gushed Victor.

On the evening of the ball, I'd spent several hours on my hair, nails and make-up to various oohs and aaahs from Victor, and I was now fairly confident I could pass for a society lady. The doorbell rang, dead on 7.30 as arranged, and there was Ernie, standing on the doorstep in black tie, a cashmere scarf draped over his shoulders. Shaved, Brylcreemed and smelling of fine aftershave, here was a man who wore a dinner jacket well. He looked at me in silence and open-mouthed for a few moments, as if he had rung the wrong doorbell and a glamorous neighbour had come out.

"Good Lord... hello, Gwen... you look... absolutely lovely... I mean... you've made a great effort with your undercover disguise..." he stammered.

"I don't scrub up too badly, do I, Ernie? And neither do you..."

263

"Well, shall we…" said Ernie, offering me his arm to walk to the unmarked car. I noticed a blush had crept up the side of his cheek.

"Cor, Miss Crockford, you look bloomin' gorgeous tonight," said PC Ingham our driver. "Mind you keep your hands off her, Ernie you old dog."

Ernie blushed even more.

Inside the grand, colonial-style Guards Club, the air headily scented with cigar smoke, expensive perfume and alcohol fumes, it was all we could do to keep a straight face as the master of ceremonies announced us as "Lord and Lady Hardley-Therre", his eyebrow raised as if he didn't quite believe us either.

Despite our made-up social standing, it was fairly easy to mill around the Guards Club unnoticed and ignored as everybody was chattering, braying and gesticulating in their own little social cliques, and didn't particularly want to start a "getting to know you" conversation with outsiders. We looked the part, certainly, with our funny name and our expensive clothes, but we didn't really feel the part.

I patrolled the riverside lawn and shrubberies of Guards Club Park, coughing loudly at rustling bushes to flush out tipsy debutantes having a fumble with young suitors raring to keep them in the manner to which they had become accustomed. An inebriated colonel type stumbled past me, muttering, "You're a fine young filly," at my bust and then fell into a rose bush.

I was bored, so I caught up with Ernie at the back of the clubhouse in Guards Club Road.

"Did you bring your ciggies?" he asked. "I'm gasping for a fag."

I took a packet of Kensitas out of my evening bag, put two cigarettes between my lips and lit them, passing him one.

"Any Teddy boy action tonight?" I asked, taking a deep drag.

"Absolutely nothing. Streets are dead."

"Do you think we need to go across the bridge and see if there are any troublemakers on Guards Club Island or over on River Road?"

"Nothing better to do, eh?"

Taking two glasses of champagne from a waiter's tray, we crossed the lawn and clanged over the ornate metal footbridge to suss out nearby Guards Club Island, flushing a few more fumbling debutantes and their beaux from the vegetation. Looking across to the boathouse, all was quiet – no gangs of youths causing mischief. The dusty paths round the little island were thick with trip hazard tree roots, and I was ruining Paulette Goddard's silk shoes.

"Shall we go back? Leave these young lovers to it?" I suggested.

Climbing the steep wooden steps back up onto the bridge, I tripped properly, banging my toes, and Ernie had to grab me to stop me falling down onto the decking below.

"Careful, Gwen! You haven't had that much to drink, have you?" he asked as we limped, arm in arm, onto the bridge.

A giggling debutante, hand in hand with a young man, rushed past us to the island, and it crossed my mind we couldn't look less like detectives if we tried.

It was a beautiful warm night, the river twinkling with light from the waning moon. I stood with my bruised toes raised and Ernie's arm still supportively round my waist, leaning on the ornate cast iron rail. We were gazing south, towards Brunel's magnificent red-brick Sounding Arch – the railway bridge spanning the Thames – just as a train passed over and whistled.

"This is nice," whispered Ernie and we moved instinctively closer together, our faces just a couple of inches apart...

Then...

"What the bloody hell...?" exclaimed Ernie.

A rowing boat was silently heading north towards us, under the Sounding Arch and towards the club. As we watched in the gloom, two young men, both wearing black bow ties, moored the boat to a tree root, and with gymnastic ability hopped up onto the bank and nonchalantly moseyed towards the clubhouse.

"I don't think they've got invitations, have they?" I said. "We'd better go and check them out."

By the time Ernie had helped me hobble across the bridge and down the steep steps the other side, the two young men were nowhere to be seen.

"I'm going to be useless if we need to chase them," I said.

We checked out the ballroom where the debutantes and their beaux were politely jiving to a band playing some rock and roll numbers – no sign of them – and through to the dining room where the remains of a buffet banquet were still laid out on a long table. I was feeling quite peckish, but all the nice things such as sliced roast meats, cheeses and salads appeared to have gone, leaving only the wobbly things in aspic untouched. *No, thank you.*

"There they are!" said Ernie, and down the end of the table, two young men fitting our description, one with his back to us, were enthusiastically tucking into a plate of pastries. As we approached, the smaller man noticed us and stopped mid-chomp. He nudged his pal who had just stuffed a whole sausage roll in his mouth. The pal turned round, and I don't know who jumped more, me, Ernie – or PC Matt Wagstaffe.

"Bloody hell, Matt, what are you doing here?" hissed Ernie.

"Mmmmf mmbp mmmfm," mumbled Matt, spraying us with flakes of puff pastry.

"Did we see you two arrive in a rowing boat?"

"Yes, we did," said the smaller man, ignoring the daggers look Matt was giving him. "Fancy a vol-au-vent?" He offered us the plate.

So as not to draw attention to this unexpected scenario (and because I really, *really* fancied a vol-au-vent) I took one and popped it in my mouth. Then I had another one.

"I didn't think you were on the undercover list," continued Ernie. "I thought it was just me and Gwen."

"I'm not," said Matt sheepishly. "Jerry here is chauffeuring tonight and thought it might be a laugh to borrow a rowing boat and go down to Bray instead of sitting in the Rolls waiting all night. Then on the way back, we felt a bit peckish, and Jerry said he knew how to get in through the Guards Club tradesmen's entrance and there would be leftover food that would only go to waste…"

"And you just happened to be in evening dress when you decided to make this detour?" asked Ernie. "C'mon, Matt, we weren't born yesterday – you'd planned to gatecrash, hadn't you?"

"There wasn't any security last year, and, well, Jerry and I thought it would be a laugh," said Matt, blushing.

Matt and Jerry are certainly more fun than 90 per cent of the people who are here legitimately.

"I ought to report you to the inspector, I really should," grumbled Ernie.

"Well, before you do, help us out with this plate of rare roast beef, brie and grapes," said Matt.

With the evening drawing to a close, Jerry returned to his Rolls to take Lord and Lady and The Miss Whatever back home, and Inspector Morton dropped in to see how we'd got on.

"Any trouble tonight, chaps?" he asked.

The three of us (yes, three – Matt had decided to stick with us and style it out as undercover duty) shook our heads and said the night had been pretty uneventful.

"No gatecrashers, or young Teddy scoundrels trying to breach the perimeter?"

Ernie locked eyes with Matt.

"No, sir, nothing untoward tonight. It all went off without a hitch," he said through gritted teeth.

"Well, jolly good. PC Ingham will run us all home now."

Matt squeezed into the back seat of the Wolseley between me and Ernie, with a big smile on his face.

CHAPTER 20

Under siege

Maidenhead with Le Mercier
Summer 1958

"Who was that *glorious* man who picked you up for the ball last night, darling?" asked Victor the next morning in the kitchen, passing me a cup of tea.

"Oh, that was just Ernie Le Mercier," I replied, cursing the blush I could feel warming my cheeks. "He's my detective sergeant at Maidenhead."

"*Just* Ernie Le Mercier," Victor repeated, smirking at my discomfort. "Well, he seemed to have eyes only for you, that's for sure. Mind you, in that Dior, even I did."

"Oh stop it!" I laughed.

Victor dropped to one knee and flamboyantly spread his arms.

"Marry me, my darling Gwen, and I'll take you away from all this," he mock-pleaded.

I'd really turned the colour of beetroot now. *Damn you, Victor.*

"Only joking, petal. I'd be a nightmare of a husband. But you did look stunning last night," he said, standing back up again.

I'd had a lot of fun last night, but the evening had left me with some feelings I really could do without. As I'd hung up the Dior gown, I'd looked at Beatific Jesus on the mantelpiece.

"I know, I know, do not commit adultery. As if I would," I said to Him.

To stop my mind wandering to places I really didn't want it to, I figured a trip to Seaford Road to drop off Mum's dress would be as good as a cold shower for extinguishing unwanted thoughts.

Mum was in the scullery, scraping at potatoes with a knife.

"Hello, Mum, guess who's sorted your dress for you."

"And not a moment too soon, Gwendoline, considering the Ladies' Night is only next week. Let's have a look then. I hope you haven't ruined it."

"Come into the parlour and I'll show you," I said.

I whisked the dress out of the garment bag and spun it round so she could see the stunning teal back that Victor had created. Her eyes lit up with more spark than I had seen in years, and she was silent for a few moments.

"That's quite nice, actually," she said finally. "You didn't do that, did you?"

"I had a go, Mum, but in the end my housemate Victor did it for me with his sewing machine. He's a costumier for the film studios, and knows what he's doing."

"Really? Hmm. Yes, well, I always said men are better at tailoring than women. I have to say, he's done a nice job."

Dad came in, drying his hands on a tea towel.

"All right, my Gwennie?" he asked, pecking me on the cheek. He took a step back when he saw Mum's dress.

"Crikey! That's a beauty, isn't it? You've done a great job," he said, his eyes twinkling in admiration.

"She didn't do it; she got a friend to," replied Mum.

"Try it on then," urged Dad.

After some tutting, Mum wriggled into the dress, and I pulled the zip, smooth as silk, all the way up to her neck. The dress flowed over her every contour perfectly, and even with hair rollers still in, she looked wonderful.

"Aww, Mum! You're going to be the talk of all the Masonic ladies in that," I said.

"Well, I hope not. I don't really like drawing attention to myself…"

"It's a perfect fit, Aggie," said Dad, "although lay off the suet dumplings this week – you want it to stay that way."

I noticed Mum's eyes flash with fury, and I made a quick exit.

On Monday morning, as I walked up to the CID office, I took deep breaths to try to control any blushing if I saw Ernie. To my relief, he wasn't at his desk, and his trilby and mackintosh weren't on the coat stand. Then I remembered him saying he was giving evidence in the magistrates' court today against four Woodlands Park Teddy boys who'd beaten up another lad at a youth club dance. It was quite a big case, with four youths accused, and 12 prosecution witnesses, so it could be a long day.

The telephone was silent, so I busied myself typing up the report of the uneventful (in criminal terms, anyway) Guards Club Ball, doing some filing and generally tidying up loose ends. I *could* go out on patrol, but I was enjoying the peace and quiet of the empty CID office.

Well, that peace and quiet didn't last long. Around mid-afternoon, I heard shouts and jeers coming from the street outside, and a hammering sound. I opened the window and leaned out. A crowd of about 30 people, some dressed in Teddy boy garb, and what looked like mums, dads, aunties and uncles, were chanting what sounded, shockingly, like "Fuck the police!", "British justice is a joke!" and "Woodlands Teds forever!" outside the police station and banging on the door. Someone was aiming a catapult at the blue police lamp.

One Ted looked up and saw me leaning out of the window. "Get back to your typing, you tart!" he shouted.

I could just see the front door from my vantage point, and was astonished, and not a little proud, when Inspector Morton came marching out of it, gesticulating at the crowd to calm down. *Brave man*. But, as the saying goes, never in the history of calming down has anyone ever calmed down by being told to calm down, and Inspector Morton wasn't going to be the first.

The motley crowd rushed towards him, pelting him with eggs, sticks and a couple of paraffin lanterns grabbed from the roadworks opposite. He turned tail and ran back inside under the hail of makeshift missiles. From upstairs I could hear hammering and banging as the crowd tried to force their way into the station after him.

SPLAT! An egg spattered against the window a couple of inches from my head, and I thought it might be prudent to come in now. I ran down the stairs into the lobby where the uniform shift had gathered, nobody willing to unbolt the door.

"What are we going to do now?" cried Matt Wagstaffe, waving his arms, clearly relishing the opportunity to clown around. "We're under siege! Under siege in Maidenhead! Of all places!"

"All we can do is wait it out," said Inspector Morton, wiping egg off his uniform with a handkerchief. "There's clearly been some ruckus in the court. My guess is all the accused have been found guilty and the friends and relatives are taking it out on the police. We never get this when people are acquitted."

"Do you think they're all OK in the court?" asked Beryl the typist, a worried frown on her face.

"I'm sure they are. The court duty officers and a couple of CID are in there – they won't take any nonsense," said the inspector who'd just taken nonsense.

"Why don't we go up to the CID office?" I suggested. "We can see what's going on from there," and we all trooped upstairs to watch from behind glass the diminishing crowd jeering and making V-signs at us.

Our Black Maria trundled out of the station yard, no doubt loaded with the prisoners off to whatever detention centres they were being sent to. A couple of Teddy boys threw eggs at it and another went to kick the tyre but missed and fell over, and it sped on its merry way up Queen Street. After a few more V-signs, and some tin can kicking, the crowd gradually dispersed and Broadway was quiet again. We all trooped back downstairs.

"Bloody hell, what just happened there?" said Inspector Morton to Cockerill, Ernie and a couple of court duty officers, as they staggered in through the station back door.

"Never seen the like before in a British court of law," said Cockerill, shaking his head and wiping blood off his lip.

Ernie dabbed at a bloody nose with a handkerchief, and my instinct was to rush over, but Beryl got there first with ice cubes wrapped in a tea towel.

"The public benches were jam-packed with friends and relatives of the accused," continued Cockerill. "It was quite an intimidating atmosphere. When even the adult witnesses gave evidence, the four accused and their supporters openly jeered and laughed at them – the chairman couldn't keep order. It was the teenage girls giving evidence I felt sorry for – they were so scared they said they didn't remember anything."

"What about the victim?" I asked.

"Oh that bugger," spluttered Cockerill. "After all that, he said he hadn't really been hurt. It was a little scrap; he'd provoked it and got what he'd asked for."

This doesn't sound right.

"And then, get this, the victim's 63-year-old mother goes into the witness box. She's got two black eyes and a plaster on her nose. The chairman asks her how she'd got her injuries, and after glancing at the accused in the dock, she says, 'I had a bad fall,' and there's raucous laughter and whoops from the dock and the public benches."

"This is dreadful!" I said. "Witness intimidation, surely?"

"What really got me was the attitude of the accused when they were cross-examined," continued Cockerill.

"They chewed gum, had their hands in their pockets, lounged all over the witness box. No respect for the process of law at all…"

I think the beaten-up 63-year-old would have got me more.

"…They claimed they were the victim's friends, and he'd fallen over a chair, not that they'd hit him with it. And the whoops of laughter from the public benches just egged them on."

"So, what were the verdicts after all that?" asked Matt Wagstaffe.

"Well, the Bench was out for nearly an hour. The chairman could clearly see through the intimidation and said it was a 'very bad case'. He sent two of them to a corrective detention centre for three months; one who was already out on licence from Borstal got three months' imprisonment; and the fourth was sent for Borstal assessment."

"Good – at least they got what they deserved," said Inspector Morton.

"That's when pandemonium broke out in the courtroom," said Cockerill. "When PC Gough and PC Boyd here went to remove the prisoners from the dock they started fighting. Their mates, especially the women, screamed abuse at the magistrates – I heard the f-word several times – and ran forward as if to join in with the punch-up. Ernie and I pitched in to help and took blows ourselves, as you can see." Ernie nodded glumly behind his tea towel ice pack. "But we subdued them and got them down to the cells. I hear you had some trouble outside in the street?"

"Oh yes, but nothing we couldn't handle," replied Inspector Morton.

"This Teddy boy violence is really getting out of control now," said Cockerill to Ernie and me in the CID office later. The dramas of the afternoon had superseded the events of the Guards Club Ball and everything was fine with Ernie again.

"It seems to have come a long way from ripping a few cinema seats and setting off fire extinguishers," I said.

"There's a kind of feral gang thing going on with them," continued Cockerill. "I blame influence from London and films like that wretched *Blackboard Jungle*[50] inciting casual violence. They seem to find that acceptable – entertaining even. If we don't stamp on this, somebody is going to get killed."

I was up uncharacteristically early at 6 a.m. the next Tuesday morning, enjoying a peaceful cup of tea, when the telephone in the hall rang. I leapt on it before the third ring, praying it hadn't woken Mrs Foskett or Victor.

"Gwen, it's Ernie. Can you get to Maidenhead General Hospital ASAP? There's an elderly lady, a Mrs Edith Kinnear, who's been beaten up and robbed by an intruder overnight. Nasty case. I need a statement from her."

---

50 An American social drama film shown in the UK in 1956 about teachers in an interracial school, with a powerful rock and roll soundtrack that had Teddy boys ripping up cinema seats again.

A 10-minute brisk walk later and I was at the hospital in St Luke's Road. A kindly West Indian nurse who reminded me a lot of Suzette led me along a corridor to a private room.

"Poor darling," she said. "The doctor has checked her over and she's quite bruised but not seriously injured. You don't expect something like this to happen to a lady in her 70s, do you? Whatever is this country coming to?"

White-haired Edith Kinnear was propped up on pillows, and, despite a lump on her forehead, and swelling under her eye and across the bridge of her nose, she managed a smile as I went in.

"Hello, dear. Are you with the police?" she asked.

"I am, Mrs Kinnear. I'm Woman Detective Constable Crockford…"

"Are you really? Good for you."

"More importantly, how are you?"

"I'm alive, that's the main thing, and I gave him what for."

"What a horrible thing to happen to you. I'm so sorry. I'm afraid I'm going to have to ask you to go over the events of last night again while I write them down in a statement."

"Of course, dear."

And Edith Kinnear began her account:

"Well, I was asleep in my ground-floor flat, and footsteps padding along the hallway woke me up. It was about 2 a.m. I watched in horror as my bedroom door slowly opened, and a gloved hand came round it. I shouted, 'Who is it? Get out of my

bedroom!' but instead of running away, he ran over to me in bed and hit me in the face with a rubber torch he was carrying. I climbed out of bed and tried to smash my window, but he jumped on me and pulled me back onto the bed where he punched me in the face. I thought I might be indecently assaulted, but then I thought what youngster would want to have an old lady like me?

"'If you keep quiet, I won't hurt you,' he said. 'I must warn you I've killed people before.'

"Well, I had no intention of keeping quiet, so I shouted and screamed, even though he tried to tie me up and gag me with my spare nightie. We probably struggled for about an hour, and he kept saying 'I'm going to kill you.' I said, 'That won't do you any favours, will it?' then he climbed on top of me, put his hands round my neck and pressed down on my throat. This is it, I thought. I'm going to be strangled. He even said, 'You're a feisty old bird, but I'm going to kill you anyway...'

"Then suddenly he stopped, and started ransacking my room, taking my handbag, purse and jewellery box out of the wardrobe and stuffing them into a holdall he had brought.

"Then he pulled all the electric wires for the telephone out of the wall and went out of the door, locking me in. Well, I opened my window and climbed out, but I landed awkwardly and cut both my knees on the gravel outside. I saw him climbing back out through the kitchen window, running across the garden and disappearing over the back wall into my neighbour's. If I hadn't landed awkwardly, I was all up for chasing him, and giving him what for, you know?

"I managed to get round to my other neighbour and he telephoned the police. Your lovely Sergeant Le Mercier came straight round with some other officers and a scary looking police dog who ran off after a scent, but didn't find him.

"Description? Quite young – 17 or 18? Spotty face, tall and slight, with high slicked-back hair and dressed in that – what do you call it – Teddy boy garb."

"That was a very frightening thing to happen, Mrs Kinnear," I said as I held the statement for her to sign. "We're going to do our utmost to catch the beast who did this. You were incredible to fight back the way you did."

"Oh I'm all right, dear. I used to live in India years ago, and I got used to chasing monkeys, leopards, elephants and even the odd human robber off our property."

"Bloody Teddy boy again!" snarled Cockerill as he went over the evidence in the Mrs Kinnear case with Ernie and me. "They've got no moral compass, no pity, no conscience, no dress sense, no respect, for the law or anything else! Bring back national service, that's what I say."

"Feel better now, sir?" asked Ernie.

"I'll feel better when the greasy, quiff-headed bastard that did this is behind bars," replied Cockerill.

Ernie put down the telephone after a long conversation and cadged a cigarette off me.

"Well, well, well," he said. "That was Essex police on the line. They're holding a shopbreaker by the name of Charlie O'Malley, and – get this – he's complaining that he's been falsely represented in the newspapers."

"Eh? How come?"

"He's admitted to breaking into a flat in Maidenhead, but denies beating up Mrs Kinnear or threatening to kill her, as has been reported. He says he just pushed her onto the bed and threw an eiderdown over her head to stop her identifying him, and told her to keep quiet."

"An eiderdown doesn't cause facial swellings or bruising," I said. "I know who I believe."

"Oh, and he regrets her injuring herself falling out of the window – that's how she got all her injuries, he says. He feels so bad he is going to give up housebreaking apparently. He's got loads of form from Essex Quarter Sessions."

Charlie O'Malley appeared at the Berkshire Assizes, and while we were expecting a lounging, swaggering, gum-chewing Ted, he was a tall, pale, quiet youth with his hair plastered down flat. He pleaded guilty to robbery with violence, thereby saving Edith Kinnear the trauma of facing him and giving evidence.

"I would have gladly done so, though," she'd said to me. "I'd have given him what for in the witness box. How dare he say he never attacked me or threatened to kill me?"

And of course, there was a sob-story from the defence in mitigation – Charlie was a good boy, he loved his mother, he went off the rails when his parents divorced and got in with a bad crowd, he wanted to apologise to Mrs Kinnear for giving her such a frightening experience, he wasn't going to do anything like this again... Perhaps the Teddy boy had a conscience after all.

Charlie O'Malley got four years for robbery with violence.

CHAPTER 21

No business like show business

Maidenhead with Ernie Le Mercier
Summer 1958

Not all my day-to-day detective work at Maidenhead involved arsonists, beaten-up elderly ladies or troubled, self-harming teenagers. True, Maidenhead was a town of enormous social contrasts: there were still people who lived in rented caravans; families in the post-war prefabs that would be rebuilt in brick as the "Bomber estate", its road names taken from World War Two aircraft; stockbrokers and aristocrats who could muster private security from the police for their swish parties with just a telephone call; and an ever-changing cast of glitzy, Hollywood stars who either lived here or swept into town for the duration of their filming at Pinewood Studios in Iver, or Hammer Film Productions just along the river at Bray Studios.

It wasn't unusual to see Errol Flynn, Peter Cushing or Christopher Lee[51] sitting outside a café, or popping into the supermarket for a pint of milk. And quite often I would wander out on patrol in the hope of once again bumping into Colonel, a huge, drooling, friendly Great Dane, going walkies. Colonel played the eponymous

---

51 The A-list actors of the day.

hound in the Hammer film *The Hound of the Baskervilles* with a ridiculous furry wolf mask stuck on his face. His 15 minutes of cinematic fame involved pushing actor Ewen Solon to the ground at the chaotic climax of the film, licking ice cream off his face to replicate a terrible mauling. I'd met Colonel a couple of times, and kept a dog biscuit in my mac pocket just in case I encountered him again, soppy old thing that he was – nothing demonic about him.

One evening, I'd been in the lounge bar of the Jack of Both Sides pub, having a check-in with the barman who was occasionally one of our snouts for more serious crimes. I was supposed to meet Ernie there, but he seemed to have been delayed. As the barman went off to serve other customers, and my glass of light ale[52] went down, I became aware of a man – easily a foot taller than me – standing by my side and encroaching a little too far into my personal space. I looked up, and recognised a familiar face; he looked down and smiled.

Is this a senior officer I should recognise? Is he one of my brother's friends? I think I've seen him in a film... or on television... Oh my goodness, it's Sid James!

I smiled and went bright red. Anyone who'd seen *The Lavender Hill Mob* or *The Titfield Thunderbolt*, or listened to *Hancock's Half Hour* on the radio, knew who Sid James was. Always the loveable Cockney rogue with a dirty laugh, he was going to become a big star with the *Carry On* films – the first of which was made at Pinewood Studios in the spring of 1958.

---

52 Uniform police weren't supposed to drink on duty, but in CID we could – to keep up the undercover pretence, of course.

"What's a guy to do to get a drink round here?" Sid asked me, putting on a bizarre American accent.

"Oh… you just need to ask the barman," I replied. "He's gone down into the cellar to change a barrel, I think."

"Can I ask you to join me, ma'am? What are you drinking?"

I can't believe Sid James is about to buy me a drink. And my partner is going to be here soon. And what on earth is happening to my heart rate?

"Oh, um, just a half of light ale would be lovely, thank you," I replied, then because I couldn't think of anything better to say, I blurted, "I think you're really funny in *Hancock's Half Hour*. I always make a point of sitting down with my dad and listening to it on the radio."

"Excuse me, ma'am? What is this Hancock Half Hour? I've never heard of such a thing," he drawled.

"Oh, so you're not… oh, um… I'm sorry. I think I've got you mixed up with an English actor called Sid James…"

"Well, I *am* an actor," he drawled, "but I'm not Sid James. Forrest Tucker at your service, ma'am." He held out a meaty hand and shook mine, crunching my joints together.

Clearly my detective's identification skills had let me down and I peered more closely at Forrest Tucker. To be fair, he could have passed as Sid James's more attractive brother as they didn't look dissimilar, although Forrest was well over six foot, and Sid never looked particularly tall in his films.

"Gwendoline Crockford. How do you do? What might I have seen you in, Mr Tucker?"

"Well, I was in *The Westerner* alongside Gary Cooper before I enlisted with the United States Army during the war. *The Yearling* for MGM post war. *California Passage*? *Pony Express* with Charlton Heston?"

I hadn't seen any of these films, but I felt it polite to nod and "mmm" along as Forrest rattled off a list of movies and Hollywood A-list names.

"So, am I right in thinking that Hammer Studios has brought you here?"

"Got it in one, Miss Gwendoline. Played the lead in *The Abominable Snowman*..."

"Ooh, that sounds chilly," I simpered.

"Haha!" boomed Forrest, "and I'm currently working on an independent, *The Strange World of Planet X.*"

I couldn't be bothered with contemporary science-fiction movies – too many rubbery effects and women screaming at things with multiple eyes, not even attempting to defend themselves.

"Oh, that's fascinating," I replied. "What's *Planet X* about?"

"So. This mad scientist and his assistant – that's me – plays about with magnetism and creates these powerful magnetic fields that draw in UFOs from outer space. Earth gets plagued by storms of cosmic radiation that break through our protective atmosphere, and all the spiders and insects turn into giant flesh-eating mutants."

So, a screaming heroine getting stuck in a giant spider's web.

"It sounds brilliant," I lied. "I guess you come along and save the world from these flesh-eating creepy-crawlies?"

Forrest chuckled. "I won't give away the ending, but do catch it at the movie theatre when it comes out – the special effects are incredible."

"I'll look out for that then."

Forrest was beckoning the barman over. "A glass of dark beer for me and something called a light ale for the lady here, if you please." He turned to me again. "So what is it you do, Miss Gwendoline?"

"Well…" I began, "I'm in the police."

"Wow! You don't say?" replied Forrest.

"She's our one and only woman detective, aren't you?" Ernie's voice cut in as he appeared behind us. "Sorry I'm late, Gwen. PC Ingham was supposed to give me a lift, but he got called to an RTA instead."

"Can I buy you a drink too, sir?" asked Forrest.

"Oh no. No thank you, kind sir," replied Ernie. "We'd better get going to The Bear, Gwen – apparently there's some intel we need to hear…"

And that was my only encounter with Hollywood actor Forrest Tucker. I've often wondered what might have happened if Ernie hadn't turned up that night.

One Friday afternoon, the phone rang in the CID office, and I picked it up.

"Police? This is Mr Payne, the cashier from Bray Studios. We've had our wage packets stolen out of the safe. Could you come, please?"

Ursula was hanging about in the lobby as Ernie and I hurried down the stairs carrying the big fingerprint kit.

"Fancy helping us take the dabs of some famous actors and actresses, Ursula? We've got a theft at Bray Studios to investigate."

"Ooh yes!" She skipped up and down like an excited teenager. "I've always wanted to go and see what that's like."

Piling into the black CID car, we headed out along the Windsor Road and within 10 minutes reached Bray Studios at Down Place.

"Look! Look! That's clever!" enthused Ursula at the BRAY STUDIOS road sign painted to look like a clapperboard.

We turned left into Water Oakley Lane and trundled past the studio outbuildings to the back of the magnificent white bow-fronted riverside house that served as the main studio.

Mr Payne met us and led us along to a modest accounts office. He showed us a splintered cupboard that seemed to have been forced open.

"Can you tell me what happened?" asked Ernie.

"Yes. I'd made up the staff wage packets this morning, then locked them in this cupboard while I popped out for a quick 20-minute lunch. When I came back, the door was hanging open and all the money was gone."

"How much do you believe was taken?" I asked.

"Exactly £2,150," replied Mr Payne, referring to a balance sheet on the desk.

Ursula gasped. "Blimey, that's an awful lot of dosh, isn't it?"

"This feels to me like an inside job," said Ernie. "It's unlikely any safebreaker would venture all the way down here into the studio complex in the middle of the day."

"Well, quite," said Mr Payne. "We're like one big happy family here at Hammer Film Productions, and I'm sure any interlopers would have been noticed coming in. It does, sadly, beg the question which one of the family chose to steal from their own."

"Well, that's what we're going to find out," said Ernie. "Gwen, can you dust for fingerprints, and Mr Payne, is there a film currently in production?"

"Yes, *Further Up The Creek,* a naval lark with David Tomlinson and Frankie Howerd," the cashier said. "It's the sequel to *Up The Creek* – that did so well at the box office they're rushing out a follow-up."

"In that case, we need to stop the filming and assemble everyone on the property together and take their fingerprints. Could you do that for me, please?"

"There's about a 100 of us on site today, officer," replied Mr Payne. "I hope you brought enough ink with you."

"I hope so too," said Ernie. "If that Matt Wagstaffe didn't replenish the ink block after the schoolkids' police station visit last week, I'll have to have words. Thirty little sets of fingerprints on cards to take home to their mums will have made a dent in our ink supply."

Mr Payne toddled off to halt the afternoon filming, I dusted for fingerprints, a colleague from our Fingerprint Department turned up to photograph what my powder disclosed, and Ernie briefed us on the afternoon's investigation.

"As you take everyone's dabs, ask them if they saw anything suspicious or out of the ordinary today. And, of course, use this opportunity to flex your detectives' instincts – let me know if anyone seems shifty or evasive and we can question them further."

We set up three tables amid a mess of huge cameras, rigging and booms in one of the spare studios, and some lighting wag trained a spotlight on us. It turned out we had plenty of ink – Matt Wagstaffe had put a full bottle back in the fingerprint bag after all – and enough kit to have a fingerprint station each. A chatty, orderly queue of extras wearing naval uniform, technicians, stage builders, and *Further Up The Creek's* director and stars assembled and snaked around the studio. Everyone amiably came forward to be questioned and have their fingerprints taken.

I noticed Thora Hird taking a particularly long time having her fingerprints taken by Ursula. She seemed to be more interested in asking her what it was like being a policewoman, than talking about her own incredible career, which by this time had already clocked up 45 films. Ursula's face was pink, and she was beaming talking to this legend.

I could hear the familiar guffaws coming. Approaching my and Ernie's station in separate queues were Frankie Howerd and David Tomlinson dressed as naval officers, and sparring wisecracks off each other.

"Shut up, David, and let this lovely lady take your prints, while I shall enjoy some finger action with this *gorgeous* young detective," said Frankie, leaning in and grinning lasciviously at Ernie, making him blush right up to his hairline.

"You know, darling," David Tomlinson said to me loudly as I rolled his little finger onto the fingerprint card, "now Scotland Yard have *his* prints..." he nodded towards Frankie Howerd who was still tormenting Ernie "...they're going to be able to solve a vast number of previously unsolved crimes."

"Oh shut your face, you grass," retorted Frankie.

"Check his pockets, officers!" cried David. "I'm convinced I saw him stuffing wads of notes down his trousers in the gents earlier..."

We were laughing so much at all this wisecracking that it was almost impossible to question David and Frankie sensibly. Anyway, I was pretty certain stars of their calibre had plenty of money and no need to rob the Bray Studios wage cupboard. Yet nobody seemed shifty or dodgy, or had seen anything or anyone untoward today. There was some grumbling that they weren't going to get paid on time, but of course that was between Hammer Studios and their insurance company. We would just log the police report to support it. Mr Payne was right – Hammer Studios genuinely felt like one big happy family.

As the cast and crew returned to their make-believe ship to resume the afternoon's filming, we took our time and particular care packing up all the fingerprint cards, there were so many of them. Ursula could barely keep still and was grinning from ear to ear because lead actor Lionel Jeffries had told her she looked "so smart" in her police uniform. I had a moment of missing my uniform. Ursula looked so polished and official, whereas in my blue mac and grey suit I may as well have been somebody brought along from the typing pool.

"Anything, ladies?" asked Ernie.

"Nothing," I said. "Nobody I spoke to seemed at all suspicious, and nobody saw anything."

"Nothing for me either," said Ursula, still with a massive grin on her face.

"We'll have to see what the Fingerprint Department come back with, then. Whoever stole the wage packets planned and executed the theft perfectly. There are no clues whatsoever to go on."

With one hundred fingerprint cards packaged and sent up to Sulhamstead HQ for analysis, and a report on the investigation typed up, I cycled back home in the crisp autumn dusk with a smile on my face. I really loved my job, my colleagues, the people I met, and I felt that I wanted to be in the police for ever. To coin our Prime Minister Harold Macmillan's phrase, I'd never had it so good.

Mrs Foskett was away for a few days, so Victor and I could play house and relax a bit. I put my bicycle in the garage and opened the front door, looking forward to the cup of tea I'd been gasping for all afternoon. Standing by the sink in the kitchen was a shirtless young man I'd never seen before, his trouser braces the only things covering his toned, tanned torso. I hesitated, then called out the phrase Dad always used when Mum was scared there was an intruder in the house.

"If there's a burglar in here, would he like a cup of tea?"

"Just made a pot actually," called back the young man. "I'm just letting it brew while I pack all your valuables into this bag marked SWAG."

There was the sound of the downstairs lavatory flushing and Victor emerged, his linen shirt unbuttoned, revealing his own toned, tanned torso.

"Well, that won't take you very long then, love," he said to the young man. "Gwen meet Giorgio, Giorgio meet Gwen."

I forced myself to look Giorgio straight in the eye as I shook hands with him.

"And put your damn top back on in front of the lady," joshed Victor, throwing an expensive-looking checked shirt at him.

"Er, hello, I–I don't believe we've met before?" I ventured. As far as I knew, Victor usually kept his friends out of the way in his room.

"Gwen is our very own Miss Marple, got a nose like a bloodhound, haven't you, darling?"

Giorgio looked puzzled. "Like Lily, you mean?" he asked Victor.

"Yep, she's an orderly daughter. Certainly keeps her room tidy..."

Giorgio shot Victor a worried look. I hadn't got a clue what they were talking about, these arty types, and part of me didn't want to know.

"But she's also fantabulosa, aren't you darling?" Victor grabbed my face in his hands and planted a kiss on my forehead. "Now let's get that tea down us or it will be stewed to buggery."

Over a cup of rather tannic tea, I told Victor and Giorgio all about our investigation at Bray Studios and the personalities we'd encountered. They seemed to know them all.

"That Thora Hird is an absolute peach to work with," he said.

"Queen," replied Giorgio, nodding.

"I think Frankie Howerd scared my sergeant, Ernie Le Mercier, a bit," I said.

"Oh that old fruit. He does it to everyone. Well known for it. Mind you, your Sergeant Le Mercier, though…"

Giorgio shot Victor another of his looks and I could feel the colour moving up my neck. *Damn feeling like this.*

"I think you've got the hots for Sergeant Le Mercier, Gwen love," said Victor, his gaze piercing me like a laser beam.

"Oh don't be so ridiculous, he's got a wife," I replied, the colour burning my cheeks now.

"I wouldn't let that get in the way of anything," continued Victor. "Gwen and Ernie sitting in a tree, K–I–S–S–I–N–G," he chanted.

"They must be in Special Branch, then," cackled Giorgio, and even I had to laugh.

"Leave the poor girl alone now," said Giorgio. "Anyway, aren't we supposed to be going up the West End for a few bevvies tonight, Vic? We'd better get going or we'll never be able to park around the Dilly."

"The Dilly?" I asked.

"Piccadilly Circus, love," replied Victor, getting up from the table. "Don't wait up for me, will you?"

And off they went, blowing me kisses.

We never did find out what happened to the Bray Studios wages, much less who the thief was. The only matching fingerprints we found on the cabinet were those of Mr Payne himself, as we would have expected. Some of his prints were smudged, indicating that the thief wore gloves.

And *Further Up The Creek* didn't match anywhere near the box office success of *Up The Creek,* but it was great fun to sit in the cinema with Hilda, whispering, "I met him … I met her… I met him…"

PART 2

CHAPTER 22

Smelly Eddie's post-mortem

Windsor with Kinch
Summer 1959

Remember "Smelly Eddie" Rooke, who we found dead under Windsor's railway arches? The coroner, agreeing with the doctor that his death was unexplained, ordered an autopsy to discover what had killed him. So, on a bright sunny morning, I met DI Cockerill outside the mortuary at Windsor's Edward VII Hospital, where he was leaning against the bonnet of his car smoking a small cheroot.

"Where's DS Kinch, guv?" I asked.

"He decided that his time on this case would be better spent searching Mr Rooke's room in Sheet Street, rather than here," said Cockerill with a wry smile.

I tried to keep a straight face myself. *He knows as well as I do how squeamish he is.*

"I supervised the unloading of Mr Rooke's body at the morgue when he first arrived," said Cockerill. "And this morning we've removed his garments, photographing them as we went, and bagged, labelled and sealed them for the lab to take a look at. Be grateful you weren't here for the undergarments…"

"Bad, were they?"

Cockerill wrinkled his nose.

"Did they find anything in the pockets?" I asked.

"Nothing apart from a single 10-bob note in his shirt breast pocket. I think we picked up most things in his little den."

"Do we know who the Home Office is sending down to do the PM?"

Cockerill looked at his watch. "No, but he should be here in about 10 minutes."

"Ooh, I wonder if we're going to get Donald Teare or even Keith Simpson," I mused.

"I remember Teare from the Straffen case," said Cockerill, blowing out a plume of smoke. "Such a gent. Just the right pathologist to investigate a little girl's death."

"He was," I replied. "I met Keith Simpson at Guys. He made the post-mortem I attended so interesting, I completely forgot about the smells and the fluids. I even had a chance to chat to him afterwards. A great man."

Cockerill nodded thoughtfully. "Well, Eddie's all undressed and on the slab ready for whoever is going to do the PM, and the mortuary technicians are on standby with the bottles, flasks and test tubes he's going to need when he gets here."

Forty minutes later, Cockerill and I were still standing outside the mortuary. And at last, in the distance, we could see an official-looking black Wolseley trundling up the drive.

"I reckon that's him now," said Cockerill. "Do you want to go in and let them know he's here? I'll do a meet and greet and bring him in."

"Yes, guv," I said as I walked into the mortuary. "Morning!" I chirped to the two miserable-looking mortuary assistants, one who was leaning against the sink, and another who was wiping down a blackboard with **HEART**, **LUNGS**, **SPLEEN**, **LIVER**, **KIDNEY** and **BRAIN** written on it.

"Morning, miss," they replied.

The white-and-green ceramic-tiled room couldn't have been more depressing if it tried – no wonder the assistants looked fed up. The steel mortuary table, on which lay a small shape under a sheet, straddled a gully in the concrete floor that connected to a grating, which then ran into the drains. A rubber hosepipe, loosely coiled round a wall tap, flopped onto the grating, and next to that in a corner were propped three hard brooms; I didn't want to dwell too much on the pink and red matter caught among the stiff bristles. At least there was some sort of bright angleable overhead lamp – some mortuaries I'd been in had only bare bulbs hanging from the ceiling.

"I think the pathologist has arrived," I said. "DI Cockerill is bringing him through shortly."

No sooner had I said that, the door to the autopsy room crashed open and a huge bear of a man with slicked back hair, a cigarette sticking out of the side of his mouth and a grubby raincoat strode in. Behind him trotted a small woman in pointy glasses, carrying two briefcases, and behind her puffed DI Cockerill, trying to keep up. The man grabbed a privacy screen on wheels and pulled it into the centre of the room.

"You can work behind that, Miss Fairbrass," he barked.

Ignoring the mortuary technicians, he looked me up and down, unsmiling.

"Well, good morning, everybody," Cockerill panted as he mopped perspiration off his brow with a handkerchief. "This is the pathologist Dr Frederick Tenterden from the Home Office..."

The two technicians flashed each other knowing looks.

"...And, Dr Tenterden, this is WDC Crockford from..."

"Yeah, yeah, hello, whatever," snarled Tenterden, waving away the surgical gloves offered by the technician. "I'm guessing this is the body under here?"

Without even removing his coat, he jerked the sheet like a magician doing that pulling-off-a-tablecloth-but-leaving-the-crockery-in-place trick, exposing the naked, purplish, wizened corpse of Smelly Eddie for all to see. Reaching up, Tenterden angled the lamp above the body and switched it on, flooding Eddie's diminutive body with white light. He took a final drag on his cigarette and threw the butt into the gully.

Seizing Eddie's mauve face with a massive, nicotine-stained paw, he jerked it from side to side.

"Extensive congestion and petechial haemorrhages on the skin of the face, Miss Fairbrass, raising the possibility of pressure on the neck, possibly strangul-ation," he boomed to his secretary behind the screen, "and a deep abrasion beneath the left eyebrow."

"He was found face down, so I would assume that purplish colour would be post-mortem lividity, due to the blood settling at the lowest point, don't you think?" ventured Cockerill.

"I'll be the judge of that once I've got the organs of the mouth, nose and neck out," snapped Tenterden.

He prowled around Eddie's body, tapping another cigarette on a silver case, before sticking it in the corner of his mouth.

"Funny-looking little bloke, wasn't he?" He sniggered, to a resounding silence, before prodding at a fuzzy tattoo on Eddie's upper arm.

"Naval tat of a proud British bulldog. Although he's lost so much muscle mass it's turned into a little pug, HAHAHAHAHA!"

Nobody joined in with his laughter.

Tenterden yanked some hair from Eddie's head and scraped at the bitten-down nails with a wooden stick, dropping the items into test tubes.

"Right, swabs," he ordered, holding his hand out to one of the technicians, who blinked back at him. "BEFORE NEXT TUESDAY!" he bellowed, making the technician jump and shove a handful at him. He poked the swabs into Eddie's mouth, ears and nose and dropped them into bottles.

"I think you all know what's coming next." He grinned. "You two, turn him over so I can swab the other orifices."

The two technicians arranged Eddie face down in a most undignified pose. Tenterden picked up a long swab and prodded around with his fingers.

"Well, well, well," he said. "I wasn't expecting that. Just look at this, everyone!"

We craned forward and peered at Eddie's nether regions.

"Look at this arsehole! Just look at it! You could drive the bloody Lord Mayor's carriage up that!" cackled Tenterden, pleased with his "wit" and looking around expectantly for our reactions.

I felt my stomach turn over, and wanted the floor to open up and swallow me. Dr Keith Simpson's words resounded in my head: "*As a pathologist, I have to remember that I am hugely privileged. I'm the last person to properly look at someone deceased... And this is why every deceased body must be treated with the utmost respect.*"

In my entire police career, I had never heard a medical practitioner come out with anything as crude as this before, and I struggled to contain my embarrassment. Cockerill's face had also turned bright red, and one of the technicians had his elbow over his mouth.

"Miss Fairbrass, here we have the keratinised and dilated anal orifice of the habitual homosexual," Tenterden called, as he inserted a swab.

"Turn him back over," he ordered, and the technicians rolled Eddie onto his back again.

"Scalpel!" he barked. The technician handed him one. "And Miss Fairbrass, a light."

Miss Fairbrass scurried out from behind the screen with a Zippo lighter, lit his cigarette and scurried back again.

Tenterden sliced open Eddie's body from Adam's apple to pubis, clipped off his ribs with shears, and delved into his abdominal cavity, all the while dropping cigarette ash over everything. He pulled out the tongue, larynx, oesophagus, trachea, heart and lungs and threw them onto the autopsy bench where, hunched over, he wordlessly rummaged about in the viscera, chopping with a scalpel, and spattering his coat with blood droplets. We had no idea what he was doing, as he clearly wasn't prepared to share his findings in a more educational way than barking them at Miss Fairbrass.

Keith Simpson would never have done that, I thought.

Eventually he said, "Trachea and oesophagus without rupture. Carotid arteries, jugular veins, hyoid bone, thyroid cartilage and cervical spine all intact, indicating it unlikely that the victim was strangled or asphyxiated, and the congestion and petechiae are more likely the result of livor mortis from the position of death."

"I bloody told you," Cockerill mouthed irritably behind Tenterden's back.

I had never felt sick at a post-mortem before, but I did that morning. It wasn't Eddie, or the smells, or the organs themselves that were making me feel nauseous. It was the sight of this obnoxious character poking, prodding and chopping away at them, in the same way that a slobbering drunk dinner guest with no table manners could put you off a perfectly nice meal.

"Aha! Probable cause of death!" proclaimed Tenterden straightening up, holding Eddie's excised heart in one hand, and in the other, a dark jellified blood clot that he wobbled triumphantly at us. I could feel the bile rising in my throat, and took a deep breath.

"An occlusive thrombus! Aka a bloody great big blood clot that completely blocked his coronary artery. You got that, Miss Fairbrass?"

"Yes, I did," came the voice from behind the screen.

At that point I excused myself, with Tenterden braying, "There's always one who can't hack it, isn't there?" and hooting with laughter as I left the mortuary.

I cursed him under my breath all along the corridor to the exit, and again as I sat on the low wall outside, inhaling the calming nicotine of a cigarette. I was cross with myself that I had appeared weak, that I was the only woman who'd had to step outside.

I knew what was coming next in the post-mortem process. I just couldn't face seeing that revolting, disrespectful man – who couldn't even be bothered to wear an apron – examining stomach contents, or peeling Eddie's scalp over his face, or manhandling the "magical blancmange" that was his brain. I remembered seeing Eddie when he was alive, pushing his pram of newspapers around Windsor, and while he probably wasn't someone you'd invite for dinner, he was still a human being who deserved some kindness and respect. And if Tenterden's "Lord Mayor's carriage" revelation was correct, perhaps Eddie had a secret life beyond the newspapers.

I stood up and dusted the ash off my skirt. I took my mirror out of my pocket and reapplied some lipstick, pressed my lips together, and flicked back some loose hair. I took a deep breath, ready to go back in, then noticed Tenterden's driver had been sitting in the parked Wolseley all this time, watching me. He smiled and nodded, no doubt used to a trickle of green-faced police officers stepping outside mortuaries for, at best, a breather; at worst, to throw up in the flowerbed.

As I approached the glass double doors in the middle of the corridor, Tenterden was striding towards them. Miss Fairbrass trotted along behind him, struggling with her jacket and two briefcases, while trying to keep her glasses on her nose. He shoved one door open and marched through, with not a backward glance as it swung shut on Miss Fairbrass and she tried to open it again with her back, her hands full. Cockerill rushed to her aid and pushed the door open for her to hurry after Tenterden, then held it for me to go through.

"You OK? I'll meet you back inside in a moment," wheezed a flustered Cockerill. "I'd better just see Tenterden and his secretary off."

I walked through into the mortuary. One of the technicians was sloshing the bucket of Eddie's viscera back into his body cavity, brain and all, while the other was listlessly stitching his scalp back over his skull with thick linen thread.

"All right, miss?" said one.

"Oh yes, I'm fine, thank you. It wasn't the blood and organs that bothered me, it was more the way Tenterden treated the body." The two technicians looked at each other as if they didn't really believe me, then launched into a tirade.

"Aye, he's a pig of a man all right, worse than a navvy," said one of them.

"He's supposed to leave us technicians £1 tip each for a PM, and does he ever, my backside..." said the other.

"And we never get our bottles, test tubes and specimen jars that he's 'just borrowed' back from him," the first replied.

"I'm amazed he was dictating Mr Rooke's autopsy to his secretary. I've heard from my mate in London that he can be doing one autopsy, and simultaneously dictating his findings from the previous one to her. So, he's talking about excising an ovarian cyst, and there's this hairy-arsed bearded bloke on the slab he's working on. Bizarre."

Bizarre indeed. Cockerill came back into the room just after Eddie had been put back into a cadaver drawer, and the technicians were hosing and brushing his last pinkish remnants into the drain grating.

"Well, that was somewhat unorthodox, wasn't it?" said Cockerill, wiping his brow.

"I can't say he was a particularly appealing character, guv. What did he say about Eddie's cause of death?"

"Well, obviously we have to wait for his full report and sample analysis to come back, but he said it's likely the coronary thrombosis in a diseased artery killed him. He was concerned about the abrasion under the eyebrow – quite a chunk of skin was missing, and he said it was con-sistent with being hit with a sharp stick or piece of wood."

"And we couldn't see anything in his den that could have caused that," I replied.

"For all Tenterden's bluff and bluster, he did explain that some sort of exertion which demanded more blood in the left heart than the blocked arteries could supply might cause sudden death a few hours later…"

"So if Eddie, with his dodgy ticker, was chased or attacked, he could collapse and die in his den a few hours later as a result of it?" I asked.

"I think we need to get back to the station, regroup with Kinch, and see where we go next with this investigation," said Cockerill.

"You got Tenterden?" Kinch whooped, leaning back in his chair. "You poor sod. If there's a pathologist to put you off post-mortems, it's him."

"You're not wrong there, Stan," I replied. "I'm usually fine with PMs, but he made me shudder far more than an autopsied body does."

"That comment about Mr Rooke's er... back passage, though... completely uncalled for..." said Cockerill, shaking his head and colouring slightly again.

"What comment?" asked Kinch.

Cockerill told him.

"Euww," replied Kinch. "Smelly Eddie a twinkle toes, though? That's a turn up for the books..."

"What did you find in his room in Sheet Street, Stan?" I asked.

"Talk about a man of surprises," said Kinch. "I was expecting a hoarder's paradise in the vein of his den, but there was barely anything in it. Just a single fold-up bed, neatly made with a sheet and a couple of blankets, an armchair, a wardrobe with three shirts and an old tweed coat in it and an empty bookshelf."

"What about his landlady?"

"She was visibly upset when I told her he had been found dead and asked for access to his room. She said he was a quiet, polite man – a little lacking on the personal hygiene front – who usually paid his rent on time, kept himself to himself, and wasn't there much. She couldn't recall him ever having any visitors."

"He would have needed to keep his rented room as no way would he be able, or allowed, to live under the railway arches," I added, "but that was probably the place he felt more at home, and made homely."

"It's that cut under his eyebrow that's bothering me more than anything," said Cockerill. "I'm going to get on to uniform to pull in the Teddy boy ringleader characters from Cookham, Maidenhead and Windsor who were kicking off that weekend. See if they seem shifty or if they know something they want to get off their chests."

"Do you think we'll get anything out of them, seeing that they might be staring down the barrel of a manslaughter charge, guv?" asked Kinch.

"Have you got any better ideas, Stan?" retorted Cockerill irritably. "Someone, somewhere knows why Eddie the newspaper seller died late one night under the railway arches with a cut on his face, and we're going to find them."

CHAPTER 23

Talking to the Townswomen

Windsor with Kinch
Summer 1959

Kinch and I spent a headache-inducing couple of days re-interviewing Teddy boys. We'd devised a neat and tidy plan with the uniform section to bring in members of the various local Teddy boy gangs known to have been causing a ruckus on the weekend before Eddie was found dead. To avoid conflict at the police station, we decided we would interview members of just one gang at a time, but of course police work is never neat and tidy. Some Teds were at home, some at work, some hanging around the streets, and some living dangerously in rival territory. Uniform could only find who they could find, so the gangs got mixed up as they were brought into the station lobby.

The rival Teds jeered at and jostled each other, jabbing fingers and singing their rivals' songs to wind them up. I'd had no idea each gang of Teds had their own special song that only they could sing. One of the ways to start a fight was singing another gang's song, apparently.

Inspector Morton stormed out of his office to see what all the cacophony in the lobby was about. One Ted pointed at him and called out, "There's that bloke who ran away when we egged him," and Morton, muttering, swiftly retreated into his office.

Bringing each glowering Ted into our interview room, Kinch and I made it plain that the focus of our inquiries was not on the damage and disturbances in the town, but whether they knew anything about what might have happened to Eddie. We went over the same set of questions with each one, and received assorted answers.

"Have you heard of the newspaper seller Mr Edward Rooke, otherwise known as Smelly Eddie?"
1) "Never heard of the bloke."
2) "Yeah, he was the old geezer with the pram what the Langley Teds roughed up a while back. We never done it."
3) "Was that his real name?"

"What was the reason you were in Windsor that evening?"
1) "We was going to a dance."
2) "Hanging around outside the Beauclaire caff picking up girls..."
3) "Teaching the Pinkneys a lesson."

"So, on that night where exactly did you go?"
1) "Stayed in the town centre."
2) "Stayed outside the pub."
3) "Hung around the train station."

"Did you see anyone else in the streets that night?"

   1) "A couple of pissed-up guardsmen going back to barracks."

   2) "No coppers at all – no wonder this keeps kicking off."

   3) "Some old people who were about 30."

"Were you aware of any weapons being used?"

   1) "I've heard the Slough boys are putting razor blades in the toes of their creepers."

   2) "Someone picked up a bottle."

   3) "Didn't some lad get a bicycle chain in the face?"

"How did the fight start?"

   1) "It was pre-arranged…"

   2) "The Pinkneys lot were on our patch…"

   3) "Saturday night's the night for fighting, ain't it?"

"Did you leave the town and head in the direction of the railway arches?"

   1) "No."

   2) "No."

   3) "What railway arches?"

As Kinch let the last Teddy boy out of the interview room, he rubbed his eyes and sighed.

"We really got no new information out of the re-interviewing, did we Stan?" I said. "None of the Teds acted suspiciously, as if they were covering something up, and I can't believe so few of them knew there were even railway arches stretching away out of the town."

"Make no mistake, Hepz, there are some vicious little sods among this lot, that's for sure, but like you, I didn't get a feeling any of them would have reason to, or be capable of, killing a little old man," said Kinch. "They seem more interested in fighting each other than stealing."

"I agree," I said. "So where can we possibly go from here?"

"You remember me saying we might not have to tooth-comb all the junk in Eddie's den...?" Kinch asked, grinning as my face fell.

"Well, I'm not going to be able to do that this afternoon," I said. "I've been booked to give a talk to Maidenhead Townswomen's Guild about what it's like to be a female detective."

"Why don't I get asked to do cushy stuff like that?" asked Kinch.

"Maybe they're worried that you might offend the polite Maidenhead society ladies with your tales of blood, gore and policing rudery," I replied. "Either that, or you're just not interesting enough..."

"Very well, Hepz – First thing tomorrow morning, I'm sending you back to Eddie's den with the tiniest seaside bucket and spade I can find so you can start sifting through the piles of laths and timbers. I'll be along a few hours later."

I laughed. "I'd hoped we'd get away with not having to toothcomb the den, but I didn't think we'd be that lucky."

"Yeah, me too," said Kinch, yawning and stretching. "Now, off you trot and enjoy your Jam and *Jerusalem*..."

"That's the Women's Institute, Stan, not the Townswomen's Guild..."

"Whatever. Just bring me back a slice of Victoria sponge."

Giving talks to community groups such as the WI, Mother's Union, Townswomen's Guilds and school parent-teacher associations was increasingly becoming part of a policewoman's remit. Until she became an inspector, Miss Robertshaw did most of them, as she quite enjoyed public speaking and being feted as a local treasure. Word had got around that there was a woman detective in Berkshire worth listening to, and now my diary was filling up with speaking engagements. The Townswomen's Guild was my first one, and I was absolutely dreading it. My problem was, I was terrified of public speaking.

You might think this strange, as part of my job was standing in the witness box in court giving evidence. I could get pretty nervous before doing that, and more than once I'd wished I could have fallen over and broken my leg, so I didn't have to appear. But somehow the familiar rhythm, rituals and personalities of the courtroom, as well as being able to hide behind a wooden box were oddly comforting. Today would be my first time standing on a stage facing an afternoon audience of society ladies to talk about my life as a CID woman. Last night, I'd dreamed I'd given my talk, received boos of disapproval and had things thrown at me – stark naked.

I put this phobia down to an incident in my horrible junior school. One Monday, my brother Ron was supposed to be walking me to school, and instead of

313

going directly there, he took me on a diversion via the sweetshop where we got stuck in a queue. Despite me tugging his sleeve in increasing desperation, he made me wait his turn with him, and by the time we got to school, I was 15 minutes late.

I creaked opened the classroom door just as Miss Clamp finished marking the register. Thirty pairs of eyes bored into me.

"Gwendoline Agnes Crockford!" she boomed. "Good afternoon! So nice of you to bother showing up for school today. Why are you late?"

Nothing coherent would come out of my mouth. "W-well Miss... I'm sorry M-Miss... my brother... the sweetshop... a queue... made me late..."

"Sweets, eh?" Miss Clamp rose slowly from her desk and marauded around it, a wooden ruler in her hand. She pointed it at me like a weapon.

"You are late. You will be punished."

My kneecaps pulsed up and down uncontrollably. *Please don't whack me. Please don't whack me.*

"You don't enjoy poetry, do you, Gwendoline?"

My stomach turned over. I did indeed dislike poetry – all that plodding de-dum, de-dum-de-dum rhythm, and sappy rhymes like "moon" and "June". My dislike had turned into hatred when Miss Clamp made us read aloud a horrible poem about a Scottish railway bridge collapsing on a stormy night in 1879[53], plunging a train and all its passengers into a freezing river.

---

53 *The Tay Bridge Disaster* by William McGonagall is now recognised as one of the world's worst poems. It is unintentionally hilarious for adults that read it, but pretty traumatising for schoolchildren.

So the train mov'd slowly along the Bridge of Tay,
Until it was about midway,
Then the central girders with a crash gave way,
And down went the train and passengers into the Tay!
The Storm Fiend did loudly bray,
Because ninety lives had been taken away…

I'd felt sick, Winifred Parrott next to me had started crying, and some of the boys wouldn't shut up about whether the people on the train drowned quickly or slowly.

"I-I don't mind poetry, miss," I stammered, unsure of why she was asking me this question.

"Good." Miss Clamp pulled a tome of poetry off her bookshelf and shoved it at me. "Then for your punishment you won't mind learning off by heart the poem *The Lady of Shalott* and reciting it to the class on Friday morning. And woe betide you if you forget any of it."

"Y-Yes, miss," I stammered, taking the tome and scurrying to my desk.

When I got home, I opened the poetry book to find *The Lady of Shalott* was 20 verses of "shiver, quiver, ever, river, Camelot, towers, flowers, imbowers, Shalott" about some poor woman marooned on Shalott Island, yearning for a handsome knight. Attempting to escape to Camelot in a rowing boat, she freezes to death. *What was up with Miss Clamp that she made her pupils read poems about people dying in freezing conditions?*

For the next four nights, I sat alone in my bedroom memorising that damn 20-verse poem. I told my parents

I had to learn it as a special project – no way could I tell them the real reason; I'd have been punished for getting a punishment. I wrote out the story, beginning to end, in my own words, then visualised the scene described in each verse. Helpfully, the predictable aaaabcccb rhyme scheme made the words easier to remember.

Dad came in with a cup of tea for me.

"There you go, Gwennie, a nice hot cuppa to help those words go in," he said. "I'm so proud of you that you love poetry so much you've chosen it as your special project." *If only he knew.*

"And that Lady of Shalott – she sure knew her onions," he quipped, laughing like a drain. I just wanted to cry.

But I did it. I stood at the front of the dusty classroom on that Friday morning, 30 pairs of eyes staring directly at me, Miss Clamp standing beside me slapping that ruler against her palm, and began:

> *"On either side the river lie*
> *Long fields of barley and of rye,*
> *That clothe the wold and meet the sky;*
> *And thro' the field the road runs by*
> *To many-tower'd Camelot…"*

Verse after verse of this flowery pre-Raphaelite tale tumbled faultlessly from my lips, narrating my mind's eye recreation of the Lady of Shalott's sorry story in glorious Technicolor. My mouth dry with effort, I concluded:

> *"The web was woven curiously,*
> *The charm is broken utterly,*
> *Draw near and fear not,—this is I,*
> *The Lady of Shalott."*

Twenty-nine pairs of juvenile eyes stared back at me, and a few mouths hung wordlessly open.

Miss Clamp turned to me. "You can go back to your seat now, Gwendoline. Don't be late for school again."

And thinking back on it, Ron never did share any of the sweets he'd bought that Monday morning.

So I felt nine years old again, standing on a stage in an echoey assembly hall with *40* pairs of eyes looking at me this time, my kneecaps oscillating up and down, and feeling as if I was being punished. In my damp palm I clutched a sheet of notes I'd written, focusing on the more palatable aspects of detective work I thought the genteel Townswomen's Guild ladies could stomach hearing about.

"I'm delighted to introduce this month's guest speaker, WDC Gwen Crockford from Maidenhead Police Station, who is going to tell us all about her life as a woman detective..." said the chairman, Mrs Plumridge.

I stepped up to the lectern.

"Thank you, Madame Chairman. I am thrilled to talk to you today about modern day policing... blah blah training schools... Mill Meece for uniform... blah blah Hendon for detectives... observation... ballistics... crime scene role play... the training for a policewoman is exactly the same as that for a policeman... blah blah The Children and Young Person's Act 1933... If you're unlucky enough to have a female prisoner in the cells overnight, you have to stay with them on matron duty... When a child is reported missing, every officer on duty drops everything to search for him or her...

blah blah... Shoplifting... these modern self-service supermarkets are far more tempting to a shoplifter than the old-fashioned shops... but did you know that most incidences of shoplifting take place on quieter days?"

I could sense my audience shifting on their hard, wooden assembly hall seats. My sanitised account of police work, and particularly the shoplifting, was boring even me as I spoke, relying heavily on my notes. And I realised to my dismay that I had used up all my material within 20 minutes, and I was supposed to speak for an hour. I didn't have the confidence of Miss Robertshaw or even Kinch to come up with anecdotes off the cuff, and I could feel the panic rising.

I made a decision. "So, those were the basics of my police work, does anybody have any questions?"

There was a long, palpable silence, and I began to wish the stage trapdoor would open and I could drop through it.

Then a large woman in a floral dress and pearls put her hand up and asked, "Have you ever seen a dead body?"

The ladies sat up and paid attention.

"I've seen several dead bodies," I replied, grateful to be asked a question I had plenty to say about. "My first was a dear soul who had committed suicide by hanging herself."

The audience gave sympathetic "oohs" as I continued.

"Then I and another policewoman were called to the skeletonised body of an elderly pilgrim who had passed away six months before in some woodland – we had to

318

remove him on nothing more than a sheet of discarded corrugated iron – and his head fell off."

A couple of ladies whooped with laughter, then checked themselves, unsure whether their reaction was appropriate or not.

"And at detective training school, I attended a post-mortem on a gentleman who had dropped dead in the street, performed by the great Dr Keith Simpson..."

"Keith Simpson! She's met Keith Simpson!" His name resounded round the hall as the ladies murmured among themselves. He really was such a rock star pathologist that anyone who read the newspapers or listened to the news knew who he was. And I had worked alongside him.

"What is a post-mortem like?" asked a tiny lady in the front row, her chin resting on be-ringed, arthritic fingers that themselves rested on a knobbly walking stick handle.

"Well, the one thing you're probably not expecting is the smell," I replied. "Even a fresh human cadaver smells not unlike a piece of pork that's been left out of the fridge and gone off. Different body parts have different smells, and of course these get worse the more decomposed a body is. And there are often maggots on a corpse, but these are incredibly useful: modern forensic techniques are being used that determine the time of death by measuring the sizes of the maggots and the fly pupae."

"Fascinating, dear," replied the tiny lady, "but when I asked what a post-mortem was *like*, I meant, how is it performed?"

"Ooh, yes, do tell us – we'd like to know," added a ruddy-faced countrywoman in jodhpurs sitting next to the tiny lady.

Eloquently, and now in my element, I talked the ladies of the Maidenhead Townswomen's Guild through the post-mortem process. Cliché as it is, you could have heard a pin drop in the church hall as I described one in detail: initial external examination, swabs, incision from throat to pubis, clipping off the ribcage, removal and examination of the viscera, tissue sampling, peeling away the scalp, sawing off the top of the skull, and removing the jelly-like brain.

Breaking the reverential silence at the end, the tiny lady asked gleefully, "Thank you, dear. I've heard they don't put all the bits and pieces back in the right places; they just pour them back inside the body and sew it up. Is that true?"

With a queasy flashback to the aftermath of Tenterden's PM on Smelly Eddie's body, I had to agree that that was indeed the case, and the audience gave more eeeuws, aahs, chuckles and nudges.

"My brother used to work at a funeral directors, and he said that some dead bodies belch and groan," added Jodhpur Woman. "Can give you a right old scare, he said."

"Yes, I've heard that gas can build up in the stomach, gut and lungs and cause bodies to make all kinds of rude noises," I replied, "although I have never heard it."

Another woman with straggly grey hair put up her hand. "When they exhumed my Great Aunt Maud, her hair and nails had continued growing after she had been buried. What do you make of that, Miss Crockford?"

Before I could answer, the chairman, looking some-what flustered, stood up. "I fear, ladies, that we're out of time now, but if anyone would like to ask one final question about... the prevalence of shoplifting, perhaps?"

Everybody shook their heads, and my talk wound up with enthusiastic applause – no booing or missiles. A small queue formed round me at teatime, the ladies still hungry for forensic details, and making me promise to come back and give another talk very soon.

I put a slice of Victoria sponge wrapped in a paper napkin in front of Kinch when I returned to the station.

"Coo, ta," he said, unwrapping it with relish. "Give away all our surveillance secrets to the doughty ladies of Maidenhead, then Hepz?"

"Don't worry, Stan, the last thing the Maidenhead ladies want to hear about is petty thievery. They're far more interested in guts and gore."

CHAPTER 24

Back to the arches

Windsor with Kinch
Summer 1959

Kinch didn't give me a tiny bucket and spade after all, and he came with me to re-examine Eddie's den. Murder bag hanging heavy in my hand, we waited as a handyman armed with a claw hammer pulled off the boards preserving the scene. We stepped once more into that strange, cluttered, musty-smelling space where Eddie breathed his last, both of us determined to solve this mystery once and for all.

"We'd better get started shifting all this timber outside and checking every piece of it as we go," said Kinch, throwing me some thick gloves.

"I think it's worth just standing and looking for a few moments more, Stan," I replied. "Once we've pulled out all the stuff, the original crime scene is gone forever."

"I'm less convinced this is a crime scene, now, and more likely just the place where old Eddie keeled over from a heart attack."

"But that abrasion above his eye, though..."

"Yeah, yeah – you and Cocky are more fixated on that than I am," replied Kinch. "Very well then, we'll have another look around, but let's be quick as I really want to get this wretched job done and dusted ASAP."

I pushed my hands down the sides of the button-back armchair's cushion and found nothing. I rechecked the paraffin lamp for any bloodstains that might hint that it had been used a weapon – nothing.

"Give me a hand moving this chest of drawers, Stan," I asked.

Kinch tried to lift his end of the chest using the one remaining piece of moulding around its top. With a light crack it came away in his hand.

"Piece of crap!" he cursed. "Looks like somebody once took this old Victorian tat and tried to modernise it by sticking on some moulding. They couldn't even stick it on the right way up. And that must've been donkeys' years ago as there's only this one piece left."

Kinch launched the detached moulding like a boomerang, and it spun out of the den and landed on the grass outside.

"Nothing underneath this chest either," I said as we moved it by opening a drawer.

We lifted the armchair, lamp and chest outside, and prepared to roll up the threadbare oriental rug covering the floor.

"Start from the far end, Stan, so we don't have so far to drag it outside," I advised.

"It's a bit caught up under these lengths of wood," grunted Kinch, moving some timbers and tugging the end of the carpet free. As he began to roll the top corner of the carpet, he exposed a circular piece of metal that looked like some sort of lid.

"Aye aye, what do we have here?"

As Kinch pulled at the lid, a jam jar emerged from its purpose-made hole in the earth floor, and he brushed the soil off it.

"Well, well, well, Eddie's life savings," said Kinch as he held up the jar filled with a fat roll of 10-shilling notes and clinking with a few loose coins.

"Good find!" I said, feeling that forager's rush of pleasure and excitement when you stumble across something you've been looking for. "We'd better see if there are any more wonderful things under this rug!"

"All right, all right, Howard Carter[54], don't get your hopes up," chuckled Kinch. "This is probably as good as it gets."

Disappointingly, Kinch *was* right – for now. There was nothing else under the rug except slugs and woodlice. We rolled it out onto the grass and then reluctantly surveyed our next task – the woodpiles.

For the next two hours, we untangled the heap of almost identical shattered laths and timbers making up the right-hand wall, checking each piece before dumping them outside.

"If we get another job like this, I'm putting the probationer PCs onto it as part of their training," huffed Kinch, "and I'll just stand there supervising."

We'd only got halfway through the heap when I noticed something oddly familiar nestling among the

---

54 When asked what he could see when he broke through into the hitherto undiscovered tomb of Tutankhamum in 1922, Egyptologist Howard Carter could only utter, "Wonderful things!"

rough building timbers. As I reached for it, something told me to be *very* careful how I handled it.

"Look, Stan, there's another piece of moulding down here, like the one that just broke off that old chest."

Kinch stopped what he was doing and stooped down beside me.

"Certainly looks the same, just a sec..." He went outside to retrieve the piece he had flung away.

It *was* the same. As I lifted the hidden piece gingerly by its edges, I noticed a piece of organic matter concertina-ed onto its sharp end. My detective instincts screamed at me to preserve this at all costs. I looked at the spot where the chest had stood, and back to the pile, my mind performing calculations I couldn't even begin to explain out loud.

"Could you get me a polythene bag out of the murder bag, please, Stan?"

Kinch rummaged about in the murder bag. "Bugger. We're out of polythene bags."

"Whaat?" I replied. "I only put some in there the other day!"

"Yes, well, they're the perfect size to put half-eaten sandwiches in. I used the last one to take your piece of Victoria sponge home."

And you didn't think to replenish the murder bag, I thought, but didn't voice, as I didn't want to sound like my mother.

"Well, is there a large envelope we could use?"

"There's some brown paper and string – will that do?"

It's going to have to, isn't it?

"Yes please, Stan," I replied.

I laid the moulding on the brown paper.

"Unless I'm very much mistaken, this looks like a piece of human skin," I said, pointing at the matter.

"It does, doesn't it?" agreed Kinch. "So you think Eddie could have been hit in the face with it, and his assailant threw it into the timber pile?"

"I don't think anyone hit him in the face with it. I think his face hit it."

"Eh?" replied Kinch, screwing up his own face.

"We'd need to get forensics to check all this out properly," I said, "but my theory is he might have been standing near the chest of drawers when his heart packed up. As he collapsed, he caught his brow on the sharp point of this second of the two remaining pieces of moulding. It broke off, as easily as that last moulding came off in your hand, was catapulted up into the air, and by Sod's Law fell down into the woodpile where we couldn't see it – until now. The piece of flesh, amazingly, is still impaled on it. We need to get this moulding checked for fingerprints, just to rule out that it wasn't used as a weapon, and the piece of flesh needs to be matched with Eddie's head wound."

Kinch was silent for a few moments, stroking his moustache.

"It's not an impossible theory, Hepz. And I like it for two reasons: number one – it's the only one we've got so far, and number two – it gives us an excuse to stop clearing out this shithole."

Cockerill was more than happy to run with my hypothesis. Rather than poke the repellent bear that was Tenterden, I asked Dr Welby, our police surgeon, if he could deal with the piece of flesh on the end of the moulding.

"I don't see why not," he said. "It will need popping into some sterile saline to rehydrate, then I can take it to the mortuary and place it on Mr Rooke's abrasion – see if it fits. If it doesn't, no harm done. If it does, I can send my findings to Tenterden, and he can include it in his post-mortem report if he thinks fit."

The piece of skin delivered to the ever-obliging Dr Welby, I dusted the moulding with powder to see if any fingerprints came up. Apart from my own on the edges, which would need eliminating, I couldn't see anything else. Although that didn't mean the experts in the Fingerprint Department wouldn't use their mystical juju to conjure up some prints that to me were invisible.

Forensic errands run, and with both flesh and moulding now in their rightful places for analysis, I could take my long-awaited-for afternoon off. It was a while since I had treated myself to a proper wander-aimlessly-in-and-out-of-the-shops trip, and I was looking forward to ambling around, maybe treating myself to some new clothes, and even some shoes.

Maidenhead was a lovely place to shop in. From the "pile it high, sell it cheap" utilitarian vibe of Woolworths, to the Turkish carpeted, Tiffany lamp-lit, posh Biggs department store ("if you have to ask the price, you can't afford it"), and lots of other independent shops and chains in between, who needed to go to London?

I began my wanderings in the bustling high street, pressing my nose against Surplices electrical store's window, admiring the television sets, radiograms and spin dryers waiting to go to their new homes on hire purchase. ONLY £28 10s.6d. WITH A 10% DEPOSIT AND TWO YEARS TO PAY! Maybe one day I would have a home of my own rather than a room in someone else's home, and I could swan around these stores choosing occasional tables, a bureau and a cocktail cabinet to go with my brand-new three-piece suite. *Dream on, Gwen.*

Milwards didn't have the navy court shoes I wanted in my size, so I tried out what I believed to be the new shoe purveyor on the block, Freeman Hardy Willis.

"Madam, we've been open since 1956!" laughed the shop girl as she found me exactly what I was looking for. *Was it really more than three years since I last went proper shoe shopping?*

I ignored R. G. Bott and Son Menswear and hurried past. In previous years I would have loitered, looking at the shirts, ties and pullovers in the window, thinking about what would suit Henry's colouring for a surprise gift. But now I didn't need to go anywhere near a menswear shop until Christmas when I would buy Dad and Ron their annual jumpers and socks.

On a roll with my shoe purchase, I felt a sudden impulse to buy a cardigan and *maybe even a skirt*. Why not splash some of my hard-earned cash? I'd been so immersed in my work, and the (well-founded) belief that the quality clothes and shoes I bought would last, that I hadn't had anything new for ages. Webber's department store was my go-to shop of choice; not cheap, not *too* expensive, lots of choice, and good quality.

I trotted up the creaky oak staircase to the womens-wear department. On the way to knitwear, I paused by the brushed nylon nightgowns and drip-dry nylon housecoats, fingering the material, and wondering whether Mum would like one of these for her birthday. Mum had gone nylon-mad in the last year. It was so easy to wash and get dry, she had even swapped her beloved cotton bed sheets for new-fangled nylon ones. Dad complained that if you moved around in bed too quickly you could make static sparks fly, and Mum had told him off for being smutty.

I found the cotton cardigans and was in the process of deciding whether the baby blue, the mint green or the lemon yellow one would suit me best when I became aware of another shopper in the department with me. From my vantage point behind a mannequin wearing a summer dress and cardigan ensemble, I recognised her: Celia Le Mercier! A tumble of odd emotions rippled through me, and I really didn't feel like standing and making small talk about shopping, the weather, church and Ernie with her. She had that far-off gaze of somebody who believes they are alone, and even when she glassily scanned the room, she didn't notice me behind the mannequin. I thought I'd stay put until she moved on, but if she came my way I'd have to pretend to be surprised and delighted to see her.

I peeked under the mannequin's armpit to see what Celia was buying. She was down the expensive end where the cashmere was stacked, stroking a folded cream twinset on a display table.

Blimey, Ernie, you're going to have to work a fair few shifts to pay for that.

Celia picked up the twinset, glanced behind her, and quick as a flash shoved it into her shopping bag. Pausing momentarily to brush her hand over a mauve cashmere cardigan hanging on a peg, she strode towards the staircase.

Did I really see what I thought I saw? Celia Le Mercier, churchwarden and wife of Detective Sergeant Ernie Le Mercier ... shoplifting?

I knew from my numerous, tedious dealings with shoplifters and shoplifting that a crime is only committed when the thief has physically exited the store without paying for the item and has to be apprehended outside. For all I knew, Celia could be stuffing all manner of things into her bag, fully intending to pay for them at the till downstairs. Maybe Ernie had even told her about the criteria for shoplifting and she knew the legal position. But I wouldn't have scrumpled up a lovely cream cashmere twinset into a bag like that, though. What if she had a newspaper in there? The print could come off all over it. Perhaps I was being too nice. We would see.

I scanned the ground floor of Webber's from the top of the staircase and tracked Celia moving about in the cosmetics department at the rear of the store. Using the suspect-tailing technique taught at Hendon, but rarely used up until now, I sidled down the staircase and variously positioned myself where I could see, but not be seen. I even remembered the bit about avoiding mirrors, so the quarry couldn't catch a glimpse of me in a mirror, watching from behind. But Celia seemed to be floating about in a world of her own, trying sample lipsticks on the back of her hand, and dabbing sample shades of pressed powders onto her nose. A couple of times she moved towards the front till, and I exhaled. Then she moved away from the till, and it was game on again.

I secreted myself among the summer jackets, mackintoshes and leather gloves near the front entrance to the store, once again using the outerwear-clad mannequins as human-like shields for my surveillance. I could see Celia, gazing fixedly ahead and striding purposefully towards the double doors onto the high street, bag firmly over her arm.

No way is she going to stop until she's through those and out on the pavement.

They say your whole life flashes before you in the moment before you die. Even in this non-mortal situation, my mind managed to churn out an awful lot of possible scenarios – both sensible and appalling – in the few seconds it took Celia to reach the double doors of Webber's department store:

(1) I could let Celia walk out and get away scot-free. Only I would know.

(2) I could let Celia walk out, and she gets caught by the store detective, who could be any one of this afternoon's shoppers. She would get a criminal record, her name printed in the newspaper, and this would potentially ruin Ernie's police career.

(3) I could let Celia walk out, the store detective catches her, she gets a criminal record, Ernie divorces

her in disgust, protects his career and marries me...
BRAIN, STOP IT!

(4) I could intercept Celia before she leaves the store
and make her go and pay for her items. We would both
be embarrassed, but I would have done the right thing,
and legally, no offence would have been committed.

You guessed it. I went for Option (4).

As Celia was about to set foot on the doormat at the
store's exit, I called out, "Cooee! Celia! I haven't seen
you for ages!" waving to catch her attention. A bullet
wouldn't have halted her more abruptly, and she swung
round, brown eyes wide like a terrified doe.

"G-Gwen! Sorry, you made me j-jump! Er, no, it
has b-been ages, hasn't it?" she stammered, her cheeks
burning red.

My mouth went into overdrive, waffling on about
my own shopping trip, what I'd bought and what I was
looking for, giving Celia time to calm down and compose
herself. When her cheeks had returned to near-normal
colour, I asked, "And how about you? Have you bought
anything nice today?"

"Well, um, I'm trying to get my mother some slippers,
but the sheepskin ones she likes aren't out until the
winter stock comes in..." she rambled.

I looked deliberately into her bag.

"That's a lovely twinset you've got there. I'm looking
for something similar myself. Where did you find it?"

Celia's colour instantly rose again, and she stared at
me, wide-eyed, once more. She gave a little gasp, a few
seconds too late.

"Oh my goodness! I've COMPLETELY forgotten to pay for the twinset!" she gushed, pulling it out of her bag. "I was in such a hurry I must have bundled it into my bag without thinking! Silly, silly me! Sometimes I get in such a fluster that I think I'd forget my head if it wasn't screwed on!" Celia giggled maniacally, for a little too long.

"And what with Ernie being in CID and all! It wouldn't do for me to get accidentally caught shoplifting, would it?" she continued, a rictus grin on her face.

We looked each other in the eye, and at that moment, she knew that I knew. And I knew that she knew. And we both knew that wouldn't happen now.

"Er, well, the queues at the till have gone down now, so I'd better run along and get this paid for, hadn't I? Silly me with bells on," she faux-tutted.

I nodded.

"And it would be lovely if you could come round for dinner again, with Ernie and I, very soon, Gwen. It was such fun last time."

"That would be lovely, I'll look forward to it," I lied.

"Well, bye then!" she panted.

I hung around the summer outerwear section, trying to bring my heart rate down, until Celia trotted past, raising her Webber's paper carrier bag containing the twinset in a valedictory salute, then disappeared through the double doors.

After a couple of minutes, I followed her out. I'd walked halfway along the high street when I looked down, and it was my turn to gasp. In my hand was a pair of leather driving gloves with the Webber's price label of 16s. 6d. hanging off them. I turned on my heel and marched straight back to the department store to return them surreptitiously to the gloves display.

How useless, or perhaps non-existent, were the Webber's store detectives? And how easy was it to shoplift absentmindedly?

CHAPTER 25

Honeytrap

Windsor with Kinch
Summer 1959

"Well, Miss Crockford," Cockerill began, "looks like your theory of how Eddie Rooke died holds water."

Kinch, Cockerill, me and Inspector Morton sat around a large table that was scattered with photographs and files of reports, going through Smelly Eddie's case review.

"Have we got all the reports back now, guv?" I asked.

"We have. The rehydrated piece of skin found on your moulding did indeed fit Eddie's abrasion perfectly. That finding was incorporated into the post-mortem report, although it didn't affect the cause of death. The necromancers in the Fingerprint Department could find no other prints apart from yours and a very faint one of Eddie's on the moulding, so it's highly unlikely it was used as a weapon by a third party. The two mouldings were reconstructed onto the chest of drawers, and together they would have made a dangerously sharp edge for Eddie to fall onto."

Cockerill spun round a piece of paper covered with equations and dotted lines that looked like fireworks.

"Forensics and ballistics together worked out from

photographs and our information that it *was* possible that Eddie, at his height and weight, could have collapsed onto the chest of drawers, scraped his brow on the moulding, and for that poorly-glued moulding to be catapulted, skin still attached, on a trajectory consistent with where it was found in the woodpile."

"And we know the post-mortem found his cause of death to be…" Kinch squinted at the typed Report of Post-Mortem Examination signed by Tenterden "… acute thrombotic occlusion of a coronary artery."

"And we found no witnesses or potential suspects to suggest foul play," I added. "His money was still where he'd hidden it, and even the thickest of thieves would have looked under the rug for hidden cash."

"All things considered, I think we can conclude that Mr Edward Rooke died of natural causes," said Cockerill. "Poor old bugger…"

"Quite literally," said Kinch, grimacing.

"Er, well, yes, but still… nobody deserves to die alone and unattended, their body only found by a dog walker," added Cockerill.

We were all silent for a moment at Cockerill's words. Eddie Rooke had been someone's son; maybe a brother, uncle or father; a lover, obviously. A person who deserved acknowledgement. Cockerill inhaled deeply.

"So, no juicy murder investigation for Windsor CID after all, I'm afraid. But well done, everybody, especially you, Miss Crockford."

Some weeks later, I picked up my phone in the Maidenhead CID office and heard a familiar voice.

"Hepz? Stan Kinch here. Could you come over and take some notes for an interview I'm about to do?"

"What am I – a WPC again?" I joshed. "DI Dankworth made me do this all the time in Wokingham."

"No, you're not a WPC, just the best," smarmed Kinch. "Let's just say it's an interview where I would appreciate your feminine presence."

"OK, OK, flattery will get you everywhere, Stan. So, a female prisoner, then?"

"Just get over here as soon as you can, and I'll explain everything."

I cadged a lift off Inspector Morton who was heading towards Windsor anyway, and met Kinch in the interview room before the detainee was brought in.

"All right, we will be questioning a member of Her Majesty's Brigade of Guards – but of the shirt-lifting variety," said Kinch.

"I'm not sure I follow," I said.

"OK. There'd been complaints from the public that men of a certain persuasion were using the Home Park public conveniences to meet each other, and in some cases actually do the dirty in the cubicles. Of course, we can't be having that, so we sent our prettiest – PC Black – down there in plain clothes to pose as 'one of them'," Kinch made an unnecessary limp-wristed gesture, "and he reeled in a big fish – a guardsman."

"A guardsman?" I asked. That was a surprise. My preconception was that the army, and especially the elite Guards, were so unquestionably testosterone-fuelled and macho that "men of a certain persuasion" wouldn't feature in their ranks. How naïve was I?

"But how… why…?"

"This sort of thing is absolutely rife in the Guards," continued Kinch. "Some of 'em can't keep their hands off each other, or any willing civilian for that matter. But with PC Black's help looks like we may have got another off the streets, or at least out of our public lavs."

The door opened and the custody sergeant poked his head round the door.

"Are you ready for him now, DS Kinch?"

"Bring him in."

Through the door walked possibly the most beautiful man I had ever seen, and I had to struggle to stop myself staring. I estimated his height at 6 feet 4 inches (he would have had to have been at least 6 feet 2 inches to even be in the Guards in the first place), with a broad, triangular, muscled upper body atop long, lean legs. Blue-eyed and with blond hair in a sharp regulation cut, he had cheekbones you could cut your finger on, and a cute cleft in his chin. He gave me a rueful but genuine smile, revealing white teeth with slightly protruding incisors, the imperfection only enhancing his attractiveness. I inhaled furiously to keep that damn blush that was the bane of my life below my jawline.

"Take a seat, Guardsman Green," said Kinch.

Guardsman Green folded himself onto the hard wooden interview room chair, then sat up as straight as it would allow. His left knee vibrated up and down.

"I'm DS Kinch. This is WDC Crockford, who will be taking notes of this interview. You are not obliged to say anything, but anything you say may be given in evidence. Guardsman Ross Green, you are in here because you attempted to procure the commission of an act of gross indecency with one PC Eustace Black in the Home Park public conveniences, am I right?"

Green folded his bulky arms across his chest.

"I rather think that it was your PC Eustace Black who attempted to procure the commission of an act of gross indecency with me, Detective Sergeant," replied Green.

"Well, that's fine, because a police officer can legitimately do that to apprehend someone procuring or committing indecency," said Kinch, reaching for Black's crime report and squinting at it.

"PC Black states that at 20:30 on 28th June, he saw you leaning on the railings outside the Home Park gentlemen's convenience as he approached, and he asked you for a light, which you gave him. Is that correct?"

"Yes, I lit his cigarette for him."

"PC Black then went into the convenience, into one of the cubicles and locked the door. After three minutes, he heard somebody – you – enter the cubicle next to him and also lock the door. He noticed your foot appear under the cubicle partition, near his own. In the process of completing his constitutional, he moved his foot and unintentionally touched yours. Did that happen?"

"I don't believe for a moment that was unintentional," said Green.

"So you agree that your feet touched? And responded to this unintentional touch by nudging his foot twice, firmly and deliberately?"

Green didn't reply.

"PC Black then flushed the lavatory and came out to wash his hands. You did the same, and washed your hands at the adjoining wash basin. You commented what a beautiful evening it was."

"Well, it was," said Green. "There's no law against saying that."

Kinch continued reading, "He agreed with you. You then replied that you were going to go for a riverside walk, if he would like to join you. Did you say that?"

"Yes, he seemed a pleasant-enough chap to go for a walk with."

"And you walked together south down Romney Lock Road, then crossed the railway line onto Riverside Walk, where you headed north again along a secluded footpath with small, wooded copses on the left-hand side?"

"We did."

"What did you talk about as you walked?"

"Your PC told me about how he played cricket in Home Park, and I talked about my duties in the barracks."

"And PC Black then went off the path into a copse, saying he wanted to look at the river. You followed him into the copse and stood beside him. Can you remember what you said?"

I'd been furiously scribbling a shorthand account of this interview, and I was grateful for the pause as Guardsman Green put his face in his hands and sighed deeply.

"I can't off the top of my head, but I'm sure you'll remind me," he said, peering over his fingertips.

"You're gorgeous. There's nobody around. Do you fancy a bit of turn and turn about?," said Kinch in the most expressionless way he could.

"Well, thank you for asking, but there is a lady in the room in case you haven't noticed. And you're not my type."

Kinch's eyes flashed, and I couldn't suppress a smile. Guardsman Green was turning out to be a most appealing character.

"And what happened then, eh?" snarled Kinch, his lip curling.

"Your PC spun me round, and for a moment I thought everything was going all right. Then he pulled out some handcuffs and clapped them on me saying he was an undercover policeman, and he was arresting me for attempting to commit an act of gross indecency," recalled Green, "and that's how I ended up here."

"And were you?" needled Kinch.

"You've got me, Sugarpuff. Bang to rights."

"In that case, Guardsman Ross Green, I am charging you with attempting to procure the commission of an act of gross indecency with another male person, contrary to the Criminal Law Amendment Act 1885, Section 11. Do you wish to say anything in answer to the charge?"

"No," said Green.

"In that case, you are not obliged to say anything unless you wish to do so, but whatever you say will be taken down in writing and may be given in evidence."

Kinch leaned back in his chair, hands clasped behind his head.

"Off the record, Green, don't think we don't know this sort of thing is rife in the Guards. You're not the first round here to get caught and you won't be the last. But you can't flaunt your perversion wherever you like. Surely if you must do stuff like this you could do it in private with your barracks mates who are that way inclined too, if we are to embrace Mr Wolfenden and his report? Although just because Mr Wolfenden's recommendations have been accepted, they're a long way from becoming law. And believe me, the military will *never in a million years* tolerate your type in its ranks."

"Easy for you to say," replied Green. "Ever heard the expression – and excuse my French here, miss – 'Don't shit in your own nest'?"

"Of course I have," scoffed Kinch.

"You don't trust anyone," continued Green. "Least of all your own comrades in arms. Turn Queen's evidence[55] at the first whiff of trouble, they would."

"*Queen's* evidence," sniggered Kinch. I could have kicked him.

Green had a point. I knew from reading Hilda's *Against The Law* that Peter Wildeblood's airman lover turned Queen's evidence against him to save himself from prison. Wildeblood went down for 18 months just for loving a man; the one who ended up betraying him got off scot-free.

"Why would you take the risk of approaching strange men in public conveniences...?" asked Kinch.

"Cottaging, love. It's called cottaging," said Green, with nothing to lose, clearly enjoying winding him up.

---

55 Evidence for the prosecution given by a person who is also accused of the crime that's being tried. People can "turn Queen's evidence" in exchange for immunity from prosecution or a reduced sentence.

Kinch's eyes glazed over as he must have been visualising the connection between a chocolate-boxy thatched country cottage with roses round the door and Home Park's little concrete public lavatories.

"Oh, I see," he said.

"And things have been very different for... us... since Eddie died," continued Green.

"Eddie?" asked Kinch. That made us both sit up.

"Yeah, Eddie the little newspaper seller bloke. Well, at least that was his day-job. You probably don't know this, but at night, he made himself available in his little 'love shack' as he called it over in the railway arches, to 'offer relief' to me and any of the other lads who wanted it after a night out. Ten shillings a pop."

Well, that explains the notes in the jam jar.

"Good Lord!" said Kinch, wrinkling his nose in disgust. "But he... he was... people called him Smelly Eddie for a reason."

"You didn't even notice that after you'd had a few pints," continued Green, "and you could always flick through some of his *Health and Strength* magazines to get the blood pumping, if you get my drift..."

"I still don't understand the appeal," said Kinch, shaking his head.

"We could trust him," continued Green. "And his love shack was secluded on the outskirts of town – your lot rarely patrolled out that far. And in his funny little Eddie way, he made an effort. He'd light the paraffin lamp, he'd ask us how we were, about our day, and he'd remember things about us. There was even a little thrill if we bought a newspaper from him in town: we'd look each other knowingly in the eye as co-conspirators with a big secret. A secret that stuck two fingers up at the Establishment all around us and the law that drove what we are underground."

Kinch was silent. He took out his cigarettes and offered me one, then after a short pause, to Green as well, pushing his silver Zippo lighter towards him.

Green drew the smoke deeply into his lungs, and it came out in puffs as he spoke again.

"So when Eddie died, the safe option for scratching the itch, so to speak, went with him. Men like me had to take our chances down the traditional, risky routes. We didn't realise how spoiled we were to have Eddie. You don't appreciate something until it's gone, do you? I miss the old fruit."

I sensed that Green was tearing up, and I was in danger of doing so too, something I didn't want to happen in front of Kinch.

"So when did you last see Eddie?" I asked.

Green wiped his eyes with the ball of one thumb.

"It was on the Saturday night before he was found dead on the Monday. There were some stupid little Teddy boy types trying to pick scraps with each other in town and I couldn't be bothered with it. My mate went back to barracks early and I fancied a walk to clear my head and a visit to Eddie."

"How did he seem to you?"

"He said he was tired, and he'd been a bit breathless that day. He cursed getting older, and said he really ought to pop into Boots and get some milk of magnesia for his indigestion when he was next in town. He'd often joked in the past about having a dodgy ticker."

"You know that a heart attack killed him, don't you?" said Kinch.

"That doesn't surprise me," replied Green, stubbing out his cigarette in the ashtray. "Because he seemed out of sorts, we just sat chatting that night. I didn't ask him to do anything and instead we had a laugh at the latest *Health and Strength* magazine. I tucked a 10-bob note in his shirt pocket anyway and got up to leave, and he tried to chase after me to give it back, but I ran. I glanced back and he was a silhouette against the lamplight coming from the arch, waving. That was the last time I saw him."

Green's eyes moistened again and there was nothing left to say. Kinch got up and went to the door to fetch the charge officer and complete the formalities of Guardsman Green's arrest.

I popped into the lavatory then and had a little weep myself that morning. I was finding it increasingly difficult not to let myself get personally affected by the unravelling backstories of the people we investigated. The tale of Eddie and Guardsman Green was more affecting than most, even though what they had been doing was completely against the law.

As I dabbed my blotchy face with a cold wet paper towel, I took some comfort in the thought that Eddie, with his double life, had probably enjoyed his last few hours on earth in the company of a stunningly handsome and kindly young man. Guardsman Green, by contrast, would be looking at up to two years in prison, and whatever the army wanted to do with him themselves.

Prostitution itself – money in exchange for a sex act – has never been illegal, and the armed services had always been major clients of sex workers. Sailors had "a wife in every port", soldiers of the Napoleonic era had their own entourage of women following them around on campaigns, and airmen – well, they rarely had to pay for it.

Hilda believed that every population would naturally have a proportion of people who were, as she called them, gay, with the same needs as those who weren't, so we shouldn't be surprised, but more radically, we shouldn't discriminate. And having read *Against the Law*, and met Guardsman Green, I couldn't help feeling, once again, that the current law was an ass.

CHAPTER 26

A woman's place is on the phone

Maidenhead with Le Mercier
Autumn 1959

Ernie brought me a cup of tea and a chocolate biscuit.

"What's all this in aid of?" I asked.

"Celebration and commiseration," he said.

I looked at him quizzically.

"I'm moving on. Got a transfer to the Norfolk Constabulary," he blurted.

"Oh," was all I could say. The walls of the CID office seemed to close in, and at that moment cosiness and certainty went out of the window.

"It'll be even more oo-arrr oo-arrr than it is round here, I know. Sheep worrying, sheep rustling, farmyard thefts, drunken farmhands, fishing people out of the Broads. I can't wait." Ernie screwed up his nose.

"Why Norfolk of all places?" I asked, not really knowing much about it apart from it was supposed to be flat, agricultural, and my brother made jokes about the locals having webbed feet.

"Celia wants to be closer to her mother and sister in Swaffham. She's never really settled or found her niche here, finds Maidenhead a bit snooty. And expensive! I can barely keep up with financing her shopping sprees on our Webber's account…"

"Well, it can be, granted…"

Ernie lowered his voice. "She'd also like us to, er, um, have a baby," he said, blushing. "Not much joy on that front so far, but she thinks a quieter pace of life in the country might help that, er, aspect along."

Ernie, you would be such a great dad. I'd never seen him be vindictive, unkind or rude – and he had always supported me as a colleague. *Just summon up the biggest smile you can, Gwen, and wish them well.*

"It might be just what she needs, Ernie. I'm so sorry you're going, but I wish you and Celia all the best, really I do. When are you leaving?"

"Today's my last day, actually. We're having a few beers in the police club later. You've got to be there."

"Goodness, that's all a bit sudden!"

"Been in the pipeline for a while, but I haven't been able to say anything. To be honest, I don't really want to go."

And I don't want you to go either.

"I'm sure once you get there, you'll enjoy it. And it's not as if you haven't had experience of a rural constabulary."

"I know. And, as the saying goes, 'Happy wife, happy life'."

I really hope so, for your sake, Ernie.

"Have you got any idea who's replacing you?" I asked, changing the subject before reality sunk in. It wouldn't be me as I'd have to do sergeant's exams, and nobody had asked me.

"Cockerill's got some bloke from out of county coming in, apparently. Hasn't told me anything about him."

So, with Cockerill, Morton, Wagstaffe and Ursula, we gave Ernie a send-off in the police club with several light ales, some backslapping, a game of snooker that I let him win and a chorus of "For He's a Jolly Good Fellow". At the end of the evening, we stumbled upstairs to fetch our mackintoshes from the CID office coat stand together for the last time. Closing the door, we paused on the deserted landing.

"Come here, WDC Crockford," said Ernie, and we hugged for longer than we should have, then he planted a lingering, beery kiss on my lips.

"You're a great girl," he slurred, holding me at arms' length to look me up and down one last time. "My partner in crime – shee what I did there? You've been a joy to work with... I've loved every shecond. Perraps I can encourage the Norfolk Constabulary to shtart recruiting women detectives. Throw a tantrum until they give me one, but you can bet she won't be as great as you... maybe you could move to Norfolk too..."

That's just the drink talking.

I walked him to the front door of the station and waved him off with the rest of our colleagues. And that was the last I ever saw of Ernie Le Mercier.

The next day, I'd just finished listlessly tidying away the files Ernie had left on his desk when Cockerill swept into the CID office with two unfamiliar men. I couldn't help giving them the detective's visual once-over, judging them against Ernie, and even Kinch. The first, wearing a loud dogtooth three-piece tweed suit, had salt-and-pepper reddish hair and blotchy pink skin that looked as if it would peel off if any direct sunlight shone on it. The second man, in a dark grey suit, looked way younger and thinner, with a 1940s short back and sides, horn-rimmed glasses and a prominent Adam's apple.

"This is our very own woman detective constable, Gwen Crockford..." said Cockerill.

I stood up, ready to shake hands as two pairs of eyes skimmed my body from top to toe.

"Very nice office we've got here," cut in the older man to Cockerill. "Good big desks and plenty of storage..."

I shot Cockerill a look. *Who the hell are these people?*

"Er, it is," said Cockerill. "As I was saying, Miss Crockford, this is DS Neville Smythe who will be your new Ernie..."

I don't want a new Ernie.

Smythe finally deigned to hold out his hand, and it felt damp and pudgy as I shook it, and we muttered the usual introductory platitudes.

"...and this is DC Andy Quirke who is going to help us swell the ranks of CID and work alongside you, Miss Crockford."

It was Quirke's turn to shake my hand. It was bony but at least dry.

"So, is this mine?" asked Smythe, stroking Ernie's leather-topped kneehole desk.

"Er, yes, that's where DS Le Mercier used to sit," I replied.

Quirke contemplated the rickety desk in the corner like a disappointed schoolboy. It was still propped up on the tatty paperback copy of *Scotland Yard* by Sir Harold Scott, and still piled high with box files, wire baskets of yellowing paperwork, and that ancient Imperial typewriter. At least we'd moved the mop and tin bucket since 1957.

"Ah, yes, we're going to need to organise another desk now we've got another DC, aren't we?" said Cockerill, reading Quirke's face. "Can't we use that one in the other corner, Gwen?"

"Well, I tend to keep that one clean and use it for forensic purposes, when we have evidence to look through that doesn't need to go to the Met's laboratory."

I'm not giving up my evidence table.

After that awkward 'where have you come from what have you been doing before this' introductory conversation, Cockerill whisked Smythe and Quirke away on their tour of the rest of Maidenhead police station.

As he exited, Smythe poked his head back round the door.

"If you could just get that desk cleared off so it's useable for DC Quirke until his proper one arrives, Miss Crockford..."

I listened to their footsteps diminish down the stairs and out through the back door, then I grabbed my handbag and angry-smoked a Kensita, glaring out of the window at Smythe and Quirke being introduced to PC Ingham in the vehicle yard.

"Two teas, for Andy and I, Gwendoline. One with two sugars, one without," ordered Smythe on his first morning as my detective sergeant.

Who am I? Joan the tea lady?

Ernie had never asked me to make tea; if anything, he'd been the one to make it for me, and Kinch and I rarely had time for tea.

I didn't argue, not today anyway. I just went into the little kitchenette and made their tea, contemplating what unpleasant, yet undetectable, substance I could put in it. Back in Wokingham, somebody once put a pig's eyeball in PC Higgs's tea, and he had only discovered it in the bottom of the mug, half-cooked, as he drained it.

Maybe keep that one in reserve.

I put one cup on Smythe's desk, then squeezed round to Quirke's to deliver his. Another big desk had made the CID office cramped, and more than once I laddered my nylons snagging them on rough wooden edges.

The phone rang.

"Detective Sergeant Neville Smythe, Maidenhead CID, speaking."

It was as much as I could do not to scrunch up my face and mime his irritating nasal voice.

"Shop breaking, you say? King Street? They could still be in the building? We'll be right there."

This sounded exciting. A chance to screech round in the CID car and catch some villains red-handed! Quirke and I leaped up and grabbed our coats off the stand as Smythe finished the call.

"And where do you think you're going, Gwendoline?" he said.

"To apprehend those shop breakers…"

"Oh no you don't. Far too dangerous a situation for you to be in. Anyway, we need somebody to stay in the office and man the phones…"

"But I…"

"I'll let you analyse any evidence we gather and bag it up for Scotland Yard when we get back."

And off they dashed.

Smythe eventually allowed me out to do an undercover public house observation with Quirke. These observations were a routine part of detective work, watching for violations of the licensing or betting laws, such as short measures, under-age drinking, serving liquor "beyond permitted hours", or card games played for money. Lottie, my friend in the Met, did many undercover West End nightclub stings, and part of the pretence would be to get arrested along with the offenders during a raid. Her male colleagues' favourite wind-up back at the station would be to say, "I've seen this slapper somewhere before, but can't quite place her."

I'd done a few pub obs myself with Kinch and Ernie. Berkshire not really being a hotbed of seedy nightclubs, we disguised ourselves as a boring dating couple and were as good as invisible. With Kinch, we would slip back into our "Marmaduke and Hepzibah" routine, and he would take the opportunity to have a few too many pints on his detective duty allowance. With Ernie, we could just chat for hours, having to remind each other that we were supposed to be looking out for licensing violations.

So, one evening, Quirke and I arrived at the Beehive Inn in White Waltham, where we'd had reports of underage drinking. All we had to do was sit at a table near the bar to watch for youngsters buying drinks, and not draw attention to ourselves. I felt we looked more like a mother and her apprentice-in-his-first-job son rather than a couple in our first flush of romance. Our conversation, which wasn't allowed to be anything to do with police work in case it blew our cover, certainly bore that out.

"What do you like doing when you're not, er, working, Andy?"

"Sleeping, mainly."

Silence.

"Have you got any hobbies?"

"I like reading."

Silence.

"Ooh, so do I. What sort of books?"

"Science fiction.

Oh God, I can't stand science fiction.

Silence.

"Who are your favourite authors?"

"Isaac Asimov and Ray Bradbury."

"I don't know them. Are they good?"

"Yes, they're good."

Silence.

And so, this conversation, or rather the silences, went on for the next three long, long hours. Ernie and I would have whiled away the time looking at the other punters, weaving outrageous, hilarious backstories for them, but I couldn't imagine Andy Quirke joining in with that. No underage drinkers came in, and we drove back to the station in... *silence.*

Another day, Smythe and Quirke quick-exited the CID office to investigate a decomposed body found on some wasteland. As they left, Smythe handed me a piece of paper with an address written on it.

"Cheque fraud case in Cookham. Can you go and investigate that today for me?"

I can, but don't bloody come running to me when you can't hack the stinky post-mortem and send me to it instead.

I'd been to enough PMs to know that one on a decomposed body would test even the strongest stomach, and I wasn't in the mood to do somebody else's dirty work.

Still, there were worse places to be than having a cup of tea in a pretty Cookham cottage hung with vast original oil paintings. The artist, Mrs Judd, wearing overalls stiff with paint and reeking of linseed oil, explained what had happened.

"Well, my dear. My handyman, Sidney Jordan, popped round, and I asked him if he could put up some shelves for me. I went out shopping and left him in the house. When I got back, he was gone, but he had left a note saying he's had to pop to the village hall... something about arranging his daughter's wedding reception.

"When Sidney got back, he said that the hall treasurer had cancelled the reception and he wanted him to pay a 30s. cancellation fee. He said he didn't have that money on him – could I lend him some? He would pay me back at the end of the month, so I wrote out a cheque for 30s. in his name. So far, he's only paid me 7s. And I'm not going to let the remaining 21s go in lieu of payment for his work, as the shelves fell down and smashed a valuable vase."

My next port of call was the village hall treasurer.

"No, Detective Constable, I never received any such booking for a wedding reception in that name or any other," he said. "Neither did I ask for 30s. as a cancellation fee. Mrs Judd has been had, I fear."

That was enough to obtain an arrest warrant for Sidney Jordan on a charge of obtaining money by false pretences, and I called at his house with it tucked inside my mackintosh.

"That's right, officer, I did *borrow* 30s.," said Jordan, a shifty-looking man in his late forties. "I did mention my daughter to Mrs Judd, but that she was going away on holiday, and I needed the 30s. to pay some caterers for a 25th wedding anniversary party I was having at my house, not for a wedding reception! I don't know why she's gone and called the police on me. I said I would pay it back in two weeks, and I've already paid her 7s. I think she's going a bit doolally."

I couldn't make any sense of his mitigating story; hence Sidney Jordan accompanied me to the station. After ringing the caterers he had named, who had no 25th wedding anniversaries booked, I had no choice but to charge him with obtaining a cheque by false pretences. He was committed for trial at Berkshire Quarter Sessions.

"Superb result that your cheque fraud man got six months in prison," said Smythe a few weeks later. "We'll put you on all our fraud cases from now on."

Great. Just what I'd dreamed my police career would lead to, investigating cheque swindling and white-collar crime. Not.

I cycled back home to Sperling Road in the drizzle, with a frown on my face. I wasn't sure I loved my job any more, I didn't like my new Maidenhead colleagues, and I felt that I didn't want to be a detective forever.

From a distance, I could see Victor's stylish Ford Consul parked up on the pavement, its boot and doors wide open. Giorgio and Victor were running back and forth in the rain trying to tessellate boxes, suitcases and the Singer sewing machine into its awkward interior *and* be able to get the doors closed before everything was drenched.

"What on earth's going on here, Victor? Are you leaving?"

"Hello, Gwen darling, yes I am. I've left you a note just in case I didn't see you."

"This is a bit of a surprise?"

"Believe me, it was a surprise to me and Giorgio, but the biggest surprise was the one Mrs Foskett got. She came home early and found me and Giorgio, in, shall we say, *flagrante delicto*. Then she threw us out."

I must have looked blank and uncomprehending as I processed yet more unwelcome news, because Victor continued.

"Oh for God's sake, Gwen, she found us in bed together! We're *omi-palones*[56]! Twinkle toesies! Queers!

---

56 *Omi-palone* means "gay man" in Polari. Polari was a secret, informal language mainly used by gay men to recognise and communicate with each other when homosexuality was criminalised (pre 1967). Victor's and Giorgio's conversation was peppered with Polari, such as "lily" = Lily Law (the police), and "orderly daughter" (police again).

Do you want to go for the jackpot and arrest us?" Victor held out his wrists for some imaginary handcuffs.

Instead, I took his hands in mine. "I'm not going to do any such thing, Victor. I couldn't care less what you get up to in your own room. You've been a good friend to me, and I'll bloody miss you." I could feel my voice catching in my throat. "And let's face it, you're the only man who ever made my mother happy…"

"By remodelling her Ladies' Night dress? I meant to ask, how did that go down?"

"She felt like a queen all night, even upstaging the Worshipful Master's wife. She moaned about the other wives going on and on about how lovely it was, where did she get it from as they wanted one too, but with my mother you can't have everything."

"I'm delighted. It honestly didn't take me that long, and I'm still a regular at Mr Munshi's for my fabrics."

"Vic! I'm getting drenched to the bones here! We need to go!" called Giorgio, trying to get the overstuffed car boot to close.

"Look, I've got to go, my darling," said Victor. "But we're heading for the bright lights of the big city for the next decade. London in the 1960s, that's where it's at. I'll write!"

Victor seized my cheeks in his hands and planted a huge, wet, theatrical kiss on my lips.

"Stay fantabulosa, Lily Law!" he called, jumping into the driver's seat, and roaring away in a cloud of exhaust fumes.

Bugger, I thought, *is there anyone left that I actually like?*

I put my bicycle down the side of the house and walked through the open front door into a pungent miasma of bleach. My mackintosh left a puddle on the hallway floor as I hung it on the coat rack, and my stockinged feet left footprints on the swirly carpet as I walked upstairs.

Mrs Foskett was furiously hoovering Victor's mattress, her entire arsenal of cleaning equipment – mop, bucket, Ajax powder, dustpan and brush, Clorox bleach, Dettol antiseptic – on the landing. She stood up as I approached, wiping her heavily perspiring brow with a yellow duster.

"He was a nice man, Gwen, but I'm afraid I couldn't put up with that sort of thing, not under my roof. Any other landlady would probably have dobbed them in to the police, but he didn't deserve that, really. You're not going to do anything, are you?"

"Mrs Foskett, I'm very much of the opinion that what consenting adults do in their own home, behind closed doors, is none of the law's business. And Victor is a friend. So, no, I'm not going to do anything."

Leaving Mrs Foskett to her scrubbing and sterilising, I went into my room to put dry pyjamas on.

"This is all your lot's fault, this is," I complained to Beatific Jesus on the mantelpiece, as I flopped down on my bed, angry and sad.

"But at least *you* had the guts to say, 'judge not, lest ye be judged'."

CHAPTER 27

The grass is greener

Maidenhead with Smythe
Winter 1959-60

The Christmas season was approaching, and Smythe and Quirke were out of the office more than they were in, apparently checking up with their snouts scattered among the local pubs. I was "manning the phones" again and typing up the report of a bicycle theft that Smythe had sent me to investigate.

I typed:

> *Mr Finlay: "I don't care how old Venners is. Anyway, he's not that much older than me. He stole my bike deliberately – again – and I want to press charges…"*

> *Mr Venners: "I genuinely thought it was my bicycle left propped against the hedge, officer, so I used it, then put it in my shed. Finlay has had some sort of vendetta against me for years. He didn't need to call the police."*

This is nonsense, I thought, pushing my chair back from the desk. No more than a silly neighbour dispute that any beat officer worth their salt would have sorted out, but now CID was involved, it would probably go to court. I wondered if I could quietly lose the file (like I sometimes did for dead-end cases where there was zero chance of catching the thieves, such as the disappearance of gardening tools, or clothes from a washing line) but Mr Finlay seemed the type who wouldn't let it lie.

I lit a cigarette and looked out of the window. I noticed WPC Heather Newman in the distance, walking hand in hand with a small child towards the station. A woman, presumably the child's mother, rushed up to them and swept the child into her arms, hugging him. Their lengthy, animated conversation concluded with the mother hugging Heather as well.

Now that's what I call community policing.

Although I'd probably read too much into what I'd just seen, Heather stepping in may have prevented a lost child from being run over, falling in the river, or (God forbid) being abducted, sparing CID a tragedy to investigate. Protection rather than detection, the primary remit of the uniform branch. I bet Heather could have sorted that nasty Mr Finlay out without troubling Smythe, too.

I picked up the phone and dialled Kinch's number.

"What can I do for you, Hepz?"

It was good to hear that familiar Brummie brogue again.

"Got any juicy cases you could rescue me with?"

"Ha! Things not so rosy with old Smythey, then?"

"Things have been better. I did more detective work when I was a probationer WPC. The first whiff of a vaguely interesting case, and he and Quirke dash off together, leaving me to answer the phone."

"Have you had a word with Cocky about it? He appreciates your abilities and I'm sure would put the two of them straight if you asked him."

"I don't want to seem to be that stereotypical moany woman, you know, Stan?"

"What, like my missus?" He chuckled. "She's a stereotypical moaner. But she always gets exactly what she wants – love her."

"Well, what I really want right now is a juicy case over at Windsor. Anything going?"

"Not unless you want to help me unpick a 'conspiracy to avoid purchase tax' case against eight men to the tune of around £1500," said Kinch.

"Oh God, no. That makes my pensioner bicycle non-theft case sound positively exciting. But you will ring me if you find another dead body, won't you?"

"Rest assured, I wouldn't want anyone but you on my murder squad, Hepz," replied Kinch, "and when I see Cocky, I'll put in a word."

Since the arrival of Smythe and Quirke, and because of their frequent departures, I increasingly gravitated towards the WPCs' office, for company as much as anything. Either Heather or Ursula would usually be in there if they weren't out on patrol, and sometimes I was able to catch up with Inspector Robertshaw as well, even though she was no longer my boss.

Despite the fact that CID members are not senior to any uniformed police officers of the same rank (which meant Heather, Ursula and I were all constables, and on the same wages), I realised that Ernie, Kinch and I, with Cockerill floating in and out, had probably formed a somewhat elitist CID bubble that tended to see ourselves as a "cut above" the uniform branch. I hoped I'd tried to work equitably with Heather on cases such as wayward Pepita Cantley-Davis, and Ursula on the Bray Studios wages theft, and I couldn't help feeling we were missing a trick by not being joined up enough with our uniform colleagues. After all, they were our eyes and ears on the streets.

"So what do you actually *do* in CID that we don't do in uniform?" asked Ursula one slow afternoon, when I was avoiding typing up yet another shoplifting report. "Apart from your ridiculously long hours, wearing what you like, and spending half your day playing snooker in the police club..."

"Cheeky," I replied. "I only spent an hour on snooker, and only when Ernie was here. I don't any more..." My voice tailed off.

Ursula smiled, and continued, "It seems to me that we do just the frontline work, then we hand the more serious crimes over to you, and you do the donkey work gathering the evidence and investigating, while we go out on patrol and do it all again."

"We certainly take on the investigation of the more serious crimes you attend – robberies, burglaries, arson, sexual offences, fraud, serious assaults, suicides and murders. But then you lot are generally first on the scene, and we rock up later once the blood and screaming have stopped. And of course you and Heather do a lot of juvenile care or protection cases, and liaising with the probation and social services, just like I used to."

"I'd really like to know more about CID though," said Ursula. "What actually happens when the fingerprints get dusted, when clothes from a crime scene 'get sent to Scotland Yard', how they know that a bullet has been fired from a particular gun. And you know what – I'd even like to go to a post-mortem…"

If it was up to me, I'd happily send Ursula off to a post-mortem, but that was a decision for a higher brass. After all, I'd been sent to one with WPC Pattie Baxter early on in our Wokingham police careers and it had shaped me as a police officer. Ursula had given me an idea, though.

I got up to go back to another solitary afternoon in the CID office.

"Oh well, back to the coalface and another exciting shoplifting report to file," I said.

"Aaargh, shoplifting!" cried Ursula. "It's never-ending! But talking of juveniles, can I run something past you?"

"Yes, of course."

"I've been having calls from a worried mother. Her four-year-old daughter came home crying from playing in the park, and all she would say was there was a man that she didn't like who was 'scary'. Apparently, she's been having nightmares about him and wetting the bed and the mother is worried she may have been interfered with. I looked around the park, and I include it in my patrols, but I couldn't see anyone who looked dodgy. Anything I can do?"

"This slightly reminds me of a case I had with a 'problem family' in 1954. The little girl had witnessed her father sexually abusing her sister, and in order to charge her father, I had to get her to tell me what he had been doing. I discovered that if you spend time with a child, playing with their toys, they'll sometimes act out and explain what has happened to them. I would suggest you wear plain clothes to see the little girl, and if possible be in the room with her on your own. I've found children are often more likely to tell a visitor things than their own parents. You might need more than one visit, though."

"What a great idea! Thanks, Gwen," said Ursula, eyes sparkling. "I'll give it a go and let you know how I get on."

Tedious shoplifting report filed, I riffled through my Rolodex card index under D and dialled a London number.

"Dr Laurie Dixon, Scotland Yard Forensic Science Laboratory speaking," said an avuncular voice on the other end.

"Dr Dixon, it's WDC Crockford from Maidenhead here. We met on the Cookham caravan fire case."

"Ah yes, Mrs Flint the fire starter, who got off on some late evidence." He chuckled. "What can I do for you?"

"Well, I'm wondering if there's any way you could do me and the women police officers of Berkshire a favour?"

"Oh, that was absolutely bloody brilliant!" enthused Ursula, bounding into the police club bar late on a winter afternoon with Heather. "Thank you for setting up such a fascinating day out, Gwen!"

Using my contacts, and with Inspector Robertshaw's blessing, I had organised a guided tour of New Scotland Yard, the Fingerprint Department, the Forensic Science Laboratory, and the Black Museum for all the WPCs in Berkshire so they could get a feel for the technological advances in forensics and how criminal investigation departments work.

"You found it useful then?" I asked.

"Amazing! The amount of evidence that can be revealed with infrared and ultraviolet..." Ursula started giggling, and I knew exactly what she was giggling about.

"I'm guessing they showed you how semen stains glow in the dark under an ultraviolet lamp?" I asked. This was one of the Forensic Science Laboratory's party pieces – fascinating, and slightly risqué.

"All I could think about was how many teenage boys would be relieved that this technology isn't available to their mums," said Ursula.

"I wondered who donated the stains," I replied, and we shrieked with laughter.

"I still can't understand how on earth those fingerprint experts know where to search for a match among those millions of prints in their fingerprint library," said Heather. "Then they sit on those uncomfortable stools with their magnifying glasses poring over sheets and sheets of prints. They must have extraordinary memories – and very bad backs."

"I still think they are chosen for their superpowers," I replied. "Did you get to go into the Black Museum? I specifically asked if you could all have access."

The Black Museum in New Scotland Yard's basement

was only open to police officers, not the public, as its contents were considered too horrifying for general consumption. As a result, it had built up a reputation as some sort of chamber of horrors, and of course, that was the one place the WPCs were most excited to visit.

"I was really looking forward to that, and I don't want to sound ungrateful, but it was a bit rubbish compared with what it was hyped up to be..." admitted Ursula.

My thoughts exactly. A creative curator could do wonders with all these important historical artifacts.

"...I mean, the individual things in there are interesting, but they're all jumbled together in a crappy basement."

"Ooh, I don't know, Ursula," said Heather. "I found those photographs of Jack the Ripper's victims absolutely haunting, and the wax heads of executed criminals were macabre."

"Is Himmler still there?" I asked.

"Yes, his wax head is stuck on the shelf with the rest of them," said Heather, "but I didn't feel sorry for him."

And the learning opportunities just kept coming. A few days later, I opened a memo from Inspector Robertshaw.

> *Dear Miss Crockford,*
> *You are invited to an illustrated talk at Reading*
> *Borough Police HQ by Inspector Jenny*
> *Timberlake on her experiences as superintendent-*
> *in-charge of the British Police Unit Women's*
> *Detachment during the Cyprus Emergency, May*
> *1958 – May 1959.*

This sounds interesting. Jenny Timberlake, as well as being Reading Borough's first female inspector, was the only policewoman in Berkshire to be sent to civil-war-torn Cyprus. I was fascinated, and a little nervous to see what I'd missed out on because I'd been too scared to put my hand up and volunteer for the Cyprus Police in 1956. Heather, Ursula, Miss Robertshaw and I trooped off one evening to Reading Borough's HQ in Valpy Street, where we sat on hard wooden chairs in front of a projector screen.

The formidable figure of Inspector Jenny Timberlake trundled into the room like a small tank. I noticed she was wearing her General Service Medal with Cyprus bar in recognition of the work she'd done on the island. Very much in the Barbara Denis de Vitré mould, she had the air of one of those capable women you'd be jolly grateful to see if you were in a crisis; she would deal with that, and then make sure everybody had a cup of tea afterwards. No wonder she'd been in such demand for Cyprus.

Inevitably, Inspector Timberlake's first slide was a map of the island of Cyprus, and she explained why the British police were out there. To cut a long story short, the Greek Cypriots wanted Cyprus to be independent from their British colonisers, and unite with Greece (*enosis*). Of course, Turkish Cypriots weren't having any of this and put up resistance. A Greek terrorist group, EOKA, conducted armed, coordinated campaigns against British rule, targeting the military, police and government installations in Nicosia, Famagusta, Limassol and Larnaca. In addition to their Greek Cypriot officers, the Colonial Police had created a reserve force made up of solely Turkish Cypriots to combat EOKA's paramilitaries, which only served to heighten tensions between Cyprus's Greek and Turkish communities. The British Army and British Police Unit were caught in the crossfire of fighting resistance to colonialism as well as traditional Greco-Turkish antagonism, and suffered many casualties as a result.

A sweet-faced, smiley woman in Metropolitan Police uniform appeared on the next slide.

"This is the lovely Winifred Barker from the Met," said Inspector Timberlake. "In 1957 it was considered just about safe enough for Winifred to take 50 policewomen out there with her to patrol Ledra Street in Nicosia, or 'Murder Mile' as it was known. Her remit was to try to make it less murderous."

The following slides showed a smiling British policewoman posing for a photograph with several adorable mop-haired children, as some bewildered-looking Cypriots stood staring behind her; the same policewoman casually directing traffic in sunny Ledra Street; and lastly, one of her sitting in a family house on a low settee, drinking black tea out of a glass rather than a cup.

This looks as if it would have been fun and *worthwhile*. I felt that leaden stab of regret that I hadn't put my hand up to go somewhere more exotic than Maidenhead. With the British Empire crumbling, Colonial Service postings were becoming few and far between, and I'd probably missed my window of overseas travel opportunity.

"As you can see, we did exactly the same things in Nicosia that we would do in Reading..." Inspector

Timberlake cast her eyes round the room "...or Wokingham... or Maidenhead... We just attracted a lot more attention. The inhabitants weren't used to seeing a woman doing a man's job, but their staring was more curiosity than hostility."

"A bit like Whitley Wood[57] in 1958 then," called a wag from the back, and some of the Reading Borough crowd giggled.

Inspector Timberlake continued, "In fact, we were welcomed with open arms into both Greek and Turkish family homes, enabling us to understand and deal with domestic problems that were referred to us."

The next slide showed a British policeman with a gun in his hand.

"The men were armed, but we weren't," she explained, "and I must say, as a woman, I felt safer without a gun – nobody can take it off you and use it against you, and you don't have a shooting on your conscience for the rest of your life."

An image then flashed up on the screen that reminded me of those horrible antisemitic Nazi propaganda posters of World War Two. John Bull[58], who had been drawn with an alarmingly stereotypical Jewish face, was hugging sacks of money over a coffin filled with dead Cypriot children, while a handsome EOKA "freedom fighter" pointed both his finger and a gun at him.

---

57 Whitley Wood was one of the more deprived areas in the Reading Borough Police catchment.

58 A political caricature personifying England or the English, John Bull was a stout, middle-aged white man wearing a top hat and a union flag waistcoat.

"This was the kind of EOKA propaganda we were up against," said Inspector Timberlake. "The idea that we were murdering Cypriot children for money."

The mood in the room dropped as Inspector Timberlake showed us a slide of a man's legs lying on a dusty street, his upper body out of frame, with a distraught woman crouching beside them.

"This is one of our Turkish Cypriot police colleagues, cut down in front of his fiancée by EOKA terrorists."

It was the next slide that got us all. Two policemen, one clearly a sergeant with three chevrons on his arm, lay shot dead on a Nicosia street, their heavy, inky British uniforms incongruous in the Mediterranean heat compared with the linen shirts and trousers of the Cypriot onlookers. At first glance they looked like Matt Wagstaffe and Henry Falconer. It was the first time I had seen a photo of dead bobbies, and it felt deeply wrong.

"I regret to tell you that the Cyprus Emergency to date has meant that 18 British officers, 29 Greek Cypriot officers and 25 Turkish Cypriot officers have made the ultimate sacrifice. Shall we stand for a minute's silence to remember our fallen colleagues?" asked Inspector Timberlake.

We stood with our thoughts and in silence. I felt, on balance, it probably had been a wise decision to stay put in the UK, even though no British policewomen had been killed. If I'd gone to Cyprus, I would have missed the opportunity to join CID, and while British policewomen were bumped up a rank in Cyprus (I would have been made a sergeant), they were bumped back down again on their return.

"I don't want to leave you on such a depressing note about Cyprus though," said Inspector Timberlake after the minute was up. "There are good things going on. Archbishop Makarios for the Greek Cypriots and Dr Küçük for the Turkish ones, are talking, looking at making Cyprus a republic. It's likely Makarios will be president of the Republic of Cyprus, with Küçük vice president. Let's hope between them they can bring peace and stability to the island."

A final slide showed Inspector Timberlake with a smiling Cypriot woman in police uniform.

"I've also had the privilege to be able to train some wonderful Cypriot women police. We built up a tremendous relationship with them, which not only furthered women's work, but also gave the men an insight into the protective and preventative aspects of policing. And, for the first time, real appreciation of what the status of women *can* be. I sometimes think we could do with a bit more of that round here."

A ripple of laughter ran round the room as she paused to round up her talk. "I have every confidence that our Cypriot colleagues will be able to protect and serve their communities as brilliantly as you all protect and serve your communities here in Berkshire."

And we all applauded heartily.

Ursula and Heather took the train back to Maidenhead, while Inspector Robertshaw offered me a lift in her car as I was going to Wokingham to stay with my parents that night.

"Marvellous woman, that Jen Timberlake," enthused Miss Robertshaw, who had a bit of a thing about high-achieving women officers. "It's women like her who make all the difference in this world."

"She certainly is. Were you ever tempted to go out to Cyprus, Miss?" I asked.

"I thought about it, but I'm not good with the heat. And anyway, I'd just been promoted to inspector, and I wanted to get stuck into that role. How are you finding CID?"

I hesitated for a moment too long. Miss Robertshaw would have picked up on that.

"Yes, I'm enjoying it. I've had some interesting cases and I like working with DS Kinch, and Ernie Le Mercier before he moved. Inspector Cockerill is a decent guv'nor."

"Hmm. A little bird tells me that with the new DS and DC you're not getting a look in on the interesting cases."

"Was that little bird Ursula by any chance?"

"Might have been. She said she rarely saw you when DS Le Mercier was there, although you included her on the Bray Studios wage packets theft, which she really appreciated, by the way. Now, you're often in the women's office."

"I'm trying to encourage more crossover between uniform and CID," I replied. "There's a perception that CID exists in an ivory tower, when we should really all be working together."

"Good luck with that. Most detectives like being in an ivory tower and won't want the status quo to change.

Anyway, this is about you, Gwen. Where do you see your police career going?"

"Of course I would love to be promoted to detective sergeant, although I can't see that happening any time soon."

"I hate to break it to you, but CID promotions, even if you're a man, are few and far between. You've done exceptionally well getting to DC, but I would question whether you'll get the opportunity to rise to DS. If you want to advance in your career, have you thought about being promoted back into uniform? I would encourage you to think about taking your sergeant's exams, and I would support your application wholeheartedly."

I hadn't thought about it, but maybe I should.

CHAPTER 28

The uniform decider

Maidenhead with Smythe
Winter 1960

"Here's your cocoa, Gwennie," said Dad, handing me a comforting pre-bedtime mug of frothy brown stuff. Mum had got bored with me and Dad talking about Inspector Timberlake's Cyprus experiences and had taken herself off to bed.

"I'll bet you wouldn't have minded being armed, though, love, what with you being the Wokingham police shooting team's top scorer for so many years."

"I wouldn't want the responsibility, Dad. As Jenny Timberlake says, someone could grab your gun and use it against you, and I couldn't live with myself if I killed someone, however legally protected I would be in the line of duty."

"I wonder if we'll ever get to the stage of arming all our police officers, like they do in America?" mused Dad.

"Oh, I really hope not. With firearms, you have to demonstrate ability, and some officers simply don't have that. If every officer has to carry a gun, what do you do with those who don't pass the training? Or are simply not of the right character to carry a weapon? Give them one anyway? Create a station of gun haves and have nots? By all means have properly trained firearms officers who could be called out, but bobbies patrolling the streets with Webleys? I think not."

And this was to be a view I held all my life: the police should not be routinely armed, for all the above reasons.

"That's my Gwennie. A girl who knows her own mind," said Dad as he got up to retire to bed. "Lock the front door when you go up, love. Night night."

"Night, Dad."

I wasn't remotely tired. I was buzzing with energy from being in the presence of doughty Inspector Timberlake who had achieved so much. And even Inspector Robertshaw's chat, which, while being disappointing regarding CID, had got me thinking. Distractedly, I flicked through the pages of the newspaper, stopping at the Announcements section when something caught my eye:

ENGAGEMENTS

PC Henry Falconer, of Wokingham Police,
to Cynthia Rowland,
physiotherapist at Wokingham Hospital

So he did fancy smug Cynthia, the annoying physiotherapist who helped get him back on his feet (and eventually his damn motorcycle) after his accident, after all. *Oh well, good luck to them*, I thought, determined not to let it bother me. *I made the decision to end it.*

I lit a cigarette and opened a window so that Mum with her bloodhound nose wouldn't know I'd been smoking in the house, then sat down on the tatty settee to have a word with myself.

What are you doing with your life, Gwendoline? It's 1960, you're 30, you're single, with no one on the horizon any more that you remotely fancy. You're getting on a bit, maybe not for marriage so much, but probably children now. Perhaps it's time to fully embrace that police career, follow in the footsteps of the brilliant Barbara Denis de Vitré, the inspirational Jenny Timberlake and even comfortably familiar Inspector Robertshaw. They're strong, they're achievers, they're well-respected – and they're in uniform.

You have to be honest with yourself: fascinating as CID can be, you're not going to be given the high-profile cases. You hope things'll get better, but will they? It's unlikely that you're going to achieve the dizzy heights of detective inspector or even sergeant. And if you're not going to have a family of your own, do you really want to spend the rest of your spinstery life doing pub obs and investigating cheque frauds and shoplifting?

I took a pencil and paper out of Dad's bureau and made a list:

UNIFORM
Predictable shifts
Prevention of crime
In touch with the public
Be a better policewoman with CID knowledge
Experience to train WPCs
Promotion prospects good
Working under Inspector Robertshaw again
No more forensics

<u>CID</u>
Unpredictable long hours
Detection of committed crime
Kudos of being the only woman detective
Out of touch with the public
Promotion prospects poor
Working with Smythe and Quirke
Not working with Kinch or Cockerill
Forensic work

I wasn't sure that the list was particularly helpful. Hilda said it was always a good idea to sleep on a conundrum, as your unconscious brain works it out, apparently. I flapped a tea towel at the open window to shoo away the last plumes of cigarette smoke into the freezing night, turned the key in the front door lock and went up to my childhood bedroom. When I awoke the next morning under the same candlewick bedspread that had been on my bed since 1933, I still had no idea what to do.

You knew it was serious when Inspector Cockerill himself came in to brief a new case.

"Stop what you're doing, you three. We've got a child death that might be suspicious and it's all hands on this case. A little lad was found unconscious at the bottom of the stairs but was pronounced dead on arrival at hospital. His father swears he has no idea what happened to him."

I felt my pulse quicken. On the one hand, how horrible that a child has been found dead. On the other, a death, maybe even a murder, to investigate would at last be the classic detective work I'd signed up for.

In the car on the way to a council estate, Cockerill continued to brief us.

"The child's name is Oscar, six years old. His father says he popped out to buy a loaf of bread and when he came back in, he found Oscar collapsed at the foot of the stairs. He shook him and slapped him but couldn't get him to wake up, so he ran to the phone box and called for an ambulance.

"Oh God, what if he'd had a head or spinal injury?" I said.

"Sometimes people panic and do the wrong thing," said Smythe.

"The ambulance men arrived but sadly couldn't do anything for him."

We pulled up outside a non-descript council house alongside some uniform patrol cars sparking and crackling radio messages from HQ, and dodged under the ropes keeping nosy neighbours away. Entering the house, I saw WPC Heather Newman in the front room comforting a sobbing woman, presumably Oscar's mother.

She's in good hands with Heather.

Inspector Morton appeared from a back room. "He's in here, DI Cockerill," he said, waving us into a dining room sparsely furnished with a tatty melamine camping table, some wooden stools and a couple of deckchairs.

The father, perched on a stool and rocking back and forth, looked up, and coal-black, shark-like eyes met mine. In that second, it was 1953 again and I was back in that condemned slum house in Wokingham's Rose Street. I recognised the man sitting in front of me now.

"May I ask your name, sir?" said Cockerill.

"S-Saul. Saul Felton," he murmured.

I was right.

"And can I ask what has happened here this afternoon?"

"It's been... horrible. I-I went out to get a loaf of bread to make some jam sandwiches for me and Oscar. When I come back, Osc was lying at the bottom of the stairs, not breathing or nothing. I shook him and I slapped him and I punched his chest... I didn't know what else to do. When I realised I couldn't get him round I ran to the phone box and rang for an ambulance. The ambulance men came and they couldn't get him round neither so they took him straight to hospital... and well, you know the rest."

"DC Quirke, could you take a formal statement from Mr Felton, please?"

Quirke looked at me in mild panic.

"Can't Gwe— I mean yes, guv," he replied.

"Gwen, can you come with me?"

We went into the kitchen, hands in pockets, not touching anything as all good crime scene detectives do. There wasn't much to touch anyway, just a couple of battered saucepans on the cooker, some green crockery in a glass-fronted wall unit and two wooden spoons in an earthenware jar. A loaf of bread, still in its paper bag, sat on a board.

"Guv, I know this man, Saul Felton," I said. "He was on probation in Wokingham for child cruelty, then breached it by beating his wife, but she withdrew the charges."

"I know him too, unfortunately," said Cockerill. "When he left his wife he moved to Maidenhead with one Nora Salter – a widow with two children – and then she had Oscar. One Christmas Eve while Nora was out with Oscar he set about her two older children, beating the boy with a walking stick, and throwing the girl against the cooker, gashing her face."

"Oh God, that's dreadful," I said. "The violence had escalated from what he did to his sons Carl and Dennis in Wokingham."

"He didn't get away with it that time. He got two years in prison: 18 months for cruelty to Nora's children, and six for beating his wife Dorothy in breach of his probation order. Psychiatrist at Fair Mile[59] said he had a psychopathic personality with a sadistic streak, especially when his self-control was impaired by alcohol. Yet still Nora took him back when he got out."

Why do women take back these horrible, abusive men?

"This is sounding suspicious, isn't it, guv?"

"It is. It'll be referred to the coroner, of course, who'll order an inquest, and we'll only really know what we are dealing with after the post-mortem. In the meantime, if you and Smythe can do some house-to-house, see if anyone saw or heard anything."

Smythe and I went up and down the street, questioning the neighbours.

"I saw a man run to the telephone box and back to the house, but didn't think anything of it," said one.

"I didn't know anything about it until the ambulance arrived at midday," said another.

---

59 Berkshire's psychiatric hospital.

"They're a funny family – *they're not married, you know,*" whispered one woman with hair curlers in.

"We don't like their sort round here," proclaimed a stout, middle-aged man.

"I saw Mr Felton cycling towards the town, but I didn't see him come back," said a postman.

"Yes, a man of that description came in and bought a split tin loaf this morning," said the bakery assistant.

As we returned to the house with our sparse witness statements, the police photographer was leaving with Cockerill and Quirke.

"Let's get back to the station and see what we've got," said Cockerill.

Crammed into the CID office, which was serving as a makeshift incident room, Cockerill ran through everything we knew so far about Oscar Felton's death.

"Nora had gone out to her job, cleaning one of the big houses in Maidenhead, while her two other children had gone out to play. Oscar stayed at home with his father. At around 10.30, Felton was seen heading on his bicycle towards the town, but nobody saw him return. The first inkling that anything was wrong was when the ambulance arrived at 12, the ambulance men attempted to revive Oscar, and took him to hospital. Felton claims he came in with the bread and found Oscar collapsed unconscious at the foot of the stairs, tried to shake and slap him awake, then ran out to call 999 at 11.45, which is corroborated by a neighbour. We found nothing disorderly in the house that would suggest a fight, a scuffle or a struggle. Any questions so far?"

I put my hand up. "Was there any drink in the house? Or empty bottles?"

"We didn't find any. What are you thinking, Gwen?"

"From Saul Felton's history, he flies into psychopathic rages when he's been drinking. I guess he couldn't have been drinking in town as the pubs open at 11.30, which wouldn't have given him time to have a pint, cycle home, try to revive Oscar and ring the ambulance at 11.45."

"He didn't smell of drink when I took his statement, guv," said Quirke.

Cockerill continued, "I don't think drink is a factor here, Gwen. There's not a lot more we can do on this until the post-mortem results come back. Thank you very much for your efforts so far, everybody, and have a break now."

As the CID office emptied, Cockerill pulled me to one side.

"Would you mind attending Oscar Felton's PM with me? Smythe and Quirke aren't keen..."

Most blokes aren't, are they? It was on the tip of my tongue to ask if we could invite Ursula along too, but I decided a child was probably too distressing as a first one for a young WPC. Tough cookie that Ursula was, she would be better off at the PM of some elderly person who had died in their sleep.

"Yes of course, guv. Will Tenterden have to do it? There's a suggestion this is a suspicious death, so won't we have to get a Home Office pathologist in?"

I couldn't bear the thought of that oaf hacking away at little Oscar Felton's body.

Either Cockerill read my mind, or he had the same thoughts as me. "I don't think we need to drag Tenterden into this one, do we?" he said. "It's only a *suggestion* that it's suspicious. I'm happy for Dr Stokes, the consultant pathologist at Cliveden Hospital, to do it."

The next day, Cockerill and I arrived at Cliveden Hospital mortuary, which was lighter, brighter and cleaner than other ones I had been in. Dr Stokes, a softly spoken, slight man with thick white hair and kind eyes behind half-moon spectacles, led us through to the autopsy room, where his assistant waited with a notebook and a camera with a flashbulb attached.

I felt an unfamiliar prickle of perspiration on my forehead as I looked at the small sheet-covered shape in the centre of the table. For the first time since training school in 1951, when we were about to be shown a dead body in a funeral director's morgue, I found myself dreading what I was going to see under the sheet, and my heart pounded.

Cockerill, grey-faced, avoided my gaze.

Dr Stokes gently pulled back the sheet to reveal the thin, pale body of Oscar Felton, who belied the traumatic nature of his death by looking as if he was asleep on that cold metal table. My stomach lurched at his smallness and vulnerability. The only thing I could focus on was how beautiful and thick his sandy eyelashes were above his cheeks.

"Hello, young man," murmured Dr Stokes. "What's happened to you, then? Let's find out."

I felt my eyes welling up at his sheer humanity, and

deliberately didn't blink so that the tears drained down my nose, rather than ran down my cheeks.

"There's extensive bruising on his body..." dictated Dr Stokes to his assistant as he conducted a visual external examination and the flashbulb popped.

Of course there is, he's a child of Saul Felton, I screamed inwardly.

"...although it is consistent with a boy of his age who roughs and tumbles outside, climbing trees and getting into scrapes," he continued. "The undeveloped bruising on his face and upper body indicates that it occurred at about the time of death and is consistent with someone in a panic trying to slap him awake and clumsily attempt to administer first aid."

Dr Stokes took swabs, hair samples and nail clippings, and of course Oscar had to be examined for signs of sexual abuse. Dr Stokes did this so discreetly that we only knew he'd done it when he dictated, "No signs of sexual interference."

He then held his hand out to the mortuary technician. "May I have a scalpel please, Mr Dunn?"

I had been to enough post-mortems to know exactly the procedure, from the first incision to the final stitch, and I had felt a little sick at the thought of this process happening to Oscar. However, I could only watch in admiration as Dr Stokes's long fingers and gentle, confident scalpel work excised and examined what he needed to without seeming to violate Oscar's body.

As Dr Stokes dissected the throat area, he paused and asked for a pair of forceps. "I think I can see the probable cause of death here. There's something impacted in the air passages, across his glottis. You might want to take a look, officers."

Lodged deep in the child's throat was an orange boiled sweet, which I recognised as a cough candy twist, horribly ironic in the circumstances.

Dr Stokes wiggled out the sweet with his forceps and dropped it into a kidney dish. "Due to the sudden nature of this child's death, and the lack of cyanosis[60], I would suggest that vagal inhibition due to choking on this sweet killed him before asphyxia developed," he said.

"What's that then?" asked Cockerill.

"Well," said Dr Stokes, peering over his glasses, "the vagus is the longest nerve in the body's autonomic nervous system. It helps regulate many things including heart rate and blood pressure, and transmits messages to several organs, including the heart. When the function of the vagus nerve is inhibited, for example by pressure on the neck, and in some cases choking, a cardiac arrest can happen simply because there are no signals coming down the nerve to the heart. So it stops, and death is sudden. It's a much quicker, less distressing death than asphyxiation. Oscar wouldn't have known much about it."

We sat in the CID office trying to envisage the last few minutes of Oscar's life.

"So it's possible that Oscar, home alone, was eating a sweet upstairs, felt himself choking and tried to get downstairs and out of the house for help, but didn't

---

60 A blue tinge to the skin due to asphyxia.

manage it and either collapsed on the stairs or just inside the door?" suggested Smythe.

"I don't think he would have had that much time to think about whether he was choking. The vagal inhibition could have kicked in at the top of the stairs and he fell down them, already unconscious," said Cockerill.

"If the father was anyone else, I would agree with you," I said, "but Felton has a history of flying into rages and attacking his children. What about: Felton came back from the shop, and Oscar, who had a sweet in his mouth, enraged his father somehow. Felton attacked him, maybe shook and slapped him, causing Oscar to inhale and choke on the sweet, which killed him suddenly due to the vagal inhibition?"

"Or threw him down the stairs with a sweet in his mouth and he choked at the bottom?" suggested Quirke.

"He needn't even have fallen down the stairs," I said. "The pathologist said that some of the bruising was normal for an active boy of his age and the rest of it consistent with someone trying to slap him awake and clumsily attempt to administer first aid at the point of death. Surely falling down the stairs would have left marks? I still think Felton could have attacked him downstairs."

There were so many scenarios, all of them plausible, but ultimately, only Oscar Felton would have known what happened to him that morning.

An inquest into Oscar Felton's death was held the following week. Inquests are not like criminal trials – they have no prosecution and defence, although they do call witnesses who, on oath, give their version of events to the coroner. Saul Felton stuck by his story that he found his son collapsed at the foot of the stairs when he came home. Our police evidence didn't find anything to contradict his version of events, despite his criminal record of psychopathic cruelty. The pathologist's report gave the cause of death as cardiac arrest due to vagal inhibition caused by choking on a boiled sweet.

Oscar Felton's death was recorded as accidental.

CHAPTER 29

Carry on sergeant?

Maidenhead with Smythe
Spring 1960

"GET UP OFF THAT CHAIR, CROCKFORD, AND MAKE A START ON THE NEXT CADAVER!" roared Tenterden at me, shoving a bone saw into my hands. "YOU HAVEN'T GOT TIME TO LAZE ABOUT!"

Three more sheet-covered cadavers were lined up in the mortuary for me to dissect today. Exhausted, I dragged myself to my feet.

"But sir, I need a scalpel to make the first incision; a bone saw won't do it!" I pleaded.

Tenterden, still wearing his blood-spattered mackintosh, turned to lean against the sink, flanked by two gaunt-looking mortuary technicians, the three of them puffing on huge Cuban cigars that filled the room with eye-wateringly acrid smoke. They pointed at me and laughed maniacally.

He sneered. "Well, you're going to have to do your best, aren't you?"

Cockerill and Kinch were locked outside, their noses pressed against the glass doors, peering into the mortuary.

"Do what he says and just get on with it, Hepz!" mouthed Kinch, helplessly.

I reluctantly approached the next cadaver and stretched out my hand to remove the sheet. With a shriek, Oscar Felton's corpse sat bolt upright and screamed into my face, "YOU KNOW MY DAD MURDERED ME, BUT YOU DID NOTHING ABOUT IT!"

It was my turn to shriek and sit bolt upright, in my bed in Sperling Road, covered in perspiration. I took some deep breaths to pull myself together, then shakily reached for my cigarettes.

Calm down, Gwen. It's only a dream. A pretty nasty one, but a dream all the same.

Since Oscar Felton's inquest, I'd been having this recurring nightmare far too often. And I'd managed to add yet another phobia (besides water and public speaking) to my mental fear repository: boiled sweets. I'd always assumed that a choking incident could be rectified with sharp slaps on the back, followed by the Heimlich manoeuvre if that didn't work; but the phenomenon of instant death through vagal inhibition added an extra layer of horror. In the unlikely event that I ever had children, they would be forbidden to eat boiled sweets, or accept one if someone offered it – and from strangers of course, but that was a whole different set of neuroses I didn't have to develop now.

Even though the forensic and police evidence found to the contrary, I still couldn't shake off the belief that Saul Felton had had some sort of hand in his son's death. It bothered me. Is there any way that some community policing could have prevented this death? Maybe a regular patrol past the house so Saul Felton felt he was on police radar and had to control himself? Maybe if an officer had seen Oscar with a bag of cough candy twists, they could have warned him of the danger of choking if he ran about with one in his mouth… maybe… if… perhaps… if only…

I had a couple of days of annual leave and spent the first one moping around in my room, unable to get the image of Oscar Felton on the mortuary table out of my head. I usually enjoyed post-mortems, but this one had really got to me, and I wasn't sure I wanted to attend another one anytime soon. Was it because he was a child? Am I feeling unfulfilled maternal urges? I liked children and I didn't come across that many in my detective work. *Live ones, that is.* Brain, please give me a break, will you?

I remembered that I hadn't seen my friend Hilda Bloom for ages. We often chatted on the telephone but the last time we'd actually gone out and done something together was the cinema to watch *Further Up The Creek*, and that was more than a year ago. I hadn't realised how quickly the months and years could go by when you're constantly working long hours, as you did with CID.

"Why don't you come up to Maidenhead for the day tomorrow?" I asked my dear friend on the telephone. "We could mooch around the posh shops; I'll show you the tricks of the shoplifting trade. We can go for an amble along the river down to pretty Boulter's Lock, where I promise we can do some celeb-spotting, and after that have afternoon tea at Skindles Hotel. How does that sound?"

"That sounds like a perfect day. I can't wait," said Hilda.

"Come to mine about 11."

A day with Hilda would be just what I needed.

Mrs Foskett had gone to work, and I was in the kitchen adding a few more chocolate drops to the cake I'd baked in anticipation of Hilda's arrival. I rubbed my scratchy eyes; screaming Oscar Felton had woken me at 4 a.m. again, and I had a headache and a non-specific leaden feeling that I couldn't place. At two minutes to 11, I heard the distinctive sound of a Morris Minor engine outside and I went to the front door and opened it.

There was Hilda, wearing her light spring tweeds, her spectacles on her head, striding towards me with a large bunch of freesias – my favourite flowers. I opened my mouth to say, "Hello Hilda," – then burst into floods of tears.

Hilda put her handbag and the freesias by the garden wall, wordlessly wrapped her arms round me and just hugged and hugged me until I'd made a substantial wet patch on her shoulder.

I tried to say "Sorry, this is so embarrassing," but no words would come out.

All I could hear was Hilda's voice saying, "It's all right *Liebling*, it's all right, just let it all out," rubbing my back.

Somehow, we ended up in the kitchen and Hilda was making *me* a cup of tea and arranging her flowers in a vase while I tried, somewhat unsuccessfully, to pull myself back together.

"I-I don't know what came over me, H-Hilda," I sobbed. "I was so looking forward to seeing you and now I'm a mess."

Hilda peered at me over her glasses.

"You are not a mess. There is something going on. What is it?"

And over three cups of tea, two slices of chocolate cake and seven cigarettes, it all came tumbling out.

"My favourite DS, Ernie Le Mercier, left, and things haven't been the same since that... I really don't like the new DS and DC they've brought in... They give themselves the interesting cases where there's a chance of conviction and I get the crap dead-end boring ones ... but then we got a child death, and I went to the post-mortem, and although it turned out to be an accident, I can't get it out of my mind..."

"Child death?" asked Hilda.

"Oh my goodness... you would know the family! Your colleague Terry Fulford was Saul Felton's probation officer... Carl and Dennis's horrible father!"

Hilda listened, wide-eyed and her hand over her mouth, as I outlined the Oscar Felton case and my unease about Saul Felton.

"You could not have done anything more, Gwen. Yes, Felton is a dreadful man – those poor, poor children – but if the inquest has ruled it to be an accident, you have to accept that and move on."

"I know that, Hilda," I replied, blowing my raw nose yet again on my handkerchief. "I think I'm going soft in my old age. I used to be able to deal with all manner of child care or protection cases, and I could switch off when I got home. But I'm finding now that it's *when* I get home and close the door that the horrors creep up on me. And I'm waking early with nightmares about Oscar Felton."

"This is not good, Gwen. This sounds like symptoms of soldiers' battle fatigue from the war. I'm sensing maybe you are not enjoying the CID work as much as you used to?"

"I don't know where CID can take me, Hilda. Miss Robertshaw says there's pretty much zero chance of getting any CID promotion, but there are uniform promotion opportunities for women. She's said she would back me if I wanted to take sergeant's exams... and I went to a talk by Jenny Timberlake about all the marvellous work she did in Cyprus... stupid me being too scared to put my hand up for that, I missed an opportunity there... probably because I was going out with Henry Falconer... That turned out well, didn't it? And I liked someone, but he was married – nothing happened, you understand, it was probably all in my head..."

Goodness, it's really all tumbling out now.

"...And I look at our senior policewomen, Miss de Vitré, Jenny Timberlake, even Miss Robertshaw – they're just, impressive, you know? And the Maidenhead WPCs, Heather and Ursula, they keep their eyes and ears open and prevent crime before it happens; whereas in CID we just pick up the pieces after the crime has been committed... I think my heart is in prevention rather than detection, you know, Hilda, like we used to do when I worked with you at Wokingham..."

Hilda looked at me kindly over the top of her glasses, her head tilted to one side.

"Then I think you know yourself what you need to do, Gwen," she replied.

"I need to speak to Miss Robertshaw about those sergeant's exams, don't I?"

"You do. But first, you need another one of these." Hilda refilled my teacup from the pot. "Then you must go upstairs and put a cold flannel on your face. And after, you will give me that guided tour of Maidenhead."

And I did. Hilda and I swanned in and out of all the posh shops (even Biggs with its inch-deep Turkish carpet), walked along the river to watch the pleasure boats rising and falling as they navigated through Boulters Lock one by one, and ended up at Skindles Hotel for even more tea, with dainty sandwiches and French fancies to soak up the tannin overload.

"Oh my goodness, is that Bud Flanagan[61]?" asked Hilda, pointing to an elderly gentleman taking afternoon tea with two ladies.

I looked round. "Yes, it is – he's often in town. He lives at Riverside in Bourne End, which got burgled once. See, I promised you celebrities!"

Being with Hilda for the day was just the tonic I needed. I hugged her again as she was about to get in her car, without leaving a massive tear stain on her shoulder this time.

---

61 A famous singer, comedian and leader of "The Crazy Gang", an anarchic pre-war entertainment troupe, and one half of Flanagan & Allen, whose wartime songs such as "Run Rabbit Run", "We're Going to Hang Out the Washing on the Siegfried Line", and "Underneath the Arches" kept morale going in the darkest hour.

"You need to get out more, Gwen. Do something that is not police work. I have an idea for something we can do very soon, and I'll be in touch. But first you must speak to Miss Robertshaw. Promise me you will?"

I knew Miss Robertshaw was due in the women's office the next day, and I wandered in on the off-chance. She wasn't there, but Ursula was typing up a report.

"Ah, Gwen," she said. "I was going to come and see you. You remember me talking to you about the little girl who'd been frightened by the 'scary man' in the park?"

"Yes, I do."

"Well, I did what you said and went round to see her in plain clothes, and we played with some toys. She had a knitted lion that she pretended kept hiding behind trees and jumping out at her saying 'Boo!', nothing more sinister than that. And interestingly, we had a couple more reports about a man jumping out and saying 'Boo!' to children. One of the mums recognised him as Albie Crain, a local lad who's educationally subnormal[62]. I went round and had a chat with him and his nan, who he lives with, and explained that although he thinks it's great fun to jump out, it does frighten some children. I *think* I got through to him and he shouldn't do it again."

"Ah that's brilliant, Ursula. It is a useful technique to use with young children, and I'm really pleased it wasn't sinister after all."

---

62 An unenlightened 1950s expression for "learning disabled".

I heard footsteps coming up the stairs and Miss Robertshaw appeared in the doorway.

"Aren't you due out on patrol soon, Miss Meeke?" she said.

"Yes, Miss Robertshaw, just finished this report and I'm out of here." Ursula grabbed her tunic and hat off the peg and bustled out.

"Take a seat, Gwen," said Miss Robertshaw indicating the spare chair. "She's a good girl, that WPC Meeke, very capable."

"She is, miss. I've worked with her on a few jobs, and she's always got stuck in enthusiastically."

And she tells me you told her about the work you did with the Carroll family – with the toys?"

"It was a useful technique when I was a WPC back in Wokingham. I haven't had any reason to use it since, but I thought it might help Ursula. She said that it helped to identify Albie Craine as the 'scary man', and no harm done."

"Dear Albie Craine," said Miss Robertshaw, rolling her eyes. "Completely harmless, of course. And that's what I've always liked about you, Gwen. You work out your own way of doing things and then you're willing to include and teach others. I've heard nothing but good things about you, not just from Heather and Ursula, but from Inspector Morton and DI Cockerill as well. I've known you for nine years now, and you have a unique combination of uniform and CID experience that will get you very far in the police force, I believe. I really think you should take your sergeant's exams."

"Well, miss," I replied, "that's what I wanted to talk to you about."

Hilda and I sat on the top of a double-decker London bus crawling through the traffic on our way to a matinee at the Finsbury Park Empire theatre.

"So, what's this play about that you're so keen for us to see?" I asked.

"It's called *A Taste of Honey* and it was written by a 19-year-old girl called Shelagh Delaney," said Hilda. "It's been referred to as a 'kitchen sink drama'..."

"Don't tell me it's three hours of somebody doing the washing up," I said, and we both laughed.

"No, there's a refreshing new wave of playwrights and filmmakers who are tackling uncomfortable themes, highlighting social issues, and setting their scenes in the sorts of homes that you and I are used to visiting with our care or protection cases, Gwen. *A Taste of Honey* is apparently controversial, ground-breaking and gritty. That's all I'm going to say for now."

We trundled along in the bus in companiable silence, people-watching the stylish Londoners thronging the streets below.

"You know what I *haven't* seen today, Hilda?"

"No, what?"

"Teddy boys. I haven't seen a single one, or even the tiniest quiff for that matter. The young men have grown their fringes out, and seem to be favouring these short, fitted suits, polo neck jumpers and boots that look more Italian to me."

"You're right, Gwen," said Hilda. "I haven't either. It's 1960 after all, and rock and roll is as good as dead. It died really when Buddy Holly, Ritchie Valens and the Big Bopper went down in that plane crash last year. Elvis Presley has gone all soft, and I can't imagine anyone starting a pub brawl to a Cliff Richard song."

"Well, I'm not sorry to see the back of the Teddy boys," I said. "With their silly, exaggerated velvet collars and cuffs, long jackets that made them look idiotic, drainpipe trousers so tight they could barely sit down…" *Goodness, I was really channelling my inner fashion critic now. Victor would be proud.* "Those little sods have caused me enough aggro for the last seven years. I know you think reaction to their antics was just moral panic, Hilda, but I beg to differ. It'll be interesting to see what the next generation of juvenile delinquents will be like."

"And there will be some, you can be sure of that," replied Hilda. "Oh look – we're here."

Hilda and I clumped down the bus stairs and up the steps into the Finsbury Park Empire.

Three hours later we clumped down the steps of the Finsbury Park Empire. I was buzzing with righteous anger, yet slightly feeling that I'd just seen something I shouldn't have, like finding a copy of *Frolic* magazine in your dad's potting shed.

Oh for goodness sakes, Gwen, get over it. It's 1960 and you're 30.

The tale of unmarried teen Jo – who has a volatile relationship with her single mother, becomes pregnant with a young black sailor's child, gets thrown out and ends up sharing a flat with a homosexual art student – smashed many of the previous decade's taboos. Used to happy endings, I struggled with *A Taste of Honey*'s downbeat one, which was also left wide open to speculation and discussion, which meant, of course, that Hilda was in her element.

"You know that is the very first time a gay man has been openly portrayed on the stage?" she enthused. "Can you imagine that even being considered when the Wolfenden report was commissioned in 1954?"

"I can't," I replied. "Although I am sensing a slight shift in attitudes towards, er, *gay* men, so that Geoffrey the art student can even be allowed on the stage."

"And I was so happy that a West Indian actor played Jimmy the sailor," continued Hilda. "I feel quite uncomfortable when you go to see a play, and actors have boot polish on their faces to make them look African or Indian."

"It was all rather convincing, wasn't it? It certainly rang true to a lot of social issues that we've encountered."

'We chewed over what we thought could happen to Jo and her baby all the way back to Reading on the train, and promised that we would go and see a lot more "kitchen sink dramas" at the theatre or the cinema.

A couple of weeks later, I arrived bright and early at Sulhamstead HQ. Despite studying late into the evenings, I felt bright and fresh. It was a while since I'd had a nightmare about Oscar Felton, and I had been sleeping better. I took my place at a school desk in the assembly hall filled with uniform policemen, nodding and smiling at a few I knew. I looked down at the exam paper in front of me and cracked my knuckles.

Examination Booklet for
Promotion to the Rank of Police Sergeant

"You can all open your examination paper now," said the adjudicator.

Question 1
A woman walking her dog has found the body of a man lying in a public park. The circumstances indicate that it is a murder, although the perpetrator is unknown. Describe in detail what actions you would take and how you would organise your PCs.

I picked up my pen and started to write.
Easy peasy, I thought, a big smile on my face.

Acknowledgements

I am so lucky to have many lovely people who supported, advised and encouraged me as I wrote *Calling Detective Crockford*.

Special thanks must go to: Pippa Wilson for suggesting I write my mother's story in the first place; and Caroline Hopkins, Wendy O'Mahony and Fiona Murray, who have been a huge and enthusiastic support as I wrote and published the Crockford series.

Tony Chapman and Michael Meehan, formerly of the Hertfordshire Constabulary and CID in the 1960s, and Julie Currie, formerly of the Metropolitan Police, for their procedural advice; DI Helene Miller (Metropolitan Police) and Amelia Schmidt (BSc Forensic Anthropology, Dundee University) for advice on forensics. Roger Crowhurst for his description of The Metropolitan Police Training School, Hendon, in the 1950s. Designer Simona Marletta for her fashion expertise; Tim Lucas for his knowledge of motorcycles; and my critical readers Paul D'Alessandro, David Ledesma, Alex Talbot, Matthew Chatfield and Liz Benamri for their unflinching honesty.

My inspirational agent, Kate Hordern of KHLA, for her continuing vision, sage advice, guidance and encouragement throughout the planning and writing of the *Crockford* series; and my ever-supportive, oldest friend Catherine Cotter.

Welbeck's lovely commissioning and project editor, Beth Bishop, and her team, for continuing to recognise that the story of policewomen in the 1950s, and one female detective in particular, is worth telling; my copy-editor Victoria Goldman and my proofreader, Kate Michell, for picking up things I'd missed and James Howarth for his legal read.

Professor Louise Jackson, whose book *Women Police: Gender, Welfare and Surveillance in the Twentieth Century* continues to be the bedrock of my research, for kindly sharing proofs of her book, *Policing Youth, Britain 1945–70*, with me.

Newspaper quotes came from clippings found in my mother's papers that had neither source nor dates with them. To the best of my knowledge and research, these came from the *Wokingham and Bracknell Times*, the *Maidenhead Advertiser* and the *Windsor Express* of the period.

The Berkshire Record Office for being as helpful as they could be with the sparse Berkshire Constabulary archives; the Baylis Media Archive for background research; and The British Library for being a monumental research resource.